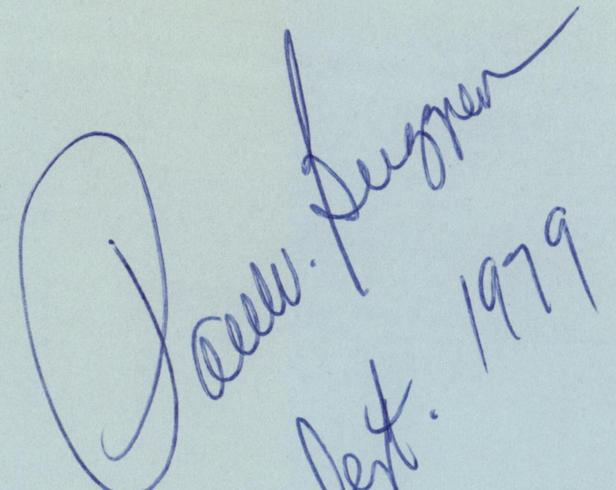

IMMIGRANT

EXECUTIVE

TRAVELER

MY STORY

Birger Swenson

Immigrant Executive Traveler

MY STORY

By Birger Swenson

1979
Augustana Historical Society
Rock Island, Illinois

Augustana Historical Society
Publication No. 27
Ernest M. Espelie, Editor

ISBN: 0-910184-27-5
Library of Congress Card No: 79-50724

Printed in the United States
WAGNERS PRINTERS, INC.
Davenport, Iowa

TO MY WIFE

LYAL

FOREWORD

The story of the poor lad who works his way to success and high position is a familiar one in America. Less often is the subject of such accounts a person who comes from a foreign land and finds his place in the field of religious publication. Birger Swenson not only "made good" but in the process became a lay leader in the church and a highly respected member of the religious press in the United States.

In reading his autobiography, I am impressed by his good-natured curiosity which led him to ever new experiences in his widening world. He later became a master of the camera and preserved the scenes of his travels, but even without the camera he was ever eager to meet new people, see new places, accept new challenges. There is thus a singular consistency in his life and his record. All who knew him enjoyed his stories—it is appropriate that in this book he tells the story of himself.

Yet it is more than the story of Birger. As we follow him, we catch glimpses of historic significance. His early travels brought him to the places across the land where Swedish immigrants settled. His years at Augustana College recall a period many alumni will enjoy in recollection. The parish life of the Augustana Synod is reflected in his accounts of visits throughout the nation. After he became director of the Book Concern, he knew the cultural and devotional life of his church as few others. And his later chapters reveal a spirit of genuine concern about the welfare of an American community.

Since retirement he and Lyal have rediscovered the world, from pole to pole, from Scandinavia to Africa, the Far East, the South Seas, and South America. The story of this modern Viking is one that the Augustana Historical Society is happy to publish.

Conrad Bergendoff

ACKNOWLEDGMENTS

This autobiography has been written as a result of suggestions and encouragement from a number of friends. Two friends in Karlstad, Sweden, Dr. Sigurd Gustavson, director of Emigrant-registret, and Sture Stålfors, editor of *Nya Wermslands Tidningen,* suggested a number of years ago that I write an account of my early years in the United States. As I pursued this suggestion, I was encouraged by another friend, Dr. Conrad Bergendoff, president emeritus of Augustana College, to write a complete life story. I am deeply appreciative of the valuable support he has given me in this writing venture. Without his encouragement there may not have been a life story.

I am very grateful to Ernest Espelie, former librarian of Augustana College and editor of Augustana Historical Society publications, for his helpful criticism and professional advice and for the final reviewing and guiding the manuscript through publication. My thanks go also to Mary Belle Espelie for assistance in reviewing the manuscript and in proof reading. My gratitude is extended to Perry Mason, director of publications, Augustana College, who carefully supervised the typesetting and key lining for this volume, and to Gustav Magnusson, former production manager of the Augustana Book Concern, for technical assistance. I also thank Sarah Johnson and Lucille Marlier for typing the manuscript.

I appreciate the service of Robert Pope and W. Samuel Bjorkman of the *Argus* staff for photographic help in processing travelogue illustrations. Permission was gladly given for including travel interviews by Larry Heintz of the *Argus* and Julie Jensen of the *Times.*

A special and very deep appreciation goes to my wife, Lyal, for encouragement and help in many ways. She typed the manuscript as the writing progressed. She is very much a part of my life story.

Writing my story has been a pleasant and rewarding experience.

CONTENTS

I

FINDING MY WAY IN A NEW LAND

This story has its beginning in the village of Averstad in Östra Fågelvik Parish, Värmland, Sweden, on July 31, 1895, when my twin sister, Signe Maria, and I were welcomed into the family of Sven and Johanna Spetz Svensson. We grew up in a family of nine children, four girls and five boys. However, my parents were asked to rear another girl along with their own, thus making five daughters and five sons. Nine had two or more Christian names, but I was given only one—Birger.

All of us attended Spånga school, located about two miles from our home. During my school years, I had only two teachers. The teacher in the lower grades was a woman whom we always addressed as "Mamsell." The teacher in the upper grades was Alfred Sundin who was also, for a time, organist in our parish church. Sometimes on a Friday afternoon after school, he would go to the church to rehearse the hymns for the following Sunday. I was asked to tramp the bellows for the organ. I became very fond of this teacher, and we kept in touch during the years that followed. I always called on him on my visits to Sweden. I saw him last in 1967, shortly before his death at the advanced age of ninety-three.

My school days began at the age of seven and continued through the age of twelve. During my thirteenth and fourteenth years, I attended continuation school for six weeks each winter. I was confirmed at the age of fourteen on August 8, 1909, in Östra

Fågelvik Parish Church. I still treasure the notes I took of the lessons the pastor, Hans Peter Norman, gave us during confirmation instruction, the subject of which was "Jesus Christ is our pattern according to the Ten Commandments."

My father operated a small farm on which he produced much of the food for our family of twelve, such as vegetables, wheat, rye, oats, chickens, pigs, and cows. The cultivation was done with horses. Flax was also harvested, and looms were kept busy weaving cloth. A by-product, called *vadmal* (homespun) was made into cloth for men's clothing. Practically all the clothing for the family, except shoes, was made in the home. During the winter evenings with light from kerosene lamps, the women folk were busy knitting and sewing while someone was reading aloud—not only books of Swedish authors but also translations from French, English, and German.

There was not sufficient work on the farm for us as we grew up; therefore, we had to look for opportunities for work elsewhere. At the age of eleven, I started to work away from home during the summer months. I worked in a brickyard located at Skattkär, about three miles from home. The working schedule was from 6:00 a.m. to 6:00 p.m. with time out for breakfast at 8:30 a.m., for a half hour; lunch at noon for an hour; and afternoon coffee at 3:30 p.m. for a half hour. The working day was ten hours, six days a week. My job was to put away freshly pressed roof tiles for drying. My pay was one and a half crowns a day. Often I brought food from home for two or three days and slept on top of the kiln so I would not have to rise so early and walk to and from work each day.

During the summer of my thirteenth year, I worked in a sawmill. The hours were the same, but the pay was better, two crowns a day. At fourteen, I hired out as a farmhand to a man by the name of Victor Larson, who lived in the village of Grän. I stayed with him for two years. In the winter he cut timber which I hauled to a sawmill in Skattkär across the bay of Lake Vänern. My horse, Guldbrand, was a couple of years older than I and more knowledge-able. Whenever I was hauling a log between the stumps to the sleigh for loading and would stumble and fall, Guldbrand would stop, look back, and wait for me. After leaving the farm of Victor Larson, I teamed up with my brother Ragnar and spent the winter cutting timber. I made enough money to order my first tailor-made suit.

A neighbor, Paul Larson, who had been in the United States for five years, was home for a visit, and we were always ready to listen to him. "America fever" was spreading fast among us. Ragnar and I asked father if he would permit us to go to America and also lend us money for transportation. I was sixteen years old and my brother was eighteen. Father agreed to help us. Neither of us had a definite goal, but adventure and a brighter horizon beckoned us.

Although my brother and I had been away working for others, we had spent considerable time in our home. Now when the time was approaching for us to leave for the United States of America, we realized that it might be years before we would see our parents, brothers, and sisters again. My parents had been firm disciplinarians, but understanding. Of great importance to my parents was engendering in us a respect for the church and its teaching. During severe weather in the winter, when we could not attend church services, father would read from the Bible, the Psalmbok, and the *Postilla* (a collection of sermons). Mother would lead in singing hymns. One could often hear her hum a familiar religious tune as she moved about performing her daily household tasks. Table grace was customary, and anyone of us might be called upon to say the blessing. We were always grateful for our parents' guidance and example.

The day came for our departure. We were a group of five, namely, the brothers, Paul and Anders Larson, Bror Anderson, my brother Ragnar, and I. All met different adventures in the new land. With the Larsons we kept in close contact for years, but we lost touch with Bror Anderson. As of this writing, I am the only one living.

We were to sail west from Gothenburg, the second largest city in Sweden. I had never been in a large city before. Fortunately we had arrived a day early, enabling us to do some sightseeing. We attended a theater performance and saw some of the night life.

We embarked March 8, 1912, and traveled by ship to Hull, England, and by rail to Liverpool. There we had to wait for several days. Thirty to forty men and boys slept in one large room, all awaiting a ship. In the open-air courtyards outside our quarters were young girls who could speak half a dozen languages. They tried to entice us into stores to buy things. I bought a raincoat. The first time

I had it on, I perspired, and it fell apart, as it had been glued together.

Finally, the *R.M.S. Ivernia* arrived. We sailed on March 13th. Equipped for the journey with some hardtack and a brick of horse meat (which, according to friends was a good preventive for sea-sickness) my brother and I were on our way to the land of adventure and promise. Traveling as steerage passengers, we found sleeping accommodations adequate but not exactly comfortable. The dining room had long rough tables with benches rather than chairs. The food was not always to our liking, but we had our hardtack and horse meat. Perhaps we could not expect better service in view of the cost of the trip. I had paid the Cunard Steamship Company agency in Gothenburg the sum of 181 crowns. This was the total price of the ticket from Gothenburg to England, Boston, and Proctor, Vermont —in U.S. money less than forty dollars.

Our first sight of the North American continent was Halifax, Nova Scotia. After a brief stop there, we sailed to our destination, Boston, where we arrived March 25, 1912. This was just three weeks before the catastrophe of the "unsinkable" British *R.M.S. Titanic*, which struck an iceberg and sank with a loss of 1,500 lives on April 15, 1912. We were happy to land, and we were eagerly looking forward to the adventures which this great land had to offer. It did not take long to go through immigration procedures. We had plenty of time as the train for Proctor was not scheduled to leave until late afternoon. We decided to take a walk. We all agreed that we needed a haircut, and we found a barber shop. As the barber had just about finished the last one of us, a U.S. immigration officer appeared. He took us back to the railway station in a horse-drawn carriage. We were still under the watchful eye of the U.S. government until we boarded the train for Proctor.

Upon arrival in Proctor, Paul Larson took us to acquaintances whom he had met on his first journey to America. But we were five, and there was not room for that many. My brother and I had to separate. He went to one boarding house, and I to another operated by a widow who had four boarders. I was to share a bed with another Swede. The price per week for board, room, and laundry was four dollars. I spent a dollar a week at the company store all for bananas, which were new to me.

We obtained work the very next day at the Vermont Marble

Company. The marble was quarried in Rutland and shipped to Proctor for cutting and refinishing. It was used for building and fine architectural work. My job was to help make boxes for shipping the finished marble. We worked ten hours a day, six days a week at $1.50 per day. There were many Swedish people in Proctor, and we enjoyed our stay there.

After three months in Proctor, we decided to join our brother Robert, who had arrived two years earlier and who now had a good job as a carpenter in Chicago. Upon our arrival in the big city, a travel assistant at the railroad station provided us with a guide who for two dollars took us by street car to the house where our brother was living. He was rooming with a family by the name of Swanson at 1102 West 59th Street. Finding no one at home, we left our meager belongings at the door of the second story apartment and went out to look for something to eat. We found a bakery with good looking frosted rolls in the window. We were pleased at the low price, but we soon learned the reason. They were hard and stale. In another window we found some red apples. We bought some, but we did not find them as tasty as we had expected. It was our first taste of tomatoes. We were learning fast.

My brother Ragnar obtained a job with a construction firm, and I with a small bakery which was a part of a grocery store operated by a family named Fisk. Mrs. Fisk was both a good cook and a good manager, and also operated a restaurant. I lived with them and shared a room with a husky Swede, a cement finisher, whom everyone called Starke Swan. The baker was a Danish fellow. Our hours were from 9:00 p.m. until noon the next day. We worked every night except Saturday. The pay was nine dollars a week.

After a few months I succeeded in obtaining a day job with Swift Packing Company, painting railroad stock cars that had been rebuilt. The pay was better, but we had to work out in the open in all kinds of weather. The crew of painters to which I belonged was made up of young fellows—all native Americans. The superintendent for the whole project was a second generation Swede. The boy who had acted as foreman for the painters' crew resigned. The superintendent wanted me to take his place. How could I who could not speak English even think of acting as a foreman? He said, "You do not have to speak. You just work and the boys will follow you."

Illness, however, prevented me from following through on this suggested experiment.

I became very ill with typhoid fever and spent many weeks in a hospital. This hospital, South Shore by name, was owned and operated by two young doctors. The care was excellent and the total cost for the doctor and the hospital was ten dollars a week. The year was 1913.

Our social life in Chicago centered mostly in a study group, a temperance organization called the Good Templars. This small group of young immigrants was very active. We tried to learn English by attending five-cent silent movies. Each Sunday afternoon we would meet to study Swedish literature. Often we were asked to review a book or recite a poem. My favorites were stories by Selma Lagerlöf and poems by Gustaf Fröding and Esais Tegnér, author and poets of my home province of Värmland.

One member of our study group was employed by the well-known Swedish weekly newspaper, *Gamla och Nya Hemlandet*, which at that time was edited by Anders Schön. The owner was C. S. Peterson of the Peterson Linotyping Company. He was born in Daglösen, Värmland, and active in civic affairs in Chicago. This young friend offered me a position with the paper as a subscription salesman. The job appealed to me. I was soon engaged in work that eventually was to take me over the United States and parts of Mexico. My first territory, however, was Chicago. At that time thousands of Swedish girls worked as domestics in apartments and houses located along Lake Michigan, all the way from Hyde Park on the south side to the suburbs north of Evanston. I found the work interesting, and I was successful in bringing in a good report each week.

My travels in Minnesota which followed were most interesting and rewarding. On Arlington Hills in St. Paul, I found Swedish people in almost every house. Most of the business men on Payne Avenue were of Swedish descent. Here I also met a neighbor boy from my home village in Sweden, named Uno Anderson, who had emigrated to the United States several years before I did.

My surprise came, however, when I visited Lindstrom and Center City, about fifty miles north of St. Paul. Here not only those of Swedish heritage, but also the Irish spoke Swedish.

The hardware store in Lindstrom was owned and operated by a man by the name of Lenz. He immediately became interested in subscribing to *Gamla och Nya Hemlandet.* Instead of paying cash, he proposed trading an article for a subscription. He said he had a goat in the backyard that he was willing to trade. He suggested we go out to look at the animal. It was an Angora with long, beautiful hair. When Mr. Lenz was called to the telephone, a farmer came along and asked what I was doing. I told him I was trying to catch the goat. "By the way," I said, "would you like to buy it?"

He did not know what to offer, but I asked him for $2.50. He bought the goat. When I returned to the store, Mr. Lenz asked, "Did you catch the goat?"

"No, I sold it," I said.

"You did what?" he said. Then he started to laugh and continued to do so for a long time. I soon discovered that others were laughing too. The next day as I was calling at various homes and introduced myself, people would smile and ask, "Are you the one who sold the goat?" I had no trouble in winning friends and selling subscriptions in Lindstrom.

My stay in smaller towns and communities would be of only a few hours duration. It was different in Duluth, which had a large Swedish population, mostly in the west end. Many were first generation immigrants. This was also the case in Superior, Wisconsin. I spent many weeks in these two cities. It was winter time with lots of snow and often bitterly cold.

During my stay in Duluth, I had the opportunity to meet and hear Olle i Skratthult, who also was a native of Värmland. He had an amateur group with him, some of whom were readers, others singers, musicians, and folk dancers. The best entertainer was Olle himself. Strange as it may seem, he did not even have to open his mouth to make his audience roar with laughter. Olle and his group always drew packed houses.

A letter dated January 14, 1914, from Mr. Skytte, business manager of *Hemlandet*, informed me that I had succeeded in adding about one thousand new subscribers in Duluth. He further wrote me that he wanted me to consider starting on a western trip as soon as I had completed my work in Superior. He also outlined changes scheduled for the paper on March 1. The size of

Hemlandet was to be increased from sixteen to twenty pages with one page printed in English. The paper had been published weekly at fifty cents a year. The price would be raised to one dollar per year. This change would mean more money for me. My commission would be fifty cents for each new subscription and thirty cents for each renewal.

It was springtime when I returned to Chicago the first week in April 1914. The weather was quite different from that which I had experienced in Minnesota and Wisconsin. I was happy to see my brothers again and also to welcome my sister, Hilma, who had left Sweden on October 2, 1913. I enjoyed my two-day visit with them before I began my westward journey which was to be an adventure lasting two-and-a-half years.

In preparing for the trip, I obtained from the *Hemlandet* office a list of subscribers living in a given territory. This list together with a ten-cent map from a Woolworth store would help me to become familiar with towns and places to visit.

My mode of travel was by train. If I had difficulty making myself understood, I would write my destination on a slip of paper and hand it to the ticket agent. Then came the problem with the conductor. If I misunderstood when he called the name of the next stop, I either got off too early or rode too far. There were times when I spent the night in a railroad station. At daybreak I would seek a place for breakfast and then as soon as possible look about for prospective subscribers.

Practically all the small hotels in rural America were operating on the so-called American Plan. The charge was two dollars a day for three meals and lodging. If I did not understand the menu or the waitress, I ordered ham and eggs. That I knew how to order; sometimes I had it three times a day.

My first stop in Nebraska was Omaha. Here I met people who were still talking about the tornado which had struck March 13, 1913, the previous year. A hundred persons were killed, and property damage was in the millions. *Hemlandet* subscribers related how the storm completely demolished their homes and that belongings were later found miles away.

The first and second generations of immigrants were numerous in Omaha. They were prominent in business and had built quite a few churches. Members of the Augustana Lutheran Church had established the Immanuel Deaconess Institute and Training School in 1901. This institution included a home for deaconesses, a hospital, a home for invalids, and a home for the aged. These immigrants of the Lutheran faith had also founded a school in Wahoo, Nebraska, called Luther Academy.

Since the state of Nebraska is rich in grass and grain, agriculture is its mainstay. Lincoln, the capital, is located in the heart of the farm belt. Swedish immigrants were found in many of the farm communities, such as Wahoo, Oakland, Osceola, Axtell, Minden, Holdrege, and even two Swedish named cities—Stromsburg and Gothenburg. The only means by which I could visit farmers was by a horse-drawn carriage. With livery stables available in most towns, one could hire a horse and carriage for two dollars a day. Many Swedish farmers were sometimes reluctant to pay cash for the price of a subscription. A chicken, on the other hand, was another story. So it was that I quite often found myself with a crate full of chickens, which I promptly traded at the local poultry store for cash. I was thus able to pay for the subscription cost, plus the cost of the horse as well as room and board for the day.

War had now broken out in Europe. I found people everywhere discussing it. In many farming communities sympathy was with Germany, but this attitude changed as war spread in Europe.

As I was ready to leave Nebraska for Colorado, I received the following letter from Charles S. Peterson, the owner and publisher of *Gamla och Nya Hemlandet:*

Chicago, Illinois
September 30, 1914

My dear Mr. Swenson:

It is with much regret that I notify you of the sale of *Hemlandet.* While the public seems to have appreciated our efforts to give them a good paper and while the subscription list was going up rapidly, I felt that unless I could give my whole time to the paper, it would be hard to run it, and therefore I reluctantly disposed of it.

In bidding you goodbye, I wish to express my appreciation of your services, and thank you for the hard and very successful work you have done for *Hemlandet.*

I have recommended you highly to Mr. F. A. Larson of *Svenska Amerikanaren* if you wish to continue in that line. I will be glad to speak to Mr. N. A. Nelson of the *Scandia Life*, if you want to try that.

With best wishes for your success, I am
Very truly yours,
C. S. Peterson

The sale of *Hemlandet* to *Svenska Amerikanaren* was a surprise to me. *Hemlandet* was started in Galesburg, Illinois, in 1855 by T. N. Hasselquist for the edification of Swedish immigrants of the Lutheran faith. After 1874 when the Augustana Synod began publishing *Augustana, Hemlandet* became more political. Thus after fifty-eight years as an independent paper, it was to continue to serve the immigrants in the merged paper, *Svenska Amerikanaren-Hemlandet. Svenska Amerikanaren* began publication in Chicago in 1866. With the merger, the combined circulation reached 70,000. It was now referred to as the largest Swedish weekly. It is interesting to note that 10,000 of the 70,000 subscribers lived in Sweden and were recipients of gift subscriptions from immigrant relatives.

The owner and publisher of the new paper, *Svenska Amerikanaren-Hemlandet* was F. A. Larson. The editor-in-chief was Oliver A. Linder, assisted by Frithiof Malmquist, Hedvig Westerberg, and the poet Jakob Bonggren.

Somehow I was sorry to see *Hemlandet* discontinued as an independent paper. I had become very much attached to it. However, the merger of two well-known papers should be a great help in my work as a subscription salesman.

Colorado, the land of the towering Rockies, was next on my schedule. Denver is the largest city and also the capital. It has a delightful climate with dry, invigorating air. Many tubercular persons from all parts of the United States came because of the climate. The Swedes had built an institution for the treatment of tuberculosis and named it the Swedish Sanitarium. The support came from Swedish organizations from all parts of the country. One day in a restaurant, I met two young men from Chicago whom I knew. They had come to Denver to enter the sanitarium for treatment, and were looking forward to their stay with confidence.

In seeking prospective subscribers for *Svenska Amerikanaren-*

Hemlandet in this state, I found them in many walks of life. The cities had offered the immigrants various kinds of work — the building trades, housework, business, and professions. The farms were also varied. Besides grain and cattle there were large sugar beet farms around Longmont, Loveland, and Greeley. Swedes were found in mining towns like Cripple Creek, Victor, and Leadville.

I spent Christmas, 1914, in the once fabulous Cripple Creek. Gold and silver mines were still operating there. This mining town was lively during the holidays. It was not in any way a Swedish Christmas celebration for me; yet I had a certain satisfaction in observing how life is and how festivals are celebrated in a mining community. It was my second Christmas away from relatives and friends.

The ride by train through the Rockies to Utah was both an adventure and one of scenic wonders. My destination was the state capital, Salt Lake City, which is also the Mormon world capital. The city has some very impressive buildings built by the Church of Jesus Christ of Latter Day Saints. In a beautiful setting stand the Mormon Temple and the Mormon Tabernacle.

I had little time for sight-seeing, but I did have the opportunity to see the state in my endeavor to look for prospective subscribers to *Svenska Amerikanaren-Hemlandet.* I traveled extensively for many weeks visiting towns, such as Ogden and Logan, as well as farm communities. I also visited many mining towns, the largest of which was Bingham Canyon. This town has the largest open-pit copper mine in the United States.

I was surprised to find so many Swedish immigrants, not all of them of the Mormon faith. In many communities, I found Lutheran and Mission Friend churches. All were very friendly and encouraging to this solicitor.

Idaho had about the same distribution of Swedish immigrants, as I visited a number of towns, such as Pocatello, Blackfoot, Idaho Falls, and Boise, the capital. Spring had come early as I arrived in Portland.

Portland is the largest city in Oregon, located one hundred miles inland on the Willamette River near its junction with the Columbia River. It is one of the major ports on the west coast. It is also a beautiful city, known as the "City of Roses." A rose festival is held in early June each year.

I was barely settled when I became ill and felt I needed medical attention. Being a stranger in the city, I did not know a doctor. I had, however, obtained a copy of *Oregon Posten,* a local Swedish paper. Through it I learned of a doctor, named Swenson. The hotel clerk contacted him, and he responded promptly. He diagnosed my illness as pneumonia and took me to the Emanuel Hospital immediately. This hospital, located on the west side, had been founded three years earlier in 1912. A large old residence served as the hospital. Years later a new hospital complex was erected on the east side of the river. This eventually became the largest hospital in the Augustana Lutheran Church. It was interesting to me to be in this new hospital in 1941 as a member of the *Lutheran Companion* tour. This time, as a guest of the hospital, I had the pleasure of meeting the nurse who, as a student nurse, was assigned to care for me when I was a patient in the first hospital unit in 1915. She was now a prominent staff member in charge of the pediatric department. I have always gratefully remembered the kindness shown me by the doctor and the hospital staff.

It has been estimated that about 100,000 Swedish immigrants settled in Oregon and Washington. Many settled in cities, others became lumberjacks. I enjoyed meeting these first generation immigrants in Portland as I resumed my solicitation work after my illness. I observed that they were thrifty, hardworking people, and were prospering in their newly found land. I also visited places where these Swedish immigrants were clearing the forest and building homes in such places as Vennersborg, Washington, and Carlton, Oregon. It was a slow process for them as they had so few tools. Often when they had cut the timber, burned the underbrush and branches, they had to leave the stumps and try to cultivate around them. Eventually they had a clear field where they raised vegetables and grain. As I wandered about, I often had to ask for overnight lodging. Here among the Swedish settlers, I was kindly treated and given a place to sleep, sometimes in a loft.

There were also many new communities along the Columbia River, such as St. Helen's, Kalama, and Svensen, which, judging from the spelling, was named for a Dane or a Norwegian. The town of Svensen was located about a mile from the Columbia River. I still remember my visit to this town. When I was walking from the boat landing to the town, I unexpectedly found a bear in the middle of the road. Both of us stood a minute or two facing each other. Then to my relief, the bear climbed a tree.

Astoria is a seaport at the mouth of the Columbia River. It was established as a trading post by the John Jacob Astor Fur Company. Now it is an important port and also the home port of a salmon fishing fleet. I found many Swedish immigrants engaged in fishing.

As *Svenska Amerikanaren-Hemlandet* had a subscription salesman who was covering the state of Washington, I was asked to work toward California. I boarded an ocean steamer in Portland and sailed down the Columbia River bound for San Francisco. There were, however, a number of coastal towns that I wanted to visit. My first stop was Coos Bay-North Bend on the Pacific Ocean. These places had large sawmills where a number of Swedish people were employed. These were isolated communities where I found good friendly prospects.

As I boarded an ocean steamer again, I was eagerly looking forward to my next stop, the coastal town of Eureka in northern California. My mother had a brother, Gustav, who had immigrated to this area in 1888 but had not been heard from for some time. I remembered having seen a picture of three men lying end to end in a cut of a giant redwood tree, my uncle having been one of them. Evidently, he had started out as a lumberjack.

As I had no knowledge of my uncle's whereabouts, I began to ask all the Swedes I met, "Do you know a man, named Andrew Gustav Spetz?" I soon found a lead. A housewife told me that her young mail carrier's name was John Spetz. I gave her the name of the hotel where I was staying and asked her to have him contact me there. In the evening when I returned to the hotel, I found a young man named John Spetz waiting for me. It was a pleasant meeting for both of us. I learned from him that his parents lived in Arcata, a town twelve miles north. The following Saturday afternoon I went with John to visit his home. I found that my Uncle Gustav and his wife, Marie, had a large family—three sons and seven daughters. The meeting was a surprise for all of us. I stayed with them for four days. Often during those days, I reminisced with my uncle and aunt about Sweden. My mother was very happy to learn that I had met her brother and his family. Since those days, I have kept in close touch with these relatives, corresponding with several of them.

In 1954 after attending a church convention in Los Angeles, my wife, Lyal, and I drove north to call on all members of my uncle Gustav Spetz's family, some of whom were living in the bay area of San Francisco, others in their home town, Arcata. Phil Spetz and his wife, Frances, are still living in the parental home on Buttermilk Lane. Only John ever visited Sweden.

My next journey on the coastal steamer took me to San Francisco. I had read and heard much about the disastrous earthquake and fire of April 18, 1906, which almost completely destroyed the city. An estimated seven hundred persons lost their lives. Now, in 1915, the city had been rebuilt. It was celebrating the opening of the Panama Canal with the Panama-Pacific Exposition. The city also had many other points of interest for the thousands of visitors who came to the exposition — the famous Mission Dolores, Golden Gate Park, the unique cable car system, Fisherman's Wharf, and Chinatown with its Oriental architecture, tea rooms, and temples.

The exposition grounds were located at the Presidio, near Golden Gate Park. It was my first experience to visit an exposition of world-wide interest. I was proud to find that Sweden was participating. The Swedish building was impressive as well as the various exhibits in it. The Swedish people on the west coast were all celebrating in various ways. I well remember San Francisco Swedish Day held June 24, 1915. The Swedish Singing Society on the Pacific coast as well as other groups participated. It was a most successful event.

A large number of Swedish immigrants had settled in San Francisco as well as in the neighboring cities of Oakland, Berkeley, Richmond, and Alameda. I spent several weeks calling on prospective subscribers to *Svenska Amerikanaren-Hemlandet*. In the settlement around Ebenezer Lutheran Church, there were many Swedish business establishments. *Vestkusten* was published here by the editor and owner, Alexander Olson. Wherever I went, I found the people most friendly and cooperative. I grew very fond of San Francisco and its suburbs. The time came, however, for me to depart as there were many other Swedish communities in California I hoped to visit.

As I traveled south, I visited a number of towns, such as Modesto, Turlock, Fresno, and Kingsburg. Most of these towns were surrounded by fruit farms. A large number of Swedish immigrants were fruit growers, specializing in grapes, figs, lemons, grapefruit, oranges, apricots, peaches, and melons. These fruit farms were not large, but they looked prosperous. These fruit growers had comfortable homes, some even having automobiles, which were not too common in 1915. Many of them supported churches, such as the Augustana Lutheran Church, the Mission Covenant Church, the Swedish Baptist Church, and the Swedish Methodist Church—all bilingual. The first generation immigrants commonly used Swedish; therefore, good prospects as subscribers.

The cities on the Pacific coast that I had visited thus far, such as Portland and San Francisco, were not large, neither was Los Angeles. They were, however, destined to become great cities on the west coast. In each of these cities, I found a new mode of transportation. Anyone owning an automobile could operate his car as a taxi. These cars were called jitneys with a fare of five cents. Many car owners would operate their jitneys in the evenings or after work. For me these jitneys provided a good and reasonable way of getting about.

The Swedish people were fairly well distributed over Los Angeles as well as suburban towns, such as Pasadena, Long Beach and others. These immigrants were employed in various trades, in business, and in professions. They found their social life in churches and lodges. I became acquainted with the Good Templars, a lodge which had a study group similar to the one I had attended in Chicago.

The Swedes had also found their way to San Diego, located on the very southern tip of the state of California. I traveled from Los Angeles to San Diego in a jitney. We had tire trouble three times. After the inner tube had been repaired, I had to help pump air into the tire. In San Diego I found the Panama-California International Exposition of 1915 in full progress. During a few days there, I was able to call upon many Swedish people and introduce them to *Svenska Amerikanaren-Hemlandet.* I also had time for some sight-seeing. Besides visiting the exposition, I traveled to places like Point Loma and Coronado Island. As San Diego is close to Mexico, I visited the border town of Tijuana, where I first saw a bullfight.

As I headed east, I was to enter Arizona, which had become a state in 1912. It has a variety of climates, the southern area, preferred by Swedish immigrants, being warm and dry. I found quite a number of Swedish people in Phoenix, Tucson, Douglas, and Bisbee.

Bisbee, a mining town, is where I spent my fourth American Christmas. The place was crowded with an influx of visitors for the holiday. The small hotel was filled; I had only a cot in a hallway. This was nothing unusual as I often had to accept accommodations that were less than comfortable. I saw no Christmas trees nor any other Christmas decorations; however, Bisbee had a festivity of a kind. A community turkey dinner was served at the school. A special event for the youngsters was a race similar to a soap box derby. It was the first contest of that kind I had seen. Parents were cheering their youngsters, and all present were most enthusiastic. Prizes were given to the winners. Besides Swedish immigrants in Bisbee, there were a number of Swedish-speaking Finns, who also could be interested in *Svenska Amerikanaren-Hemlandet.*

My experiences in Douglas were rather unusual. The town is located on the Mexican border with Aqua Prieta, Mexico, on the other side. After I had made contact with all possible prospects, I decided to explore the other side of the border. I asked a U.S. border guard whether I was permitted to visit Aqua Prieta. His reply was, "Yes, you are, but at your own risk." I soon discovered that the town was occupied by soldiers under the leadership of Francisco "Pancho" Villa, a revolutionary leader. As I walked up and down the streets, I saw not only soldiers but also women and children. I learned that when a Mexican soldier goes into service, he regularly takes his family with him. The wife prepares the food and cares for the children. These soldiers and their families were not permanent residents. People of the town lived in adobe huts; the soldiers and their families lived in temporary quarters such as tents and box cars. I saw a military train arrive with soldiers and their families not only in box cars but on top of them as well. I obtained a picture of a loaded box car, which was reproduced in *Svenska Amerikanaren-Hemlandet.* After a couple of very interesting hours of wandering about, I returned to the United States side. No one interfered with my visit. Afterward when I related my experience, the people seemed to be of one mind, namely, that they wished that Theodore Roosevelt would be our next president. Only then would Mexico be quiet.

Heading east again, I reached El Paso, a city in Texas on the Rio Grande River across from Juarez, Mexico. Here before any solicitation work, I had to find a tailor as my trousers needed mending. A Swedish fellow was operating a tailor shop on the first floor of a hotel. He invited me to sit on the table on which he was mending my trousers. Then when I heard the noise of someone at the door, I quickly stepped down from the table and grabbed a copy of *Svenska Amerikanaren-Hemlandet* as a substitute for my pants. I was properly covered when a somewhat surprised female entered. The tailor was helpful in giving me a start to find prospects. I was surprised to find so many Swedish immigrants in this southern border city. I was also pleased the way they readily conversed with me in Swedish. They appreciated the opportunity to subscribe to *Svenska Amerikanaren-Hemlandet.* Several advised me to cross the border to see the points of interest in Juarez. I found quite a considerable difference between the two cities. Late in the evening of the second day, I boarded a train for the long journey to Austin, Texas. I was accustomed to coach travel and had no trouble sleeping in a coach chair.

Arriving in Austin, the capital of Texas, I was told that I was in the heart of Texas, the largest state in the Union. It had a rich and varied heritage, having flown the flags of six nations; namely, Spain, France, Mexico, the Republic of Texas, the Confederate States of America, and the United States of America.

One of the first persons I met in Austin was Rev. Gideon Olson, pastor of Gethsemane Lutheran Church. I called on him one evening and learned that he was conducting a class in English for newcomers, Swedish young people. After the class in his study, he kindly gave me some information about the city and where to find prospects. He also suggested that I see a business man, Carl T. Widén, who could speak Swedish fluently though he was born in Iowa. I found him a very congenial fellow and very knowledgeable about Swedish immigration in Texas.

Texas at this time had about 5,000 Swedish immigrants, most of whom seemed to have settled in and around Austin, although there were large numbers in Williamson and Travis counties. In Travis County one village was named New Sweden and another Lund. Other settlements in these counties were Palm Valley, Round Rock, Manor, Elgin, Taylor, Georgetown, and Hutto. All the farmers were cotton growers. It was a pleasant surprise to hear even the second generation speak Swedish, as well as some of the Negroes. Some of the blacks had taken Swedish names, one having the name of Larson.

Mr. Widén also informed me that the first immigrant to settle in Texas was Swante Magnus Swenson from Barkeryd Parish in the province of Småland, who had arrived in 1838. He became a large landowner and brought many relatives and friends over to Texas. After the Civil War, he settled in New York as a banker. In Texas his sons and agents turned many of his cotton plantations into cattle ranches. Swenson also brought over an uncle, Swante Palm, in 1844, who was considered to be one of the best educated immigrants among the Swedes.

The Swedish immigrants promoted education through their own institutions. The Swedish Methodists owned and operated Texas Wesleyan College in Austin, and the Swedish Lutherans had a similar school, Trinity College, at Round Rock. There was also a Swedish newspaper published in Austin, *Texas Posten,* which paper is still being published in 1978.

Galveston is a seaport on the northwestern tip of Galveston Island at the entrance to the Galveston Bay, an inlet of the Gulf of Mexico in southeastern Texas. Here a few Swedish immigrants had settled, some as sailors and others as fishermen. They seemed to enjoy their island town, but they were still interested in their homeland and were eager to know about the paper I represented.

My next stop was Houston, located on the Houston ship channel fifty miles from the Gulf of Mexico. Although the city was not large at the time of my visit in 1916, it was destined to become the largest inland port in the country and the largest city in the South. Since Swedish immigrants were not numerous here, I found few subscribers. As I often did, I went to the telephone book to seek the names of Swedish people. Setting out to call on these people, I came to the address of an Amanda Nelson. When I rang the doorbell, it was answered by a large black woman. I told her I was seeking a person named Amanda Nelson. She said, "I am Amanda Nelson."

There was no sale. Evidently some blacks who had worked for Swedish people had become so attached to the family that they adopted the family name.

There were cotton and rice farmers in the countryside around El Campo and Lyford, which I visited. Then I proceeded north to Dallas and Fort Worth. These cities, too, were not large in 1916, nor were there many Swedish immigrants in them. I continued to Oklahoma City. Here there was a Swedish community, small but very active. There was an Augustana Lutheran Church. These immigrants had good homes and seemed prosperous. The Swedish language was in general use. The largest business establishment was the Aurelius-Swanson Lumber Company. The Aurelius brothers were very helpful to me. As a result, I succeeded in adding a few more names to the subscription list.

As I moved north into Kansas, I learned that a large number of Swedish people had settled there, especially in the Smoky Valley in the central part of the state. In traveling about, I found places named Smolan, Falun, and New Gottland (meaning "a new good land"). I was told at the time of my visit in 1916 that ever since the spring of 1869 when Dr. Olof Olsson set out from Värmland with a large group of men, women, and children and settled in Lindsborg, people from that province were still in the majority. Shortly after his arrival, Dr. Olsson organized Bethany Lutheran Church. In 1879, Dr. Carl Aaron Swensson came to Lindsborg as pastor of this church. Two years later he organized Bethany College. I remember how impressed I was to see Dr. Swensson's statue in front of the main building.

I soon had the pleasure of meeting the president of the college, Dr. Ernest F. Pihlblad, whom I learned to know and admire through the years. Another man that I well remember was Birger Sandzén, the artist. He was born in Sweden and had studied under Anders Zorn. I called on him at his studio and was pleased to receive his order for a subscription to *Svenska Amerikanaren-Hemlandet*. When I handed the artist a receipt with my signature, he looked at it and said, "Birger. Your name is Birger." Then he turned to a number of lithographs and woodcut prints on display. Pointing to them, he said, "It is not often I meet someone by the name of Birger. I would like to give you one of these prints." I selected a woodcut print entitled, "Sunrise on the Smoky River." I still have it and treasure it. Years later I was able to purchase one of his oil paintings of the Smoky River.

Lindsborg was not a large town, but the majority of the population was Swedish. All were very friendly whether I met them in homes, business, or on the street. I remember how a number of business men would meet at a downtown bakery for afternoon coffee. Lindsborg was a good town for this solicitor.

The larger town of Salina, twenty miles from Lindsborg, had many Swedish immigrants. While I was there, I stayed at a boarding house operated by a Swedish family. Among the boarders were two young women who had recently arrived from Sweden. Having learned the trade of cigar making in Sweden, they had set up a small tobacco store. There they manufactured cigars by hand. At the time of my visit, a local election was scheduled. I was amused to observe candidates coming into the cigar store to obtain a supply of cigars for distribution to prospective voters in the town and the countryside. These young women had a flourishing business. I, too, was lucky. My time spent in the store meeting people resulted in winning many subscribers.

The Swedish population in Kansas was quite large, and immigrants were found in many settlements. Among those I visited were Scandia, Mariedahl, and Manhattan. A greater number of citizens of Swedish origin was found in larger cities like Topeka, Kansas City, Kansas, and Kansas City, Missouri. The immigrants from Sweden contributed much to the development of these cities.

A letter from the home office awaited me in Kansas City. Fred Bolling, the office manager, informed me that F. A. Larson, the owner of *Svenska Amerikanaren,* had bought the Swedish paper published in Kansas City, Missouri. This situation meant that the entire subscription list of the local paper had been transferred to the list of *Svenska Amerikanaren;* therefore there was no need for me to stay on there. Even though my visit was short, I had time to meet many immigrants and observe that Swedes in these two cities were doing very well. There were a couple of large building firms with Swedish names. There were first and second generation Swedes among the doctors and lawyers. I remember with gratitude a young lawyer who assisted me in cashing a check from the home office.

St. Louis, located near the junction of the Mississippi and

Missouri Rivers, is the largest city in Missouri. It was midsummer when I arrived. I attended two festivities, one sponsored by lodges and one by churches. Neither of these groups was large, but active. I spent several days visiting homes and offices. Here, too, Swedish immigrants were well established.

As I entered Illinois, I was on the home stretch after more than a two-year journey through the western and southern states. Illinois had many well-known Swedish settlements. One was at Paxton. The town was new to me but not the name. I had heard Augustana pastors speak of Paxton as the home of Augustana College and Theological Seminary from 1863 to 1875. The old-timers I met would tell me how the Illinois Railroad had persuaded the churches to help build a Swedish settlement around Paxton and to bring Augustana College and Theological Seminary from Chicago. Although the college remained there only a few years, the settlement survived. I found many faithful Augustana people as well as members of other churches of Scandinavian background living there.

When I returned to Chicago, I was happy to welcome my twin sister, Signe Maria, who had left Sweden on May 22, 1915. I was also glad to see my sister, Hilma, and brothers, Robert and Ragnar. Five of the Swensson children, or half of our family, had now emigrated to America and had chosen Chicago as their home. During my two-week visit, we often managed to meet and reminisce about our home and family in Sweden. We had a group picture taken to send to our parents. We discussed future plans. My two sisters were employed as housekeepers. My oldest brother, Robert, was a carpenter, and Ragnar was a brick layer. I told them I had enjoyed my work as a subscription salesman and that my years of travel had been not only adventurous, but also most educational. I felt, however, that if I were to continue in sales work I should have additional formal education. Perhaps a couple of years would suffice. During my travels I had met a number of Augustana graduates who had encouraged me to enter Augustana College at Rock Island, Illinois. Since courses were offered for beginners in a preparatory department of the academy, I was able to enroll at Augustana. I had written to Dr. Gustav Andreen, the president, a letter in Swedish which he answered in Swedish and bade me welcome to Augustana.

II

FROM CAMPUS TO WAR CAMPS

On a Sunday afternoon in September 1916, I boarded an evening train for Rock Island, Illinois, to enroll at Augustana College. Upon my arrival, I found a small hotel across the street from the station where I obtained lodging for the night. The next morning I walked the four blocks to the Augustana campus. I was very much impressed with the buildings on the hillside, especially the Denkmann Library and Old Main with its dome. As a stranger, I had to ask my way about. The only name that was familiar was that of Dr. Gustav Andreen. I called upon him and found him most friendly. He welcomed me to Augustana and directed me to the office of Dr. A. W. Kjellstrand, the principal of the preparatory department as well as the academy.

Dr. Kjellstrand was a genial gentleman whom the older students called "Kelley." As he was conferring with me concerning my schedule, Professor Jules G. Mauritzson, dean of Augustana College, came into the office. Dr. Kjellstrand introduced me and asked his advice as to what subjects would be best for me. Without hesitation, he said, "Give him Latin." As the years went by, Latin became a favorite subject. I had five years of Latin in the academy and the college. For the first term, my schedule included preparatory English, first-year academy English, Latin, mathematics, Christianity, and physical culture. Next I called at the business office and was assigned a room on the second floor of the west wing of the men's dormitory which I was to share with another student, Enoch Sandeen, who had come from northern Sweden. He was now a student in the theological seminary. My tuition for the fall term was $35.00, and meals served in the college dining hall were $2.50 per week.

After I had lunch, I joined a group of boys sitting on the lawn east of Old Main, most of whom were younger than I. I met Conrad Bergendoff, who was my age, 21. He had graduated from Augustana College the previous year, and the past year had earned a master's degree at the University of Pennsylvania. Now he was back at Augustana to teach. I, on the other hand, had just arrived to begin my education at Augustana. During those first days as I took walks by myself, I wondered if I had made the right decision by coming to Augustana. Life as a salesman on the road had appealed to me. Having no definite schedule, I had been on my own. Here at Augustana, I had to get used to classroom schedules, adapt to study habits, and find work to meet living expenses. Although I knew there would be other adjustments to make, I was determined to get an education.

My introduction to the classroom was a mathematics class at 8:00 a.m. the next day, taught by the assistant dean, P. W. Benzon. A twenty-minute chapel service followed at 9:00 a.m. During the service the students were informed that they were to go to chapel each day as well as attend a church service of their choice each Sunday. On Monday morning each student was expected to fill out and sign a report giving the name of the church in which he or she had worshipped on Sunday.

The teacher in the preparatory English class was a red-haired girl from Moline who was a college senior. Nearly all the members of the class had had grade school experience in the United States and, therefore, had some knowledge of American history. Each student was asked to read a sentence or two from a reader. I was asked to read these words: "The Yankees were chasing the redcoats down the lane." The teacher asked, "Mr. Swenson can you tell us who those 'redcoats' were?"

I replied, "I don't know. Maybe they were some kind of birds." The class roared with laughter.

Dr. A. R. Wallin was my Latin teacher. He was a good

instructor. The Christianity teacher was Professor Sven J. Sebelius, a most sympathetic and understanding fellow. The principal of the academy, Professor A. W. Kjellstrand, taught first-year academy English. He, too, was a very patient teacher. All students were required to take gymnastics twice a week.

After a few weeks, I found that I had no trouble keeping up with other students in various subjects except English. I had difficulty with grammar, but Latin was a great help to me.

My early knowledge of Augustana College, gained from graduates I had met in my travels, was that the school was located in Rock Island, 180 miles west of Chicago on the Mississippi River. After several weeks I learned that the community included three well-known cities—Rock Island and Moline, Illinois, and Davenport, Iowa. As I moved about in them, I found that they were physically very closely connected, forming, in fact, one large urban area. As a stranger going from Rock Island to Moline, I would not at first perceive at what point I left one city for the other. Forty-sixth Street in Rock Island was also First Street in Moline. Rock Island and Davenport, though on opposite sides of the river, were bound together by a streetcar line, several railway lines, ferry boats, and two bridges.

The tri-city area, in 1916, was a large manufacturing and distributing center with a population of 130,000 people. Many immigrants had settled here—Germans in Davenport, Swedes and Belgians in Moline. There were also German and Swedish immigrants in Rock Island. Rock Island had a national reputation because of its Arsenal, government works, and its railway system, the Rock Island Lines. Moline was known for its famous John Deere plows and numerous other agricultural implements. Davenport was rated as one of the most important trade centers of the Midwest.

Augustana College had a most favorable location, about halfway between Rock Island and Moline. It was accessible both by rail and water. The college drew students from the three cities, all of the United States, and parts of Europe. The church leaders did well, I thought, in choosing Rock Island as the home of Augustana College and Theological Seminary.

As a new student on the campus, I gradually learned about the various extra-curricular activities. Besides the musical organizations, such as the Wennerberg Male Chorus, the Oriole Club for women students, the Augustana Orchestra, and the Augustana Band, there were three English and four Swedish literary societies. I joined Iduna, which was for students in the academy. The aims of the society were to study Swedish literature and culture and to foster among its members an active interest in these areas. The faculty adviser was Professor Jules Mauritzson, head of the Swedish department. I was elected secretary at the first meeting. We met each Friday afternoon.

There were also a number of Bible societies and debating clubs which met weekly. I joined the Lincoln Debating Club. Practice in debating and rebuttal gave us valuable lessons in the ability to express ourselves before a group.

The Augustana Lyceum Association was an important student institution. This association promoted two student enterprises of the college—the *Augustana Observer,* the school paper published once a month, and the Augustana Lyceum course, which all students and faculty members were expected to support. Its primary purpose was educational. During the school year, this organization brought lecturers, musicians, readers, interpreters, and entertainers to the college.

Class work and study and extra-curricular activities made time pass very quickly. I spent Saturdays in Moline and Rock Island, soliciting subscriptions to *Svenska Amerikanaren-Hemlandet.* I also ordered a number of Swedish Christmas annuals which proved to be good sales items. Among them were *Julstämning* and *Jultomten.*

I was looking forward to Christmas vacation. My sisters, brothers, and I had been invited to celebrate Christmas Eve at the home of our cousin, Adolph Swenson, and his wife, Anna, in Chicago. On the first Christmas in America for my brother, Ragnar, and me, in 1912, we had been together with our brother, Robert, at the home of another cousin, Anna, and her husband, Carl Erickson. In 1913, 1914, and 1915, I had observed Christmas wherever I happened to be during my travels. Now in the year 1916, we had the pleasure of celebrating our first Christmas together. It was a real Swedish *Julafton* (Christmas Eve). We had *doppa i gryttan* (dip in the pot), *potatis korv* (potato sausage), *kalv sylta* (jellied veal), *lutfisk* (stock fish), *bruna böner* (brown beans), *risgrynsgröt* (rice porridge), and *glögg* (Christmas brandy).

My brother, Ragnar, was still active in Good Templars; so he would not touch the *glögg.* He was told that it was permissible to eat some of the fruit that had been cooked in the preparation of the *glögg,* especially the raisins. He found them very tasty. He did not realize they were potent. After a while he began to sing *Gubben Noak* (Old Man Noah) and other Swedish ditties to the amusement of all. Although we celebrated late, we arose at 4:00 a.m. to attend *Julotta* (early Christmas morning service). For me it was a Christmas long remembered.

During my short stay in Chicago, I spent a day at the office of *Svenska Amerikanaren-Hemlandet.* I had some details to discuss with the office manager, Fred Bolling. Then I had a good visit with the editors. The editor-in-chief, Oliver A. Linder, was always friendly and eager to know what I could report regarding the attitude of subscribers toward his paper. He invited me to be his guest for lunch. He took me to a restaurant for *ärtsoppa med fläsk* (yellow pea soup with pork) and *fläskpannkaka* (pancake with pork). It was a very enjoyable luncheon hour.

I spent the remainder of the Christmas vacation in Rockford soliciting subscriptions to *Svenska Amerikanaren-Hemlandet.* Since many Augustana students had their homes in Rockford, I had the pleasure of visiting a number of them.

Back at Augustana, we soon settled down with studies and other activities. I was fortunate in obtaining work in the college dining room during the spring term. The wage was three meals a day. If we worked more than three hours, we were paid fifteen cents per hour.

Early in the spring term of 1917, Augustana won the Little Nineteen basketball championship. The tournament was held in the new gymnasium of the college. The students attended almost one hundred percent, grateful for the new building and proud of the team. The Illinois Intercollegiate Athletic Association was composed of all leading colleges in Illinois; therefore, Augustana could claim to be champion of the colleges of the state. Arthur Swedberg was placed on the all-state team as center, and "Cub" Lundberg as forward.

The 1917 spring term also brought World War I closer to Augustana College. The United States had entered the war on the side of the Triple Entente. The male students at Augustana were immediately ready to answer the call to military service. The Augustana men who enlisted, including those who were members of the college band, were mustered into service at Springfield, Illinois, on April 17, 1917. They then became members of the Sixth Illinois Infantry. Upon arrival at Camp Logan, Texas, on September 12, 1917, their regiment was transferred into the 123rd U. S. Field Artillery. They remained at Camp Logan in training until May 1918, when they embarked from Hoboken, New Jersey, for France.

The few men who remained at Augustana entered various branches of military service later. Before the end of the war, a Student Army Training Corps was established on the Augustana campus.

The Augustana Synod had its annual national convention at Augustana College and Theological Seminary in June 1917, at the close of the school year. The theme was the quadri-centennial of the Reformation. A dozen or more students were asked to help in the convention in various ways. We were housed on the top floor of the west end of Old Main. Army cots had been rented from the Arsenal, which were used not only by the students but also by many visitors. Dr. Julius Lincoln, pastor of First Lutheran Church, Jamestown, New York, brought his church band with him. These young musicians were housed in a lecture room in Old Main.

I had very little knowledge of the Augustana Synod. I learned at this meeting that the president of the synod was L. A. Johnston. Likewise I knew very few pastors and laymen, but I did enjoy attending the business sessions and listening to discussions. One of the questions to be resolved was whether or not football was to be permitted at Augustana. When a speaker expressed himself in favor of football, we in the gallery voiced our approval. At that point, the chairman used the gavel and warned us that there be no more demonstration if we wanted to remain in the meeting. To our delight football was allowed at Augustana. The program relative to the quadri-centennial offered appropriate music and challenging speeches. As a student I was very much impressed.

I had been asked by Fred Bolling of our Chicago office to visit Swedish communities in Iowa and western Minnesota during the summer months in the interest of *Svenska Amerikanaren-Hemlandet.*

I had finished my work in Sioux City, Iowa, and had moved north to Worthington, Minnesota, where mail awaited me. One of the items was a Notice of Call for military service, and to appear for a physical examination on August 9, 1917, at 4:00 p.m. Since I was already a week late when this notice reached me, I immediately returned to Rock Island and contacted Dr. Gustav Andreen. He offered to go with me to the local board. I informed the board of the reason for my tardiness and asked for permission to be given a physical examination at once as I wanted to go back to work to earn my living. The board members were reluctant, but through the influence of Dr. Andreen they consented. I passed the examination but was not called into active duty until the following April.

When I returned to Augustana College in the fall of 1917, everyone was rejoicing because football was again allowed. To form a team was another matter as so many students had entered military service. We were soon fully occupied with classwork and extracurricular activities as well as football.

Early Saturday morning, December 22, 1917, when I reported to work at the college dining room, I was called to the telephone. I was asked, "Are you Birger Swenson?"

"Yes," I answered.

"Do you have a brother, Robert?" I was asked.

"Yes," I replied.

"He was killed last night. I am Mr. Knox of the Knox Mortuary. I would like to have you come over to identify the body." To my sorrow, I found that it was indeed my older brother, Robert, born June 7, 1886, who had immigrated to the United States in 1911.

Robert had been employed for two months by Stone and Webster's construction firm which was erecting new buildings on the Rock Island Arsenal. He had not worked on Friday, December 21, but had taken a day off to fill out papers for military service at the Rock Island County registration office. When he was ready to return home to Moline after dark, he boarded by mistake a streetcar for Milan instead of for Moline. When he reached Milan and did not recognize the surroundings, he started to walk back following the track of the Rock Island Southern Railway. He reached the bridge over Mill Creek, where an electric locomotive overtook and killed him.

After consultation with my two sisters in Chicago and my

brother, Ragnar, then in service at Camp Grant, we decided to have the funeral and burial in Chicago. The service was held on Christmas Eve at a mortuary in Englewood, with Dr. A. T. Fors, pastor of Bethel Lutheran Church, officiating. A beautiful message of condolence from the student body of Augustana was read at the service. It was a sad Christmas Eve for all of us, but the warmth and kindness of cousin Adolph and his wife, Anna, at whose home we were guests, helped us in our sorrow.

I returned to Augustana after the Christmas holidays to begin the spring term, 1918, still waiting to be called into service. It was difficult to concentrate on study after my brother's death and the uncertainty of my future. After I had waited more than seven months since taking my physical examination in August 1917, word finally came for my induction. The order read as follows:

Order of Induction into Military Service
of the United States
The President of the United States
to Birger Swenson
Order Number 449   Serial Number 1022

Greeting: Having submitted yourself to a local board composed of your neighbors for the purpose of determining the place and time in which you can best serve the United States in the present emergency, you are hereby notified that you have now been selected for immediate military service.

You will, therefore, report to the local board named below at Room 400, Peoples National Bank Building, at 4:00 p.m. on the 3rd day of April, 1918, for military duty.

From and after the day and hour just named, you will be a soldier in military service of the United States.

B. D. Connelly
Member of Local Board for Division No. 1

Report to Local Board for Division No. 1 for the County of
Rock Island, State of Illinois
Rock Island, Illinois

Date—March 29, 1918

I was happy and grateful at the receipt of the call to military service. It was a relief after months of waiting, uncertainty, confusion, and oftentimes difficulty in studying. Whenever and wherever a group of young men gathered on the campus, they invariably turned to the subject of the Navy or the Army.

After the call, I knew what awaited me. It did not take me long to prepare for departure. My brother, Ragnar, was already in military service. My sisters, Hilma and Signe, were in Chicago. I bade them farewell by phone on April 3, 1918, the day of my departure.

Before I left, I wanted to call on Dr. John Ekholm, pastor of Zion Lutheran Church, of which I was a member. I had often been a guest in the parsonage. On this my last day I was happy to be a luncheon guest in the home of Dr. and Mrs. Gustav Andreen. Their son, Gustav, Jr., also present, was my classmate in the Augustana Academy. I appreciated greatly the kindness of the Andreens.

Late in the afternoon, several hundred men who were to leave for camp had assembled at the old Milwaukee Railroad station, which was located at the present site of the new Modern Woodmen building. Also in this group of inductees was a fellow Augustana student, Oscar Bohman. Classmates and friends on the Augustana campus had come to see us off. After a last goodbye to the many relatives and friends, the train began rolling westward to its destination, Fort Rosecrans, San Diego, California.

As our train ride to the west coast took several days, we had time to observe the farm lands of Iowa, Kansas, Oklahoma, and Texas, the irrigated farms and ranches of New Mexico and Arizona, and the fruit farms of California. At one or two stations, we left the train for meals. We were also given calisthenics to limber up. I remember a stop between Los Angeles and San Diego when the boys left the train to help themselves to oranges. The owner who came to greet the men had no objection.

There was time to think. I was soon to be back in California where I had spent considerable time a year and a half earlier. Now I came as a U. S. soldier. It was an adventure that I had not anticipated. I had left Sweden too young for military service. I had not expected it here, but when the call came, I was willing and ready to go. I could have claimed exemption as I was not a U. S. citizen, but I was looking forward to the day when I could be naturalized.

We were informed that the two train sections which left Rock Island had a contingent of six hundred men. They had come from Rock Island, Hancock, and McDonough counties in Illinois. Upon arrival at Fort Rosecrans, which was the coast defense of San Diego, we were taken to a new camp built on a high ridge overlooking the Pacific Ocean. Each tent was to house a squad of eight men. We were immediately given intensive training. According to the fort commander, Colonel J. R. Pourie, we had attained "a remarkable degree of excellence" in the fundamentals in less than eight weeks. Most of us were assigned to a new overseas organization, designated as the 54th Ammunition Train.

By June 10, 1918, the 54th Ammunition Train had begun to function as a unit. There were four companies—A, B, C, D—and the Headquarters Detachment. The numerical strength of the train was 146 men in each company and a Headquarters Detachment of thirty men. Each company had one captain, one first and one second lieutenant. The Headquarters Detachment had a captain acting as a major, another captain as an adjutant, and a first lieutenant as a supply officer. Such was the 54th Ammunition Train, Coast Artillery Corps.

Although training and guard duty took most of our time, we did have an opportunity to visit San Diego, where organizations such as the Salvation Army, the Y.M.C.A., and the Red Cross had facilities for serving the men. One Sunday I asked a fellow in our company, Herman Lindbloom, of Ophiem, Illinois, to go with me to attend a service at the Augustana Lutheran Church in San Diego. I was pleased to meet the pastor, Rev. Arthur Johnson, whom I knew from Augustana College. At the church we became acquainted with a number of young people. Besides attending services whenever we could, we were invited into homes and also to picnics and beach parties.

One day we were ordered to go to the base parade grounds in full uniform, including an ammunition belt and gun. We were seventy-one in number, largely Swedish and Belgian immigrants and all of us non-citizens. We were told by a representative of the Superior Court of California that we now had qualified to be admitted as U.S. citizens. I had applied to become a citizen of the United States on April 3, 1914. Now while serving in the U. S. Army at Fort Rosecrans, California, I was asked to take the oath on July 10, 1918. I was proud to become a U.S. citizen. Later I was told that a non-citizen could not be shipped to a theater of war outside the U. S. A.

Early in our training, I was designated as a squad leader. On August 2, 1918, I was appointed corporal in Company A, 54th Ammunition Train, C.A.C., by the Fort Rosecrans commanding officer, Colonel J. R. Pourie. There were other similar appointments for non-commissioned officers. Because of these appointments, we were wondering if the long expected orders were soon to come. When the order to leave came, I contacted my sister, Hilma, by phone, who was now in Pasadena. I visited with her for a few minutes to say goodbye.

On August 14, 1918, our unit entrained at San Diego bound for overseas. That day will never be forgotten. We wondered if we would ever return as the Santa Fe coaches slipped out of the station.

We left San Diego in two sections, at 4:00 and 4:30 p.m. I remember some of our experiences during the days we were traveling to the east coast. In California we passed through Santa Ana, Orange, Riverside, and San Bernardino. At Jerome, Arizona, we set our watches one hour ahead to mountain time. By the time we reached New Mexico, we had become familiar with the menu in the dining car. A typical day offered minced ham sandwiches for lunch, and hot dogs, sauerkraut, cookies and coffee for dinner. The evening entertainment in our coach consisted of a jazz band, two harmonicas, a guitar, and a fiddle. All the boys joined in singing such popular songs as "Long, Long Trail," "Tipperary," and "Oh, Johnny!" which we had learned at Fort Rosecrans. At Amarillo, Texas, Captain Chavin got us out on sunbaked streets and made us "double-time." The exercise was welcome after three days aboard the coaches.

One morning as we awakened in Eldorado, Kansas, we found ourselves in a familiar landscape of fields of wheat and corn. Then traveling through Wichita Junction, Emporia, and Ottawa on toward Kansas City, we followed the Missouri River for a couple of hours. At Fort Madison, Iowa, and at Galesburg, Illinois, relatives and friends had gathered for hours awaiting our arrival. The greetings and the partings will always be remembered.

We just touched the outskirts of Chicago, but we were close enough to get a whiff of the stockyards. Then we traveled through South Bend, and on into Michigan. At Detroit we crossed the Detroit River by ferry into the Dominion of Canada. Our half-hour march through the streets of Windsor was made memorable as the

Canadians cheered us with "Goodbye, boys. Get the Kaiser."

The next morning we were called out in a hurry to hike up to Niagara Falls. We stayed an hour seeing the sights. It was a marvelous experience. At Rochester we got off for a swim in a Y.M.C.A. pool large enough to accomodate five hundred men.

Enroute again through Syracuse and Utica, down the Hudson River, and through Yonkers Mount tunnel, we arrived off Weehawken, finally reaching New York City after seven days on the train. We crossed the Hudson to Long Island City and on to Camp Mills, our destination. Then we had a long, hot hike to our quarters.

We spent ten days, August 21-30, 1918, at Camp Mills in preparation for our overseas voyage. We underwent one inspection after another, but we did have time to see the "big city." The sixty-story Woolworth Building, 750 feet high, and with an observation tower, was the big attraction. Other buildings visited were the Flatiron and Singer buildings. We had a trip through Chinatown and the Bowery. We also had an enjoyable evening at Coney Island. The ferry trip to the Statue of Liberty was another highlight. I must not forget to mention that I saw the Ziegfeld Follies. We all agreed that New York had much to offer.

We left Camp Mills at 6:00 a.m. on August 31, 1918, and at 1:30 p.m., we were all aboard the *S. S. Lancashire.* We were anchored overnight and put out to sea at 3:00 a.m. It was Sunday.

Speaking of Sunday, I attended a communion service on the second Sunday at sea. Quite a large group of soldiers had gathered in a small dining room aboard ship. The man in charge was a first lieutenant army officer who was also a Baptist preacher. After he had given the preparatory sermon, a loaf of bread was passed along and then a container of wine. Then he repeated the familiar words regarding the body and blood of Christ. It was most impressive. Here as we sailed on a stormy sea, uncertain of our safety, if I have ever been prepared for communion, it was on this day.

The *S. S. Lancashire* was a British freighter converted into a transport. It had formerly been used to haul cattle from Australia to England. Our sleeping quarters had been thoughtfully arranged. They consisted of hammocks, strung side by side across the width of the hold. When all the hammocks were filled, they helped to keep us from falling out. When we rolled out of the hammocks, we were on top of the dining tables. The air in our sleeping quarters was so foul that I tried to sleep on deck whenever I could. If a guard or an English officer found me, he would wake me and order me to go below. A time or two I was drenched by a big wave that swept the deck.

As the *Lancashire* was a converted freighter, the cooking facilities had been installed on deck. The bread was baked in an oven on deck and the meat was boiled in a large pot, also on deck. The English must be very fond of mutton because it was served to us regularly, boiled without any seasoning. Even to this day I do not relish mutton. Every other day at breakfast we had storage eggs.

One night I was in charge of a small guard detail, just four men. We were placed near a mounted gun. Our duty was to peer through the darkness and scan the sea for any foreign object. It is strange how one's imagination can make one see what does not exist. For four hours our attention was on the sea. Sometimes someone thought he saw something, but our guard duty was uneventful. In fact we saw no submarine on the entire ocean crossing.

When we reached the coast of Ireland on the early morning of September 12, we were told that we had just missed a mine, the floating type, by a very few feet. We arrived at Liverpool at 9:00 p.m. on the same day. When we docked the following morning at 4:00 a.m., we had completed our ocean crossing in thirteen days. It is interesting to note that we had thirteen nurses on our ship and thirteen steamships in our convoy. It was estimated that the total personnel in the convoy numbered 50,000. Someone said, "Kaiser Bill, here we come. Take notice."

As we traveled across England by train to a rest camp, we were impressed by the picturesque countryside—green fields, grazing cattle and sheep, towns and villages with their rows of houses all alike. That England was at war was apparent, since we saw only women, children, and old people. The train we were on was of interest to some of the men. The equipment, such as the coaches and locomotive, was on a smaller scale than that which we find in the United States. We were fascinated by the whistle. After three shrill toots of the tiny whistle, the little locomotive would move slowly ahead. We arrived at Romsey at 11:00 p.m. and hiked up a long hill to a so-called rest camp.

Camp Woodley, where we spent the night, was certainly a rest camp as far as our stomachs were concerned. The fare was meager, but we did have the opportunity to wash our clothes as well as ourselves.

On the following day, September 15, we left this British rest camp at 9:30 a.m. and marched, each of us with a heavy pack, twelve miles to Southhampton. We appreciated a rest stop on the way where Red Cross women served us sandwiches and coffee and gave us the latest baseball news. Here we also received a greeting from King George of England:

WINDSOR CASTLE

> Soldiers of the United States, the
> people of the British Isles welcome
> you on your way to take your
> stand beside the armies of
> many nations now fighting in
> the Old World the great battles
> for human freedom.
> The Allies will gain new heart
> and spirit in your company.
> I wish that I could shake
> the hand of each one of you
> and bid you God speed on your
> mission.
>   GEORGE R. I.
> September 1918

Upon our arrival in Southhampton, we boarded the *S. S. Archangel* and sailed at 6:00 p.m. Besides a heavy pack and gun which each man carried, there were personal items such as sweaters which we were not permitted to carry with us. They had been collected at the time of departure and sent separately. Now when we were boarding the *S. S. Archangel* to cross the English Channel, we learned that these personal items were missing, evidently missent to another ship. I lost a sweater handknit by my sister, Signe.

The *S. S. Archangel* was a small crowded ship with no sleeping accommodations. It sailed with no light. I found a place to lie down in a storage bin for life jackets and had a restful sleep until we arrived in the harbor of Cherbourg, at 4:00 a.m. Before disembarking, we were served coffee and "dog biscuits," so called because they were so tough that they could hardly be soaked in coffee.

When we disembarked at Cherbourg at 7:15 a.m. on September 16, 1918, we marched five miles up a long hill to another English rest camp where we stayed two days. We were quartered in small round tents which we thought were big enough for three or four men, but at bedtime, we were ten to twelve men crowded into each of these small tents. Showers were provided, but the stream was only a trickle.

We left the rest camp at noon on September 18 and marched back to Cherbourg. As we arrived at the railway station, we saw a hospital train from the battle front being unloaded. These wounded soldiers were to be shipped to England. There were a number of basket cases. Even those of our men who were usually boisterous were sobered by what they saw. All remained very, very quiet.

Then we were loaded on box cars marked, "Forty men or Eight Horses." These were side-door cars, perhaps deluxe for horses, but not for men. Only a few could get near the door, others yelling and pushing for their turn. Those who succeeded could see France in a leisurely manner as the train moved about fifteen miles per hour. We traveled west of Paris through Tours and finally into the province of Charente. We arrived at the city of Angoulême at 9:00 p.m. the same day. We were given a friendly and enthusiastic welcome by the French people, as we were the first American troops to be stationed there. Our quarters were former artillery barracks, four stories high, well built but with no elevators. The barracks were built in a quadrangle, with buildings on three sides and gates on the fourth. Our first job was to clean up the barracks, but since the only furniture in each large room was a large coal stove, we only scrubbed the floor.

Each day the men drilled. A local truck school was organized to train drivers. Eventually 232 men in our organization qualified as truck drivers. Officers and men were sent to an advanced school at Chaumont; others were sent to a gas school.

October 27th was a memorable day. We received our first mail from home.

Good conduct cards were issued which permitted us to leave our quarters whenever we had time off. It was only a five-minute walk down town. A small church had been designated for our use. Those of us who wanted to attend a church service would line up and march through the city in formation, singing popular songs. Our chaplain was in charge.

There was a woman interpreter at camp who had spent some years in Canada. She offered to meet with four of us during the evening to teach us French. All went well for a couple of weeks. Then my friend, Henry Kruse, and I visited a small department store after class one evening. There we met two sisters, Maria and Germain, daughters of the family who owned the store. It was more interesting to practice French in talking with the girls than in attending the class in French. Of course we had to have pocket dictionaries at all times. One Sunday this family invited us for dinner. They had tried to prepare an American dinner for us even though there was a shortage of food. After dinner the girls and their mother sang the French national anthem, the "Marseillaise." Then they asked us to sing "The Star Spangled Banner." Luckily the words were given in the special French-English dictionary for soldiers. Neither Henry nor I had talent as singers, but we tried. On this Sunday afternoon, a military band was scheduled to give a concert in a park. We wanted to take the girls to the concert. We soon learned that we had to invite the mother also as the girls were not permitted to go with us without a chaperone. This custom was also observed when we called on the girls at their home. The mother was always present. We became very fond of this family. I kept in touch with them by correspondence for a couple of years. Then in 1924 when I returned to France, I tried to visit them, but I was unable to contact them. Evidently they had moved from Angoulême. Their father had been killed the first year of the war.

All Saints' Day came on November 1, 1918, a legal holiday in France. The people celebrated all day with music and speeches. Then came the long awaited day, the signing of the armistice on November 11, 1918, at 5:30 a.m. The actual firing on the front, however, did not cease until the eleventh hour of the eleventh day of the eleventh month. When the official word was received in Angoulême at noon, the people went wild with joy. They sang and danced in the streets. We saw fifteen and sixteen year-old boys dancing on tables in a restaurant. No wonder. The war was over, a war that had taken many fathers, husbands, and brothers. It is difficult to realize what many of these people had endured during the war years.

Our truck school closed, but it did not look as though we would be home for Christmas. Orders came December 3 for us to entrain for St. Sulpice near Bordeaux. Upon our arrival, we hiked with heavy packs to Beychac-et-Cailleau. It was a tired group that finally reached its destination, arriving a few at a time the following morning between the hours of 1:00 and 6:00 a.m. The battalion was placed in billets, six separate buildings scattered over a wide area. Our company was quartered upstairs in a large barn. The barnyard was muddy, some places knee-deep, for it rained almost every day in this part of France. One of our men, Edward L. Bertelsen, described our night-long hike in the following poem:

THE BATTLE OF NO COMPREE
Come on, you children, gather on my knee
While I tell you of the Battle of No Compree.
We rode in box cars on narrow gauge tracks;
We were then ordered out to sling our packs.

Our officers led us but went the wrong way;
Then we took a new road to march until day.
We walked for hours—we knew not where—
Through a dark, damp night. How the boys did swear!

The packs grew heavy. (They're an awful load.)
Then the officers decided to take a new road.
The non-coms cussed and the privates swore,
As the packs cut deeper and shoulders got sore.

We marched all night till early morn
And decided, "Every day some fools are born."
The night wore on and then came day;
We ditched our packs for a barn full of hay.

Tired we were, we slept right through,
Awoke the next morning for an army stew.
They talked of the Battle of No Compree.
Why we fought the battle no one could see.

A non-com from the ranks stepped out:
"I'll tell you boys how this came about.
The officers wanted a little show;
Where they were going they did not know."

> So we marched all night to keep from sleeping,
> And we slept next day to keep from eating.
> The Battle of Cognac was hard as could be.
> But who caused the Battle of No Compree?

We quickly adjusted to our new environment. A field kitchen was set up outside our quarters. Ditches were dug behind the barn to serve as latrines. A nearby creek provided laundry and bathing facilities.

Christmas mail, both letters and packages, arrived a few days before the holidays. It was a day for some to celebrate, but not for me. A letter from mother informed me that my father had died September 27, 1918. The letter was addressed to me at Augustana College and had been forwarded. Although my father had reached the age of eighty-one, he had been in good health. I had hoped to see him again. I spent the evening reminiscing about home and parents. I had fond memories of my father.

During the Christmas holidays, Company A defeated Company C in football at Sacole, 18-0. We were excused from both calisthenics and drilling if we participated in football. I joined this practice group. Our handicap was that we did not have proper clothing and equipment for football. All we had was denim or fatigue clothing. Not much to protect us from injuries.

A number of us participated in a Christmas mass at a little church near Sacole. The priest gave a short sermon in good English for the benefit of the American soldiers.

Three of us had contacted an elderly French woman, who lived alone in a house nearby, to do some mending for us. She asked if we could provide her with some soap as payment. Soap was allocated to us from time to time. One day we asked her if she would make potato pancakes for us if we would furnish the potatoes and salt pork, which we knew we could obtain from our mess sergeant. She said she would be happy to do this for us. She made pancakes from grated raw potatoes and fried salt pork. We had a feast. It brought back memories of winter evenings in Sweden when we enjoyed a similar menu in our home.

The war was over, but rumors and speculations were many as to when we were to return home. We finally heard reports that several organizations were moving to the embarkation camp at Genicart.

One of the military units was the regiment in which my brother, Ragnar, served. The distance from our billet to Genicart was about a two-hour walk. I asked my captain for permission to visit Ragnar. He said he was sorry as he had no authority to permit anyone to leave our billet. Naturally I was disappointed. A few minutes later, he sent for me and told me I could go at my own risk. He said, "If you are arrested, I will know nothing of your adventure." My friend, Henry Kruse, joined me. We decided not to follow the highway but to walk through the woods along the highway. About halfway, we saw five women trying to right a derailed streetcar, the track of which followed the highway. We wanted to help, but we did not dare to walk out in the open in case a military police should come along.

We finally reached Genicart, a large camp with many thousands of troops. We had, however, no difficulty in locating my brother's military unit. We found him and also Carl Okerblom, an Augustana student. We had a most pleasant reunion and a delightful visit, including dinner with them before we began our long trek back. It was dark when we approached our billet. Instead of trying to explain our adventure to the guard, we made our way slowly and as quietly as we could through a vineyard. I related our experience to the captain on the following day. I was grateful to him for letting me go.

It was January 31, 1919. Some one reported that he had seen on the desk of Captain Elmer P. Kayser at the Headquarters Detachment the official orders for our move to the embarkation camp at Genicart. Was it really true? After weeks and months of waiting were we actually going home?

The next day we said good-bye to our billets. We were off in trucks for Genicart. We will not forget our stay there: the "Mill" or the delousing, the cleaning process, the hair cuts. We proceeded to Bassans and up the Gironde River to Pouillac. We stepped off French soil as we boarded the *S. S. Mercury*. We were homeward bound at last.

Each one of us was handed the following letter from General Pershing:

G. H. Q.
AMERICAN EXPEDITIONARY FORCES

General Orders
No. 38-A   France, February 1, 1919

MY FELLOW SOLDIERS:

Now that your service with the American Expeditionary Forces is about to terminate, I cannot let you go without a personal word. At the call to arms, the patriotic young manhood of America eagerly responded and became the formidable army whose decisive victories testify to its efficiency and its valor. With the support of the nation firmly united to defend the cause of liberty, our army has executed the will of the people with resolute purpose. Our democracy has been tested, and the forces of autocracy have been defeated. To the glory of the citizen soldier, our troops have faithfully fulfilled their trust, and in a succession of brilliant offensives have overcome the menace to our civilization.

As an individual, your part in the world war has been an important one in the sum total of achievement. Whether keeping lonely vigil in the trenches, or gallantly storming the enemy's stronghold; whether enduring monotonous drudgery at the rear, or sustaining the fighting line at the front, each has bravely and efficiently played his part. By willing sacrifice of personal rights; by cheerful endurance of hardship and privation; by vigor, strength and indomitable will, made effective by thorough organization and cordial co-operation, you inspired the war-torn Allies with new life and turned the tide of threatened defeat into overwhelming victory.

With a consecrated devotion to duty and a will to conquer, you have loyally served your country. By your exemplary conduct a standard has been established and maintained never before attained by any army. With mind and body as clean and strong as the decisive blows you delivered against the foe, you are soon to return to the pursuits of peace. In leaving the scenes of your victories, may I ask that you carry home your high ideals and continue to live as you have served—an honor to the principles for which you have fought and to the fallen comrades you leave behind.

It is with pride in our success that I extend to you my sincere thanks for your splendid service to the army and to the nation.

Faithfully,
John J. Pershing
Commander in Chief

As we received this "Thank you" letter from our Commander in Chief, we also wanted to say as we took a last look at France: "Thank you, France, for lessons learned while on your shores and for having taught us that there is no place like good U.S.A."

The *S. S. Mercury* was a converted freighter. We slept on shelves of wire fabric which were arranged in rows, each row having four shelves. There was no mattress provided, only a blanket. It was not very comfortable.

We had fourteen-and-a-half long, dreary days at sea with mist, rain, and rough weather. There was much seasickness among the men. As we were following the Azores route, our destination seemed to point to Newport News. Most of the fellows stayed up all of the last night, eager for a glimpse of the homeland. We arrived at Newport News, Virginia, on February 18. To my surprise, I found my brother, Ragnar, at the dock as I stepped off the gangplank. He had arrived two days earlier. Another surprise was that my brother handed me a piece of apple pie which was a real treat to a returning soldier.

We marched to Camp Stuart, which we found to be a real rest camp and where we enjoyed some wonderful food.

After four days of final preparation and re-equipment, we boarded a ship at Newport News and sailed up the river to Fort Monroe. As soon as we had been assigned quarters, work began to break up the Ammunition Train into detachments according to territory. The 54th Ammunition Train ceased to be on the 27th of February, and its men from twenty-three states were sent to fifteen camps. Those from Illinois were sent to Camp Grant. At this camp I was discharged on March 10, 1919. Besides my monthly pay of thirty-eight dollars, I received a bonus of sixty dollars and a ticket on the Chicago and Northwestern Railway to Chicago. My military career had come to an end.

It was with mixed emotions that I said farewell to the men and officers of Company A. Many of the men had become good pals of mine. The commanding officer of Company A was a professional soldier, Captain Walter F. Vander Hyden. He had the respect of all. Our two lieutenants, Harold M. Poole and Morell S. Clarke, were also well liked. These officers will be remembered as well as the non-commissioned officers, the men of Company A, and the entire

54th Ammunition Train. During our time of service in Uncle Sam's army, we had traveled far, met with unusual experiences, and learned many valuable lessons.

I was looking forward to my visit with my sister, Hilma, and her husband, Carl Nordstrom. They had married on September 27, 1918, and had established their home in Austin, on Chicago's west side. It was a delight to see them again and to get a taste of Hilma's good cooking.

A letter from Dr. Gustav Andreen invited me to come at once to Rock Island to resume my studies at Augustana College. He promised full credit for the spring term if I would return promptly after my discharge. I lost no time. After a couple of days with Hilma, Carl, my twin sister, Signe, and Ragnar, who had now also been discharged, I was on my way to Rock Island.

Back in Rock Island, I found the Augustana campus in a festive mood. Sons of Augustana, who had been in military service, were coming back to resume their studies. The welcome mat was everywhere. I quote from an article by Dr. E. F. Bartholomew, a faculty member of many years:

> When we saw them coming forward to enlist, our hearts were heavy, not knowing what might befall them; but we had faith in them, assured that they would acquit themselves with honor, and would never allow the flag to trail in the dust. The days wore on, and we scanned with bated breath the published list of casualties, and in tones of solemn interest repeated, one to another, the names of our absent loved ones; fervent prayers from anxious hearts before the mercy seat ascended in their behalf, and words of mutual encouragement were freely exchanged. We dared not hope that all would escape injury; we knew they were brave men. But Providence has been wonderfully kind to us. Our Service Flag has but four gold stars. For this we give devout thanks. Praised be the Lord; the conflict is over, the victory is won, and, one by one, we are permitted to welcome our boys home again. Welcome! Home! Heroes of the Van Guards, Sons of Augustana, with honor bright and fame unstained, we welcome you home!

Homecoming parties and dinners were held at which the returned service men were asked to relate their war experiences. The men also adjusted to studies and activities in organizations in which they had been active. The spring term passed quickly.

III

COLLEGE YEARS

The father of Carl Okerblom, a fellow academy student, had offered me a summer job on his farm at Lynn Center, Illinois. I readily accepted as I needed work to earn money for tuition and other necessary expenses in order to return to Augustana in the fall. I was to be paid sixty dollars a month plus board and room. As a farmhand, I had to rise early each day in order to feed and groom the horses before breakfast while Mr. Okerblom tended to the milking of the cows. Then I cultivated the corn and had other chores in the field. Whenever it rained, I spent time going through the corn fields pulling up velvet weeds. At harvest time I was sent from one farm to another to help with the threshing. It was hard work, but the crew was well fed. Mr. Okerblom was short in stature and light in body, but he was a hard worker. The day never seemed to be long enough for his many duties. Sometimes after supper he would say to me, "Birger, there is a job I must do. It will take a while. Of course, you do not have to do this, but it would not take so long if you would help." I was willing to help. He would light a lantern and we would be on our way.

It was not all work, however. Orion had a week of Chautauqua, at which we enjoyed lectures and music. The young people at St. Paul's Lutheran Church had outings and picnics which we enjoyed. After church on Sunday, we were often at a home for a big dinner. These dinners seemed to come in rotation and to be a tradition. Mr.

and Mrs. Okerblom, their son, Carl, and their daughter, Edna, were friendly and kind, making my summer on the farm an enjoyable one.

I was happy to return to Augustana College in the fall of 1919. The war was over. Now I could look forward to a full year of study and participation in student activities. Although my studies had been interrupted because of the war, I was permitted to enroll in the third class of the academy. The tuition had increased five dollars. The cafeteria system had been inaugurated at the college dining hall with a college senior, Alfred Martinson, as manager. I lost no time in calling on him, and he promised me work in the cafeteria.

Student activities were numerous and varied. Open House at "Ha Shamia" (girls' dormitory, the Hebrew for "abode of the angels") had one hundred percent attendance. As most of the men had returned from military service, we had prospects of a good football team with a good beginning: Augustana 6–Illinois Wesleyan 6; Augustana 2–Monmouth 0. Billy Sunday, a former baseball player and now a renowned evangelist, visited Augustana and spoke in the chapel. On Reformation Day there was an Augustana night at the Billy Sunday tabernacle. Dr. Preston Bradley opened the 1919-1920 Lyceum Course in the college chapel. Armistice Day was observed by veterans at the Students' Union, an organization which met weekly in the chapel. In the evening the men had a pork and beans dinner at the canteen. At Christmas time the Oratorio Chorus, aided by the Tri-City Symphony Orchestra, presented a well-received rendition of the *Messiah*.

Christmas vacation began on December 18. Nearly all students went home for the holidays. A few remained and worked at various jobs. During the fall, I had been employed Saturdays at Widell's shoe store in Moline as a salesman. Besides serving regular customers, I would seek prospects among the students. On a lucky day, I would have four or five of these prospects with me on a Saturday. Prices on shoes ranged from three dollars to five dollars. My commission was five percent. Mr Widell also wanted me to help with the inventory.

Dr. L. G. Abrahamson, editor of the Swedish language paper, *Augustana*, and Mrs. Abrahamson, always remembered the students who remained in Rock Island for the Christmas holidays. They invited these students to their home for a party. A lively party it was with all kinds of games, songs, and good things to eat.

Then we had a Pershing Day at Augustana, which was brief but enthusiastic. General John J. Pershing arrived at noon January 6, 1920. He met the students and faculty in the gymnasium. After having pictures taken with Prexy, the General gave a short address paying tribute to the sons of Augustana, who had served under him during the war. He also took time to shake hands with a large number of students.

Our prexy, Dr. Gustav Andreen, always greeted us on the first day of the spring term with these words: "Welcome, we are back in the harness."

During the fall term, I had rejoined the Lincoln Debating Club and Iduna, a Swedish literary society. Our faculty adviser in Iduna, Professor Mauritzson, suggested that we study the works of Selma Lagerlöf. I made arrangements with the Augustana Book Concern to take orders for complete sets of Lagerlöf's works. Nearly all of the members of Iduna ordered sets.

The owner of the Widell shoe store asked me if I would be interested in keeping books for him in addition to working as a shoe salesman on Saturdays. As I had taken a bookkeeping course at Augustana, I was eager for some practical experience. Everything went well until I was ready to balance the accounts for the week. I found that I was short of cash. When I informed Mr. Widell, he smiled and said, "I guess I am the guilty one." Whenever he needed cash, he had gone to the cash drawer, but had forgotten to leave a memo of the amount taken. He saw his mistake. After a couple of weeks, I had no trouble in balancing the accounts. He was also a first-class shoe repairman, as well as a kind person.

Augustana College and Theological Seminary celebrated its sixtieth anniversary on April 27, 1920. The school had been founded in a small building in Chicago. Now the institution had a thirty-acre campus and a number of beautiful buildings. From a small beginning with a student body of twenty-one and one professor for all subjects, the enrollment was at present 700 with a faculty of forty-five, each professor an expert in his field.

The Little Nineteen basketball tournament was held at the Augustana gymnasium on March 11-13, 1920. Millikin finished first, Lombard, second, and Augustana, third.

During the spring term of 1920, a maintenance man was needed for Old Main. Three students applied and promised to accept the responsibility and to divide the work equally. Mr. David Beckstrom, the business manager, accepted our offer. The three students were Arthur Larson, Eugene Lothgren (my roommate) and I. As I had decided to remain in Rock Island during the summer to take a course in civics, I asked if I could be a full-time maintenance man for Old Main. My job would be to clean blackboards, chairs, floors, windows of all classrooms, hallways, restrooms, the chapel, and stairways. My job also included cutting the grass around Old Main and trimming around the sidewalks. I was to have the building ready for the opening of the fall term. For this work I was given seventy-five dollars a month.

The cafeteria closed a few days after commencement. There were no restaurants nearby, the closest ones being in downtown Moline and Rock Island. I asked Mr. Beckstrom if I might use the facilities in the canteen, the kitchen of the small gymnasium, so that I could prepare my own meals. Soon I was asked if I was willing to accept a couple of boarders. One was Arthur Swedberg, who had served with a group of Augustana students during the war and had risen to the rank of major. Upon his return, he was called by the college to be director of athletics and had served as such during the past year. Now he was house hunting. The other boarder was LeRoy Carlson, a graduate of the Augustana Conservatory of Music. With my limited experience, I was able to prepare meals to satisfy these men. The most popular item on the menu was *plättar*, Swedish pancakes. Often during the evening meal, one of them would say, "Birger, let us have Swedish pancakes for breakfast tomorrow." Art and I would sometimes, after the evening meal, reminisce and relate our war experiences. One day Mr. Beckstrom came and gave me a ten dollar bill. He said, "This is from Art Swedberg. He left the campus without the opportunity of seeing you." A week later, Art was back with his bride, Nancy. We met at the Beckstroms to welcome the newlyweds and wish them years of happiness.

The summer passed quickly, and students were returning for the fall term. Eugene Lothgren and I had a room with a Mrs. Granlund on 41st Street near 8th Avenue. Her son, Clarence, had been ordained the previous year, and a daughter, Amy, married a pastor, Harry Alden.

Since the college had obtained a full-time maintenance man for Old Main, I was no longer needed there. I was fortunate to be offered the position of manager of the college cafeteria as the previous manager had graduated in May. The pay was three meals a day and twenty dollars a month. I was happy as now I was assured of being able to continue my studies at Augustana. I asked my roommate, Eugene Lothgren, to replace me as bookkeeper and salesman in Widell's shoe store. Both Eugene and Mr. Widell agreed.

At the time of registration for the fall term on August 30, 1920, I was pleased to learn that I had fulfilled all requirements in the academy and that I now was to be classified as a college freshman. My friend, Max Rauer, who had arrived at Augustana in the fall of 1917, had also completed his work in the academy and was to be a member of the freshman class.

Max had an unusual background. He had left Germany at the age of fifteen as a stowaway on a freighter, sailing from Hamburg. He thought the ship was bound for the United States; instead, after weeks on the high seas, he landed in Australia. After a brief period, he tried again as a stowaway. This time the ship took him to South America. On his third attempt, he landed in Seattle. There he met an Augustana pastor who advised him to matriculate at Augustana College for his education. He had to work. He obtained a night job changing advertisements in streetcars, the streetcar barn being located below the campus on 5th Avenue. Max graduated from Augustana in 1925, majoring in chemistry. He became chief chemist in a large pharmaceutical firm in Des Moines, where I visited him a number of times. One of his great satisfactions was taking his family to Germany to visit his relatives and friends whom he had not seen since the day he became a stowaway.

One of my good friends in Company A in the 54th Ammunition Train had been Henry Kruse. I had spoken to him often about Augustana College. After his discharge he decided to attend Augustana and enrolled in the Commercial Department during the 1919-1920 school year. After completing the course he returned to his home town, Sheldon, Iowa, where he became a banker.

With registration completed, it was reported that Augustana had enrolled the largest freshman class in her history. It was a great moment for Dr. Andreen and the faculty to behold these young hopeful students who were to comprise the class of 1924. Their satisfaction found an expression in the words of welcome that were given by Dr. Andreen. We students had not realized what hopes a school places in its freshman classes. It was not long before we learned that there were others besides the faculty who had our welfare at heart. It so happened, however, that some of the academy graduates had already become acquainted with the wise ones the year before and therefore knew well what was to be expected. The former "academites" together with the incoming Tri-City boys, who knew well the lay of the land, quickly organized and created such a horror in the enemy's camp that our formidable foe, the sophs, asked for a truce. After this request, a joint committee met with Major Swedberg as arbitrator and upon his suggestion, it was decided that the differences should be settled in a flag rush. Swedberg's good intention and impartiality we never doubted. The sophs, however, put one over on us in that they were to be on the defensive, while the freshmen were to take the offensive in trying to capture the colors of the sophomore class. The date set for the combat was September 3 at 4:00 p.m., and the battleground was to be around the flag pole by Ericson Hall. The whole school family turned out to see the beginning of a new tradition at Augustana. Spirit ran high and pep meetings and stump speeches aroused the dullest "grind" to enthusiasm. A pistol shot was heard. Immediately upon firing the memorable shot, forty husky war-painted and ambitious freshmen charged down upon the flag pole, intent upon destroying about fifty cents worth of purple and white bunting that waved lazily in the breeze at quite a respectable distance from the ground. However, this aforesaid piece of bunting was valiantly defended by about thirty husky and determined sophomores who would rather go to school on Saturday than have the "frosh" lay their hands on these colors. When the allotted time was up, both classes suspended hostilities and each spent his last breath of strength in a wild cheer for the other side.

Even if we did not reach the bunting, we considered ourselves the champions. Our conclusion was also verified by a statement in the *Moline Dispatch:* "The Frosh outfought and outwitted the Sophs for a half hour."

We celebrated the same evening with a wiener roast at Watch Tower, our first real get-together. We reached Watch Tower by a specially chartered streetcar. Additionally we had to walk about a mile, climbing a barbed wire fence and crossing a creek by means of a log. We had a most enjoyable time toasting marshmallows, roasting wieners, and singing songs. The next day the members of the class of 1924 were better acquainted.

On the following Monday our first class meeting was held, at which time class officers were elected. They were Oliver Peterson, president; Anna Marie Van Duzer, vice president; Margaret Franing, secretary; Thure Fagerstrom, treasurer; and Mildred Bixler, chairman of the social committee. The class motto was "Ad astra per aspera" (To the stars through difficulties), the class flower, the American Beauty rose, and the class colors, blue and white.

Homecoming at Augustana was held October 16, with Augustana meeting Illinois Wesleyan in football. After an exciting battle, Augustana upset the visitors 28 to 10. Former students and graduates, now guests at Homecoming, were more than pleased by the good showing of our boys. The result of the 1920 football season was as follows: Augustana's total points, 188, the opposition's, 23. Much credit for Augustana's success was given to Coach Arthur Swedberg. Four members of our class — Wilson Duffin, Willard Larson, Reuben Pearson, and Arthur Palm — were members of the football squad.

In addition to taking a full college course, I continued to be active in Iduna. I also joined Olof Rudbeck, another literary society, and the Gladstone Debating Club. These organizations had weekly meetings. Although all of them required work, I felt that they were worthwhile.

I would not have one think, however, that our class centered its interest on athletics and extra curricular activities. The foundation of all college opportunities and activities lies in the classroom. Many of us gathered in Dr. Claude W. Foss's room for history; everyone took Christianity under Dr. Otto Bostrom and wrote themes for Professor A. F. Schersten. Others specialized in elocution, German, Latin, Greek, French, Swedish, mathematics or science.

Announcement of the annual *Messiah* concert meant that we were approaching the end of the fall term and the Christmas vacation. I spent part of the holiday period in the home of my sister, Hilma, and her family in Chicago, where my twin sister, Signe, and my brother, Ragnar, joined us on Christmas Eve.

Two surprises met the students as the 1921 spring term opened. "Prexy" Andreen had lost his beard, and the college cafeteria had been redecorated.

One of my duties as manager of the college cafeteria was to check all supplies and to take inventory at the end of each month. During the term I discovered that the owner of one of the grocery firms with which we dealt had the habit of anticipating our needs and delivering supplies that had not been ordered. This policy led to an oversupply of some items, causing frustration and misunderstanding in our staff as they said they knew nothing about delivery of such items. I talked to Mr. D., the grocery man who was also the delivery man. He did not seem to understand until I demanded that he would have to take back all items not ordered. He finally realized that I meant what I said and cooperated. From then on he gave us good service and remained a friend. Mr. D. was always alert for a sale. I recall an incident when a few of us had gone to the new municipal pool in Davenport. I had just dived into the pool. When I came up to the surface, I heard some one call, "Mr. Swenson, do you want more cabbage?" It was Mr. D., always a salesman.

I had problems also with student help. We had twenty-three part-time students employed. The understanding I had with them was that if anyone found it necessary to be absent at meal time, he or she was required to find a substitute. Quite often a student would forget this rule and it fell upon me to find a replacement. I called the students together on a Saturday morning and suggested that they organize as a group, elect officers, appoint necessary committees to assume definite responsibilities. I found them most willing to cooperate. I also soon learned that the officers of the group as well as committee chairmen were more strict than I had been. After that, I had no trouble with absenteeism. The organization was called Hashslingers' Union No. 1. It also became a popular social group. Since the cafeteria was closed Sunday evenings, the student employees would often leave the campus for an outing, well prepared with food and cooking utensils. Other students were delighted to be invited as guests at these outings.

The college cafeteria was a popular eating place, especially at noon on Sundays, not only for students but also for professors and their families and employees of the Augustana Book Concern. A typical Sunday menu was fried chicken, two vegetables, a salad, bread and butter, strawberry shortcake, coffee or milk — all for fifty cents.

The first annual Young People's Christian Conference of the Augustana Synod was held February 11-13, 1921, on the Augustana College campus with nearly 500 delegates. Conrad Bergendoff, a seminarian, was chairman of the local arrangements committee. More than 750 young people attended the banquet in the gymnasium. The dinner was prepared by the women of the college cafeteria staff — an efficient team of six women, led by Mrs. Hilda Watson. It was an inspiring and profitable conference. In the years to follow similar meetings were held in rotation on our college campuses.

A special ingathering of funds had been organized throughout the Augustana Synod for the purpose of creating a complex of buildings for the Theological Seminary, consisting of a chapel, a library, classrooms, and a residence hall. The director of the appeal was Dr. H. O. Pannkoke. March 3, 1921, became a banner day for students and faculty of Augustana, for on that day following chapel service the students and faculty pledged $30,000 to the fund.

Many congregations in our synod asked for student assistants during the summer months, especially to conduct summer Bible school in either Swedish or English. If the student knew Swedish well, he was expected to teach Swedish history as well as the language. These assistants were also asked to conduct services while the pastor was on vacation. Since the seminary did not have enough available students, many college students had opportunity for this kind of summer work. In order to help prepare the college students, Dr. Otto Bostrom offered a course in homiletics, the art of preaching. We were assigned a text from which we would choose a topic and prepare an outline. It was an interesting theological study and most helpful.

Following the Swedish custom of celebrating the first of May, the members of the Olof Rudbeck Literary Society with our faculty adviser, Professor Mauritzson, met for breakfast on Zion Hill May 1, 1921. We enjoyed a Swedish breakfast menu: *sill* (herring), *skinka och äggs* (ham and eggs), *smör och bröd* (bread and butter), and *kaffe* (coffee). It was a happy occasion on a beautiful spring day. The members sang Swedish student songs, and Professor Mauritzson commented on the first of May tradition in Sweden. Later we all had a second cup of coffee during which time, Professor Mauritzson enjoyed his pipe. It was a significant day also in that it was perhaps the last time we could have breakfast on Zion Hill, as it was destined to be cut down to make room for the new complex of seminary buildings.

Fortified by a preacher's license issued and signed by Dr. Gustav A. Andreen, I was ready for my 1921 summer appointment. The license read as follows:

PREACHER'S LICENSE

The Augustana Synod of the Lutheran Church of North America

Mr. Birger Swenson is hereby licensed by the committee on appointments, established by the Augustana Synod, to preach and have charge of the congregation in West Clymer, Pennsylvania, according to the terms of the appointment.

Rock Island, Illinois   G. A. Andreen, President
May 20, 1921   Augustana College
                                              and Theological Seminary

My summer appointment was to be the Emanuel Lutheran Church, West Clymer, Pennsylvania. The parish had another congregation, namely First Lutheran Church, Grassflat, both congregations a part of the New York Conference. As the pastor, Rev. C. T. Youngberg, was to be away most of the summer, a seminary student, Harry Erickson, had been called to take charge of First Lutheran. Grassflat and West Clymer were in a coal mining community with most of the men working in the mines. Since we were eager to acclimate ourselves, we wanted to visit a mine. A church member, Mr. Frenburg, who was a mine superintendent, and his assistant, Mr. Eld, promised to accompany us. Mr. and Mrs. Harry Erickson, Ebba Youngberg, the pastor's daughter, and I made up the party. All of us were furnished with overalls and miners' caps for the journey underground. It was a most unusual and informative expedition, although a dusty one. We were all ready for baths when we emerged from the mine.

I had room and board with a kind elderly couple, Mr. and Mrs. Oscar Carlson.

Practically my entire program was to be conducted in Swedish. Each Sunday I was to conduct morning and evening services in Swedish. The summer school for the children was also in Swedish. The school was to continue for two months, five hours a day, Monday through Friday, and to be held in a public school building. The subjects were Bible history, catechism, memorization of Bible verses and hymns, and two hours each day of Swedish history, spelling, and writing. The children numbered twenty-seven from the age of five to fourteen, some of whom could not read. While I was telling the younger children Bible stories, I had to assign reading or paper work to the older children. The children were intensely interested and to my surprise quite able in Swedish. They were also ready to ask questions. A little boy named Gunnar was always eager for an explanation. When we had the Bible lesson about Noah, the flood, and the ark, Gunnar's hand rose. He asked, "If everybody was to drown, except those on the ark, who was to bury the last one?" When we had the story about choosing a wife for Jacob, he raised his hand and said, "I do not understand. Here in West Clymer, the boys help themselves."

After school we played softball about twice a week. The West Clymer children played the group from Grassflat. Either the seminarian, Harry Erickson, or I had to be the umpire. Of course each of us was accused of partiality. At the end of two months we had a closing program in the church with almost overflow attendance. The parents and their friends were eager to learn what progress the children had made. My last number was a spelldown. Some of the older children had acquired quite a large vocabulary in Swedish.

Holidays were observed by the congregation. The July Fourth celebration was held in the evening in the church. I was surprised at the attendance. The church was filled with both young and old. After a song service, I gave a talk in Swedish on the role that two descendants of the original colonists had in making the break from England. John Morton, a fluent orator in both English and Swedish, represented Pennsylvania and was among the signers of the Declaration of Independence. John Hanson, whose grandfather had moved from New Sweden to Maryland, was elected three times as a representative from Maryland to Continental Congresses. On November 5, 1781, he was elected President of the United States in

Congress assembled. Many assume this fact to mean that John Hanson was the first President of the United States. This assumption, of course, was not a fact as he was never elected to any such office. We can, however, be proud of the accomplishments of both John Morton and John Hanson.

Pastor Youngberg returned from his summer vacation and seemed to be pleased with the work of the two students in his parish.

Pastor Youngberg had an old Model T Ford, which he called Greta. He had a new top on it, which I painted. When that job was done, he said, "Now we are ready." Together with Pastor and Mrs. Youngberg and their daughter, Ebba, we took daily trips to Penn State College and the valley in Centre County, Pennsylvania, where Penn's Cave is located. We saw Penn's Cave from a boat on an underground lake. We all enjoyed the picnic lunches that Mrs. Youngberg and Ebba had prepared for the trips.

Time came for my departure. In looking back, I felt that I had had a most profitable experience in preaching and giving talks to women's groups and to the Luther League, as well as endeavoring to visit every home in the congregation. I was heartily welcomed by these church members. Conducting the Swedish summer school with twenty-seven students from age five to fourteen in a one-room school was an adventure. Picture me trying to keep all students busy and interested at the same time. It was a real satisfaction to observe how well-behaved they were and how eager to learn. I felt that I had learned much from my summer in West Clymer as a student pastor.

At the close of a pleasant and eventful summer vacation, we gathered again within the walls of Augustana, but this time not with the awe-struck look of freshmen, for now we were sophomores. Registration began September 5, 1921. Our class now numbered eighty-nine.

We were at once impressed with the great responsibility that rested upon us, namely, our duty to care properly for the incoming freshman class. The first day was a busy one indeed of directing freshmen to various places of interest. After having done a good business selling Student Union pins, chapel seats, and the like to the freshmen, we decided to show a few newcomers the city, "where the East meets the West."

News of our activities soon reached the freshman camp and

made quite a stir. Several encounters took place between the sophomore and freshman forces, some on Zion Hill, others in the old commercial rooms and men's dormitory. Finally a peace pact was signed by a general handshaking which ended the hostilities for the year.

Among the many social activities held during the year were the wiener roast at Watch Tower, the freshman and sophomore masquerade, and the mock track meet.

If the class of 1924 had been active in school affairs during its first year, we found its members still more eager to do their share this year. We had four men on the football squad, five in basketball, four in track, and four in baseball. Debating was represented by Earl Hanson, Edwin Munson, and Cyrus Churchill. The sophomore women's basketball team took the inter-class tournament, Kenneth Conrey for the second time took the state championship in tennis, and Edwin Munson won the inter-class oratorical contest.

The class officers for the year were Earl H. Hanson, president; Mildred Nelson, vice-president; Merle Swanson, secretary; and Ogden Johnson, treasurer.

I was invited to membership in Omicron Sigma Omicron fraternity. The initiation for four of its members took place Thursday, September 29, 1921. Harold Hanson, Edwin Munson, Clifford Toren, and I were initiated. Dressed in white sailor suits and tiny hats and armed with street-cleaning brushes, the initiates started the day with the slogan: "A clean city before midnight." After having worked on sidewalks and steps around Old Main and the library between classes, the happy dozen marched down town for an evening adventure. At the Hickey cigar store corner across from the Fort Armstrong Hotel, we entertained passersby with songs and yells. There were also individual contributions. Munson took the stand and spoke eloquently on "The High Cost of Peanuts." I, as manager of the cafeteria, explained the necessity of higher prices on some items, my speech being in Swedish. Harold Hanson spoke on "Green Caps," after which Clifford Toren sang a solo, much appreciated by the audience. One of our members had a camera which he offered to a city detective who took pictures of our group. After these performances, we went to a restaurant and ended the evening's fun with a midnight snack.

My new studies were biology with Professor Hal C. Yingling and German with Professor Carl L. E. Esbjörn. For Esbjörn we had to learn and recite long poems in German. He was a strict but a good teacher.

Active in Iduna and Olof Rudbeck, I was now serving as secretary-treasurer of the latter society. I also joined the Phrenokosmian Literary Society. The Phrenokosmian was the oldest society at Augustana, having been organized September 5, 1860, when the college was located in Chicago. A large part of this year's program was given to the study of American authors.

Armistice Day was observed as a holiday at Augustana. An impressive program was held in the chapel with Dr. Joseph Chapman, pastor of the First Methodist Church of Rock Island as speaker. The Service Men's Club, which was still quite large and very active, had a get-together and dinner at the canteen.

Final examinations followed the *Messiah* concert and then Christmas vacation.

Dr. Gustav Andreen was an active member of the John Ericsson League of Illinois, which was affiliated with the John Ericsson League of America. It had been formed in honor of John Ericsson, the inventor and builder of the *Monitor*. The *Monitor* was a heavily ironclad warship with a low, flat deck and one or more gun turrets. It was the first such ship which fought the Confederate ironclad *Merrimack* on March 9, 1862. The organization was sometimes called the John Ericsson Republican League of Illinois as it was semi-political.

The 1922 annual meeting of the League was held at the Harper House, Rock Island, on March 9th. Dr. Andreen had asked me to be present during the day to take reservations and to sell tickets for the banquet which was held in the Augustana gymnasium that evening. The banquet was a huge success. The day was of great interest as well as an adventure for me. It was the first time I had had an opportunity to see and observe so many prominent Swedish Americans from Illinois, as well as a number of national leaders.

The two Swedish literary societies — Olof Rudbeck and Svenska Vitterhetssällskapet (Swedish Literary Society) sponsored two contests each year for their members. One hundred dollars was awarded the winners, fifty dollars of which was contributed by the well-known Swedish weekly newspaper, *Svenska Amerikanaren,* and fifty dollars, by Consul G. N. Swan, Sioux City, Iowa. The prizes for each group were first prize, $25.00, second, $15.00, third, $10.00.

I decided to enter the contest sponsored by the Olof Rudbeck. The judges in the contest were Dr. J. Ekholm, Editor Carl Kraft, and Dr. George A. Fahlund. The judges in the contest sponsored by Svenska Vitterhetssällskapet were Editor E. W. Olson, Editor Carl Kraft, and Dr. C. A. Lönnquist.

The joint meeting was held May 1, which is generally celebrated as Swedish day. Before the winners were announced, Dr. E. W. Olson, office editor of the Augustana Book Concern, gave an interesting speech about the Swedish language and its rich contributions to those who know it and are able to profit by its worth. At the conclusion of Dr. Olson's lecture, the winners were announced and prizes awarded. The winners in the Olof Rudbeck contest were as follows: first place, Oscar Broneer, second place, C. G. Carlfelt, and third place, Birger Swenson. The winners in the Svenska Vitterhetssällskapet contest were first place, Eric H. Wahlstrom, second place, John E. Nelson, and third place, Enoch Sandeen.

After the program, refreshments were served in the cafeteria, followed by a social time. Professor Mauritzson spoke on the value of these contests and expressed appreciation to Consul Swan and *Svenska Amerikanaren* for their gifts and interest. The Wennerberg Male Chorus presented several musical numbers.

This was my first entry in a literary contest. I was pleased to be among the winners. My article was entitled, "Selma Lagerlöf's Författarskap" (The Authorship of Selma Lagerlöf).

In preparation for the construction of a new seminary complex, excavation on Zion Hill began in October, 1921, and continued through the spring of 1922. It seemed that the contractor, Mr. B. L. Burke of the Rock Island Transfer and Storage Company, had an army of men, horses, and mules at work. Horse and mule power transported the dirt to the deep ravine between the gymnasium, the president's residence, and the college library. The cornerstone was laid on May 30, 1922. The general contractor was Bergstedt Construction Company. Soon a new home and a new day was to be a reality for the seminary.

Zion Hill was a place for student outings, during both the fall and the spring months. When the leveling began, the muse of poetry also began to work. The following poem is by Victor E. Beck.

DEAR ZION HILL

Dear Zion Hill, we love thee still
Alas! thy time soon ended.
From day to day thy sod and clay
Is with the valley blended.

Thy story bold,—'twill soon be told,
Writ upon histry's pages;
A mighty plow is busy now,
And destruction wages.

Fond memory will turn to thee,
In reverie a-dreaming
When lecture halls and wisdom's walls
With lad and lass are teeming.

And hoary head, by longing led,
To former haunts returning,
Will view a plain; for thee in vain
The heart with fervor yearning.

Dear Zion Hill, we love thee still,
Alas! thy time soon ended.
From day to day thy sod and clay
Is with the valley blended.

I was fortunate in securing an appointment for the summer of 1922. This one was quite different from the one of the previous year, as now I was going to the Immanuel Lutheran Church in Detroit, a city congregation. It was a small congregation, organized in 1919 with a chapel and parsonage, at 2555 Beniteau Avenue. The assignment was also different from the one of the previous summer in that the English language was used in the pulpit as well as in the Bible school.

An Augustana friend, Henry G. Hedlund, a seminary student, came from this congregation. His family lived only a few blocks from the chapel and did much to make me feel at home from my first day. I had a room in the parsonage and my meals in a nearby restaurant.

Each morning I led a Bible school for twenty-eight children ranging in age from five to fourteen. As the group was well-behaved,

I had no difficulty in keeping them busy. When I told Bible stories to the younger children who could not read, I assigned to the older children Bible passages, parts of the Catechism, and hymns for memorization. There was also Bible history. On Sundays I conducted morning and evening services. I also regularly attended meetings of the Ladies' Aid, Luther League, and the Sunday school teachers.

In the afternoon, I usually called on members and prospective members. I did, however, manage to attend a baseball game each time the New York Yankees were in town. Babe Ruth was the big attraction. He was famous for his home runs, but I also enjoyed watching him come in from the outfield. He would always step on second base as he was heading for the dugout.

One day shortly before the end of Bible school, I was called into the parsonage to answer the phone. I later found out that the children had arranged the phone call to get me out of the chapel basement where the classes were held. They wanted time to arrange a surprise party for me, having brought lemonade and cookies from home. They had also pooled their pennies and nickels and presented me with a gift of $1.73. I was told that the party was their own idea. I was delighted and grateful.

A closing program of the Bible school was held in the evening of the last day. The chapel was filled with parents and friends. The children did well in singing, reciting Bible verses, and answering questions on the Catechism and Bible history. My youngest pupil was Stella, five years old. Although she could not read, she was eager to listen to Bible stories. She liked the story of creation and could tell it well. She would begin, "On the first day, God created heaven and earth." At this closing program, I was proud of the way she was telling the story, loud and clear, until she came to the seventh day. Then she looked at me, but no words came. I tried to prompt her, but still no words came until I asked,

"What do you do on Sunday?" Quick as a flash, clear and loud, came the words,

"On the seventh day God went to Sunday school."

I instructed two adults for confirmation, a Mr. Nyquist and a Mr. Sundquist. I have forgotten their first names. Dr. Albert Okerstrom, pastor of Bethlehem Lutheran Church, was the vice pastor of Immanuel. He had charge of confirmation and communion.

It was a festive Sunday service. Following the service, the confirmands, Dr. Okerstrom, and I enjoyed a dinner at the home of the Sunday school superintendent, Mr. Herman Nelson.

Dr. Okerstrom and I traveled to Whitehall, Michigan, for a mission meeting which was held there July 27-30. We went by train from Detroit to Muskegon, where we were met by auto. Upon our arrival in Whitehall, we were taken to the Lebanon Lutheran Church. The evening service had just started. I was informed that I was to give the first sermon. I hurried into the kitchen of the parsonage to freshen up a bit and then went back into the church. As the last stanza of a hymn was sung, it was time for me to enter the pulpit. To my surprise, I could see only the last two pews, the pulpit being entirely too high for me. I had no choice but to begin my sermon. Of course, I could not see the people except those in the last two pews, nor could they see me. Afterward I learned that the pulpit had been adjusted for the pastor, Rev. August J. Beausang, the tallest pastor in the entire Augustana Lutheran Church. He was often referred to as the "high priest." One of the visiting pastors was Rev. A. P. Sater of Lansing, Michigan, who was very short in stature. When Sater and Beausang walked down the street together, everyone nearby would stop for a second look.

During the mission meeting, I had the pleasure of seeing several Augustana students in attendance. I stayed at the home of Mr. and Mrs. Youngquist and shared a room with my former roommate at Augustana, Enoch Sandeen. We appreciated these kind people of Whitehall.

Soon it was time to return to Augustana. Looking back, I will always have fond memories of my summer in Detroit and my work among the people of Immanuel Lutheran Church. They were kind and understanding and had a really deep interest in building their young congregation. Long to be remembered were the children and the Bible school, the Sunday School picnic at Belle Isle, the church service and picnic on Bob Loo Island, Canada, as well as the many enjoyable visits in the homes of members. I was most grateful for my summer's experience and for the opportunity to earn money for another year at Augustana.

As we returned to Augustana in the fall of 1922, we looked forward to our year in "juniordom" as a carefree and happy one. No longer did we need to stand in awe and "trembling fear" before the upperclassmen. As a good beginning to the many merry social events that year, the class met for an outing at Watch Tower. Then followed the eventful junior-senior party in the "Li'l Old Gym". The call for football candidates by Coach Swedberg was answered by thirty-five men, only six of whom were experienced players. Although the only experience I had dated back to army days, I was encouraged to go out for football. It took time and practice to gain experience. I was handicapped because my work in the cafeteria came first. Although I did not get into the fray much, I enjoyed the game and the fellowship.

Speaking of the cafeteria, I recall that each fall we had some new help both in the regular staff and among the students. Mrs. Hilda Watson was the efficient woman in charge of the regular staff. Mrs. Hannah Nelson was the meat and vegetable cook. She had served in that capacity thirteen years and was an artist in her line. Five more women made up the regular staff. Then there was the loyal band of students who put forth every effort to make the cafeteria a real service station. Among the counter crew were Herbert Quist, Frank Bonander, Henning Danielson, Emil Carlson, Ruth Nelson, and Ellen Carlson. We had another group in the kitchen with various duties in addition to those who set and cleared tables. The best feature of the staff was that all were members of the student body, working for the welfare of the whole Augustana family.

The students also helped to make the cafeteria more efficient. I recall that when Conrad Bergendoff was a seminarian he drew up a set of commandments so that the line along the service counter would move faster. Students were urged to choose their food quickly and to have their money ready for the cashier.

We had some comical situations in the cafeteria. There were some students who would borrow white jackets from regularly employed students in the kitchen and then try to get extra helpings of a favorite food from the cook, Mrs. Nelson. In her busy duties at the stove, she did not always look up to see who was asking for the food. When she did look up and realized they were intruders, she would stamp her foot and drive them away with a large spoon or fork, shouting, "You Augustana destroyers!" Surprised, they would back away and sometimes drop their dishes which would break into "smithereens." Mrs. Nelson's words, "Augustana destroyers," were appropriate.

My friend and classmate, Earl Hanson, asked if he could work for his breakfast only. I put him in charge of a gas operated toaster, a large one that could accommodate a whole loaf of bread. Earl did very well until his girl friend, Rose Anderson, came into the dining room. After she had selected her food and found a place at a table, Earl would leave the toaster to go to visit Rose. In his attention to her, he forgot the toaster. All of a sudden a thick cloud of smoke came from the kitchen, ending his visit with Rose. Years later I had the opportunity a number of times to tell this incident. He enjoyed this reminiscence more than anyone else.

The house on 41st Street where Eugene Lothgren and I had a room had been sold. We were lucky that the new owners, Dr. and Mrs. George A. Fahlund, invited us to stay.

I continued German with Professor Esbjörn and added two new subjects, Greek with Professor I. M. Anderson and chemistry with Dr. J. P. Magnusson. My English teacher was Dr. A. F. Schersten.

Homecoming was celebrated October 20-21. The highlights of the weekend were the freshman-sophomore flag rush, the Augustana-Monmouth football game, Conrey's victory over Tucker of Bradley in tennis, the banquet in the gym, and the carnival in the canteen. All in all, another homecoming had been a success.

The *Observer* had this news item in the November issue, 1922: "Many students are going home over Thanksgiving. Many others will pay their respects to the gobbler in Birger's eating emporium. It is a question who will enjoy their Thanksgiving dinner the most."

My Christmas and New Year holidays were spent in Rock Island. It was good to have time to catch up on work, both in the cafeteria and in studies.

The spring term, 1923, promised to be a busy one. My chemistry course with Dr. Magnusson required extra time for laboratory work. Classes were held in Ericson Hall near the athletic field. I also enjoyed Professor Anderson's Greek class. He taught us not only the Greek language, but also Greek culture and philosophy. He was a strict master. I felt from the very beginning that in him we had a teacher for whom we had to be well prepared.

Another teacher who followed the same principle was Professor

Esbjörn in German; however, both of these men taught not only their subjects but were also interested in their students. I will always remember and appreciate the interest Professor Esbjörn took in me. One day he asked me to remain after class. Could it be my class work? To my surprise, he asked what my pay was for being manager of the college cafeteria. The question struck me as being rather strange as he was not a regular customer of the cafeteria. I told him I was paid board and twenty dollars per month.

"Thank you," he said. That was all he wanted to know. A month later, he asked me again to remain after class. This time he asked if there had been any change in my pay as manager of the cafeteria. I was happy to tell him that now I was receiving board and forty dollars a month!

"That's fine; that's fine," Professor Esbjörn said. To this day I do not know why he took this personal interest in me, but I feel reasonably sure that he was instrumental in the adjustment of my pay. This incident was an example of the interest that Augustana professors and teachers took in their students.

Students, as they generally do, would often discuss their teachers. Sometimes they would tell stories of absent-minded professors. One of the professors in the music department at Augustana, came to class one day with a tan shoe on one foot and a black shoe on the other.

Going to the college cafeteria for lunch one day, he met another professor on the campus. After a short visit, the professor asked,

"Which way was I going when I met you?"

"This way, I think," the friend said and pointed.

"Oh, was I?" he asked. "Then I must have had my lunch."

I was still active in the Phrenokosmian Literary Society as well as in Olof Rudbeck. I became a member, too, of the Christian Brotherhood, one of the most active organizations at Augustana. Its membership consisted mainly of students who were preparing for religious work. It met every Wednesday. I was interested in the lectures by members of the faculty which were very challenging and inspiring. I was also a member of a group of students who organized the Press Club. Lectures were given by members and outsiders on such topics as journalism, news, and feature writing. The club also sponsored a literary supplement for the student publication, The

Observer. My first contribution was a World War I story entitled Home At Last, which appears in Appendix A.

In February, our class of 1924 held an old-fashioned sleighride party. Also in this month our fraternity, Omicron Sigma Omicron, arranged a valentine party for its members and their girl friends. It was a big social event for our group. There was another class party in the spring in the form of a farewell get-together at Watch Tower for seniors, our worthy opponents. The special feature of the evening's entertainment was a program in which the seniors saw themselves as others saw them.

Willard Larson headed the class this year. Laurene Asplund served as vice-president, Maude Adams as secretary, and Paul Swanson as treasurer. Our junior year was not only a year of pleasure, but also a year of hard work. With Kenneth Conrey as editor-in-chief and Earl Hanson as business manager, we not only put out the best *Rockety-I* in many years, but we were able to make it a real success financially which was proved by the fact that the junior class turned over to the Athletic Association $375.00 toward the betterment of Ericson Field.

Vitterhetssällskapet and Olof Rudbeck literary societies sponsored another contest with cash prizes for the winners. The festivities were held May 12, 1923, in the college chapel. Interest in the event brought the president of the Augustana Lutheran Church, Dr. G. A. Brandelle, as well as Dr. Gustav Andreen, and Professor S. G. Youngert, and a considerable number of students. Dr. Mauritzson spoke on the value of Swedish literature. The winner of the prize donated by *Svenska Amerikanaren* was John Helmer Olson. The winners of the prizes donated by Consul G. N. Swan, Sioux City, Iowa, were first, Carl G. Carlson; second, Bernard Johnson; and third, Birger Swenson. I was happy to be a winner once again. My contribution was entitled "Det Tragiska i Frödings Naturskildringer" (The Tragic Element in Fröding's Nature Description).

At the end of the 1923 spring term, I conferred with both the registrar and the dean regarding my credits and classification. Because of my work in the cafeteria, I knew that I had had difficulty fitting into my class schedule all of the subjects required for graduation. I needed credits in science in order to fulfill requirements in the Latin-Science course for an A.B. degree. Upon inquiry I found that I could take a course in zoology at Northwestern University, Evanston, which would satisfy my requirements. As I had almost a month's time before the scheduled opening of the summer term at Northwestern, I accepted a call issued by Dr. Peter Peterson, president of the Illinois Conference. He wanted me to canvass the territory around Tustin, Benson, and LeRoy near Cadillac, Michigan. The Mission Board of the Illinois Conference wanted to learn if the field was promising enough to place a pastor there.

The pastor of the Zion Lutheran Church, Cadillac, was Dr. J. A. Rydbeck. He invited me to stay at the parsonage until a permanent place could be arranged for me. I had already met the daughters of the family, Martha and Linnea, who were attending Augustana.

Upon my arrival, I found that Dr. Rydbeck had been called out of town and would not be home for several days. Soon a problem arose. Two men called at the parsonage to report that a man had been killed in a logging operation and that they wanted a Lutheran pastor to conduct the funeral. Martha and Linnea turned to me and said, "You will have to take Dad's place." Students were permitted to conduct funerals, but this was the first time that the responsibility had fallen to me. I spent the morning preparing a sermon. Then after lunch, I dressed in a Prince Albert coat, white tie, and a straw hat. The girls took a look at me and sent me on my way. The service was held in a funeral home. Evidently the victim of the accident had many friends as the chapel was filled. This was a new experience for me as a student pastor.

The next three weeks were busy ones. It was a real pleasure for me to visit the homes of prospective members, as well as present members in this wide territory. I had found a place to stay on a farm. The farmer permitted me to use his horse and buggy sometimes. If the horse was not available, I walked from home to home. I found the people responsive, interested, and friendly. On Sunday I divided my time between Tustin and Benson for services. At the conclusion of my stay, I sent Dr. Peterson a detailed report of each family and the location of each home. He informed me that he was well pleased with my work and report.

Arriving at Evanston to attend the summer session at Northwestern, I was happy to meet my former roommate, Eugene

Lothgren, who had graduated from Augustana in 1922 and was now taking post graduate work. He had obtained a room for us with a family named Wahlstrom, who had a son, Gustav, who later became an Augustana pastor.

The zoology class which I was to attend was held in University Hall. The teacher was Dr. F. D. Barker, a visiting professor from Nebraska University. His assistant in zoology was Joseph C. Hinsey, a young man with an M.A. degree.

The first day we met, Dr. Barker called the roll. Then he said, "This is the only time I will call the roll. Tomorrow my assistant will check the seats. If you are in the same seat tomorrow as today, you are present, otherwise you are absent." This was quite different from Augustana.

We spent three hours each day in the laboratory where Mr. Hinsey was in charge. In order to prevent students from leaving the room, the doors were locked for the period. We worked on dew worms, large frogs, and other animals which we dissected. We had to draw pictures in minute detail of limbs and segments. Both Dr. Barker and his assistant were excellent teachers. We spent some time in Lunt Library preparing assignments.

We did not have much time for sociability. We attended a picnic now and then with fellow students we had met. Then in the late afternoon when weather permitted, we enjoyed a swim in Lake Michigan. I also visited my two sisters residing in Chicago.

The Augustana Synod church in Evanston was the Immanuel Lutheran Church. I was asked to conduct services there for three weeks during the pastor's vacation period.

In the fall of the year 1923, forty-six members of the class of 1924 came back to Augustana. Registration was scheduled for September 3. Morning services were held in the newly decorated chapel.

I continued Greek with Professor I. M. Anderson, chemistry with Dr. John P. Magnusson, and Christianity with Dr. Otto H. Bostrom. I signed up for economics with Professor Oscar L. Nordstrom and fifth year Latin with Miss Margaret Olmsted.

Latin had become a favorite subject. At times I enjoyed translating things other than the lesson. The Lord's Prayer was one. Then I tried a Swedish ditty, "Gubben Noak" (Old Man Noah), which we sang to our own amusement.

Senex Noah
Senex Noah
Ille rarus vir
Cum exarciebat
Terram incolebat
Multa plura
Multa plura
Ille fecit hoc.

I answered the call for football again, but because of my work was not able to be very active. Besides football, I remained active in the Press Club, Olof Rudbeck, Iduna, Phrenokosmian, Sola Fide, Christian Brotherhood, Augustana Foreign Missionary Society, the House of Representatives, and Omicron Sigma Omicron.

At the first meeting of the class of 1924, the following officers were chosen for the senior year: Kenneth Conrey, president; Astrid Hanson, vice-president; Ruth Johnson, secretary; and LeRoy Stark, treasurer.

Archbishop Nathan Söderblom of Sweden with his wife and son, Jon Olof, arrived on November 4, 1923, for the consecration of the new, lofty, and imposing seminary buildings on Zion Hill. The complex consisted of classrooms, a chapel, a library, and a residence hall. The dedication was held November 6th. On that day we had many visitors, including representatives from other seminaries and dignitaries from other Lutheran bodies.

The academic procession was very colorful, starting at the Denkmann Library and proceeding past Old Main, the Old Dorm, and up Zion Hill. Here Archbishop Söderblom dedicated the buildings. Here also the architect, Olof Cervin, turned over the keys to Dr. Gustav Andreen. This ceremony was followed by a luncheon in the gymnasium, honoring visitors and guests.

The gymnasium was also the place for an academic program in the afternoon. The speaker was the archbishop. As the dignitaries marched in a procession again from the library to the gymnasium, I followed to take pictures. The archbishop, a friendly fellow, spoke to me and invited me to stay with him and Dr. Andreen and sit with them on the platform. I thanked him and told him I had more pictures to take.

The Press Club had only seven members, but they were very active. During this year the organization was particularly interested in short story and newspaper work. The literary supplement of the *Observer* had been the club's own production. Now another supplement was in the making. My contribution entitled Westward the Course of Empire Takes Its Way, appears as Appendix B.

I spent Christmas vacation with my sister, Hilma, and brother-in-law, Carl Nordstrom, in Chicago. During the holidays, I also visited my twin sister, Signe, and my brother, Ragnar.

It was a hot time at Augustana on January 4, 1924, in spite of the twenty degrees below zero weather. The students were celebrating a basketball victory over Knox, 26 to 23. It was also the first day of the spring term.

In this autobiography, I have mentioned from time to time my difficulty in choosing certain courses because of my work in the cafeteria. Now I was told that many of the students had not signed up for gymnastics because of their work in the cafeteria. A compromise was proposed. If I was willing to take charge of the student employees, conduct gymnastics and athletic programs on Saturday forenoons, keep a record of attendance, the college authorities would permit this special arrangement. The students were very cooperative. We started each Saturday with an hour of gymnastics, after which we played basketball. A hot contest developed between the counter and kitchen forces. Everyone enjoyed these Saturday forenoons in the gym. We received credit for gymnastics, and all had a good time.

Basketball was always a popular sport at Augustana. Coach Swedberg had developed a great team this year. Our boys had to win; they were too good to lose. Augustana won the championship of the IIAA Conference, popularly known as the Little Nineteen, by defeating Bradley in a beautiful exhibition of the cage sport, 20 to 16. Approximately 1400 spectators packed the Augie gym to see Coach Swedberg's team bring Augustana its first conference championship since the famous five of 1917.

The social calendar for the members of Augustana's Little Nineteen champions filled up at once. No less than six dinner invitations were received within a couple of days. These boys were royally entertained by the Kiwanis clubs of Moline and Rock Island, by Mr. and Mrs. Beckstrom, and others. I was pleased to be included as I had had charge of the gate at all home games.

As usual a Swedish literary contest was held in the spring. Once again I entered the one sponsored by Olof Rudbeck with cash prizes given by Consul G. N. Swan. The judges were Editor E. W. Olson, Dr. George A. Fahlund and Pastor John Ekholm. I was fortunate in winning first prize. My contribution was "Runebergs Episka Diktning" (The Epic Writings of Runeberg).

Several social events for the class of 1924 took place during the spring. Among these was the senior banquet, which was held on March 20 at the Blackhawk Hotel in Davenport. The honor guests at this occasion were Dr. and Mrs. Andreen and our class guardian, Dr. Wallin and his wife. It was a dress affair. I cannot describe how the girls were dressed, but the boys wore tail coats and white ties, procured and rented from Mosenfelder's men's store.

True to time-honored traditions, the junior class entertained the seniors at a farewell party at Watch Tower, Tuesday evening, May 20, at which time the future history of the members of the class of 1924 was revealed.

I will give a short review of the activities of the class of 1924 and of the circumstances which justify the name applied to us, "The Champion Class." The members of this class had proved themselves as leaders and boosters for Augustana and as leaders of The Lyceum, Student Union, and various other organizations. The editor-in-chief of the *Observer* for two years was a member of our class, as were also the managers of the *Observer* and of student athletics. Our class held thirteen captaincies in athletics. The state championship in tennis for four years was credited to a senior. Four of our members placed on all-state teams.

We also had the privilege of graduating during the championship year in basketball, tennis, and debate. Thus ended the history of the champion class of 1924. It had taken me eight years to reach this goal—seven years for the academy and college and one year of service in the Armed Forces of U.S.A. I know of no country in the world where one of ordinary background such as mine, that of a poor Swedish immigrant, could have achieved an education such as mine at Augustana. When I arrived, I had no money, no financial help, but I was willing to work, and the college gave me work. For this opportunity, I will always be grateful. I graduated without debt. I have also appreciated the many life-long friendships made at Augustana.

Class Day was held in the college chapel May 30, 1924, and the following program was given:

Salutatory	Clarence Berg
History	Birger Swenson
Cornet solo	Lawrence Tuleen
Prophecy	Astrid Hanson, Lawrence Tuleen
Oration	Earl Hanson
Class Poem	Elsye Tash Sater
Class Will	Elvira Person, LeRoy Stark
Presentation of Scroll	Kenneth Conrey
Acceptance of Scroll	Conrad Aronson
Class song, written by	J. Arthur Palm

The baccalaureate service was held in Trinity Lutheran Church, Moline, on Sunday, June 1, 1924. The speaker was our beloved college president, Dr. Gustav A. Andreen. The liturgists were Rev. Walter A. Tillberg and Professor S. G. Youngert.

Commencement exercises took place in the college chapel on June 4. For the graduates, it was a day long remembered. The speaker was Dr. Carl A. Sundberg, president of Thiel College, Greenville, Pennsylvania. His text was Luke 20:25, and his topic was "The Nation's Needs," stressing loyalty to Christ, to church, to country, to the Christian college, to character. The valedictory was given by Kenneth Conrey. President Andreen presented the diplomas.

My brother, Ragnar, and long-time friends, Henning Johnson and Ernfrid Johnson, had driven down from Chicago to see me graduate. I rode with them to Chicago the same day. Ragnar was driving and took me to the home of my sister, Hilma, and brother-in-law, Carl. I had on this day reached another milestone in my life's adventure.

IV
AN INTERLUDE IN EUROPE, MICHIGAN, AND SEMINARY

After twelve years of adventure in my adopted country, and having completed my college education, I wanted to return home to Sweden for a visit and to see my mother. In order to do this I obtained a loan of three hundred dollars from my friend and roommate, Eugene Lothgren. My twin sister, Signe, who was a later immigrant, accompanied me.

We began our European holiday on June 5, 1924. We traveled by train from Chicago to Detroit, crossing the Detroit River by ferry to Windsor, Canada. After an interesting trolley ride and a two-hour visit at Niagara Falls, we continued to Montreal, arriving June 7. Here we boarded the *R. M. S. Andania* of the Cunard Line. The trip down the St. Lawrence River was beautiful and full of thrills. We met Dr. Otto Bostrom and Rev. Carl Bostrom, who were also going to visit Sweden, accompanied by their families.

We sighted New Foundland and its snow-covered mountains on June 9th. From June 10-16, we were at sea. It was a pleasant ocean voyage with time for reading and games, such as shuffleboard, deck tennis, medicine ball, quoits, and bullboard. The most popular card game was rook, at which the Bostrom brothers were experts.

We landed at Tillbury Docks near London, arriving at St. Pancras station on June 17. We stayed at Endsleigh Hotel near St. Pancras Church. Even a brief visit of three days gave us never-to-be-forgotten memories. Among historic places visited were the Houses of Parliament, Big Ben, Westminster Abbey, Scotland Yard, Trafalgar Square, Piccadilly Circus, the Tower of London, St. Paul's Cathedral, and Buckingham Palace. The changing of the guard was most impressive.

On June 20, we boarded *S. S. Thule* of the Swedish Lloyd Line for Gothenburg, where we arrived June 22. Prince Wilhelm was a fellow passenger.

We boarded an afternoon train for Skattkärr. Signe amused the conductor by mixing English with Swedish in her conversation with him. Many relatives had assembled at Averstad, our home, for a happy reunion. Father had died in the fall of 1918, but it was wonderful to see mother again.

My brother, Sven, now operated the home farm and had added another. He had married Ester Karlsson and now had a child, Ulla Svenborg. My oldest sister, Amanda, was home with mother. Our youngest brother, Rickard, was employed as a map maker for the Forestry Department. Sister Annie had married Carl Johan Johansson in 1916. They had three children, Birgit, Neon, and Ingvar. They lived on the nearby Björka estate, which they had bought from the Swedish Crown.

The next few days were happy ones, visiting relatives, neighbors, my boyhood school at Spånga, and the schoolmaster, Alf Sundin. After a week at home, we went by train to Lysvik. Cousin Gustav and his wife, Anna, met us at the station. We visited mother's childhood home at Stallberg, where her brother's family was still living. A few days were spent with an uncle and aunt at Mallbacken. We also visited with relatives at Kilnäs outside of Torsby. While there, we had a bicycle ride to Ledvatten and Ransäter.

We returned to our home at Averstad on July 18. The following Sunday, I attended Östra Fågelvik Church. After church services, an election was held for a schoolteacher, generating much debate. Many had come for just this meeting. That afternoon my brother, Sven, and I saw a soccer game in Karlstad.

During the next ten days, July 21-30, Signe and I enjoyed a circle tour through Norway and Sweden. Traveling by train to Oslo, we met a Miss Norstedt and a lawyer friend, a Mr. Drakenberg. With them we had fun playing Svärte Per. We had dinner with our new found friend, Mr. Drakenberg, at the K. S. S. Club at Dronningen,

Oslo. Among interesting places visited in Oslo were the House of Parliament, the Royal Castle, and an American warship. We also enjoyed a trolley ride to Holmenkollen.

Traveling by Dovrebanen from Oslo to Trondhjem, we reached this northern city after a fifteen-hour ride. The mountain streams, snowcapped peaks, picturesque villages and farms made the trip memorable. A day was spent in Trondhjem visiting places of interest. Among them was the cathedral, built in the eleventh century in honor of St. Olaf. Late in the day we boarded a train for Storlien, a border town between Norway and Sweden, where we checked in at Järnsvägshotellet. I still remember the delicious smörgåsbord which we enjoyed that evening.

An early morning train on July 25 brought us to Åre, Jämtland. After breakfast at the resort hotel, Signe and I began the ascent of Åreskuttan. Near the top we met a couple, Mr. and Mrs. Youngren, from Germany. We had a grand view of Tännforsen from the top of the mountain.

Two special trains carrying delegates to a World Postal Congress, held in Sweden, stopped at this mountain resort, Åre, for a brief stay. Signe and I left by train in the late afternoon for Östersund, a beautiful city on Lake Storsjön.

On July 26, we boarded a train at 5:00 a.m. for a ride through Bräke, Bollnäs, and Orsa to Mora. The scenery was ever changing—mountains, valleys, rushing rivers and picturesque villages.

The next day, Sunday, was a big day. After visiting places in Mora, such as the Vasa Monument, Zorn's Gammalby, and Mora Church, we left for Rättvik. There we saw the church boats with eight pairs of oars come in from neighboring islands in Lake Siljan. All natives were dressed in national or provincial costumes. A concert was given in the Rättvik Church by *Hembygdskörerna* (local choirs) from Mora, Rättvik, and Leksand honoring the delegates to the World Postal Congress.

A day's visit to the town of Fahlun gave us an opportunity to see the copper mine, one of the oldest mines in the world. We also went to Ornässtugan, where Gustav Vasa hid from the Danes. This unique building was built in 1397.

Traveling all night by train from Vansbro through Dalajärna, we arrived in Kristineham for breakfast. After visiting the new harbor in

Kristineham, we continued our journey to Skattkärr and arrived at Averstad in the afternoon. I immediately changed clothes to help my brother, Sven, with harvesting hay.

For the next couple of weeks, I found many activities at home. I often went fishing with my old schoolmaster, Alf Sundin. I also enjoyed hunting with my brother, Rickard. Together with relatives, I went swimming in Lake Vänern, and I helped with the farm work. It was wonderful to be home. I tried to spend as much time as possible with mother. One day Signe and I took mother to Heljetorp, Väse, to visit the Svenssons, my father's relatives.

Members of the local study circle asked me for a program on Swedish-Americans. I prepared a lecture on the following subject: "Skildringar ur Svensk-Amerikanarnas historia" (Glimpses from the History of Swedish-America). I gave my first lecture in the Mission House in Böj on September 8. The audience was large and very appreciative. The next evening, I gave the same lecture at Skattkärr's Ordens Hus. At each place Mr. Sjöman, Rudolf Larson, and Agni Anderson presented a number of songs: "Barndomshemmet," "Längtan till Fosterlandet," and "Vårt Land." Their contribution to the program, I appreciated very much. I received fifty crowns for each lecture, which I donated to the local study circle.

Sunday, September 14, I preached in Väse Church, which was located in a neighboring parish. I was happy to have mother in the audience. My sermon subject was "Är hjärtat med när du offrar?" (Is your heart in your giving?). After lunch with my family at my sister Annie's home, Björka, we all went to Spånga school house, the school I attended as a boy. Here I gave a lecture on the subject: "Hur vi arbeta i Augustana Kyrkan" (How we work in the Augustana Church). An interesting question period followed.

The following day, Signe, Rickard, and I left by train for Stockholm. Our foster sister, Greta Arvidson, and her brother, Algot, met us at the station. The next three days we did much sightseeing. Among places visited were the Old Town, the Royal Palace (1760), Riddarholm Church, the New Town Hall, the National Museum, and Skansen. One evening we saw a play at the Dramatic Theater.

A church convocation was held in Blaisleholm's Church, Stockholm. I attended the Augustana Day where I met Archbishop Nathan Söderblom, Dr. Peter Peterson, Dr. L. G. Abrahamson, Dr.

Emil Chinlund, and Dr. C. J. Petri. Crown Prince Gustaf Adolf and Crown Princess Louise attended the session at which Dr. Abrahamson was the speaker.

We also made a trip to the university city of Uppsala. In the university library, we saw the famous Codex Argenteus (Silver Bible), written in 500 A.D. We also visited the Castle, the Cathedral, and the burial grounds in Old Uppsala. We returned home to Värmland on the night train. Rickard and I had long talks. Before we parted he told me that he had definitely decided to emigrate to America.

I spent most of the next day in preparation of a sermon. Rev. Erik Palin, pastor of my home church in Östra Fågelvik Parish, had asked me to preach the following Sunday. Since the church was being renovated, the service was to be held in Böj's Mission House. Although it was a rainy day, the attendance was good. My sermon subject was "Vårt Största Problem" (Our Greatest Problem). Sven and Amanda had arranged a young people's party at home that afternoon and evening.

The next two days we spent with relatives and neighbors. At home and at Björka I took many pictures of the family. We had an early birthday celebration for mother. Then came our last day at home. After saying farewell to friends and neighbors, we had an enjoyable evening at home. Before retiring, we bade farewell to most of the members of the family as Mr. Sjöman was to call for us at 4:00 a.m. He took us in his Ford to Karlstad, where we were to board a train for Oslo.

Signe and I had had a wonderful summer. As we left home we wondered if we would ever see our family again. Parting was difficult and I promised mother to continue to write often. She showed me a bundle of my letters which she had kept. I wish now I had asked her for them as they contained many of my early experiences in my early days in America. Mother was reconciled to the fact that we had to part again and gave us her blessing.

Miss Ellen Hultin, a fellow passenger on the *R. M. S. Andania,* had now joined Signe and me on September 26 for our return trip. Upon our arrival in Oslo, we checked in at the Park Hotel on Karl Johansgate. Then we called at the German and French consulates for visas. We had decided to travel through Germany and France and board our return ship in Cherbourg instead of Southhampton.

On the following day, we sailed on board the *S. S. Kong Ring* from Oslo to Hamburg. We had beautiful weather as we sailed down the Oslo fjord. We passed many small islands covered with green forest and charming, small villages. It took hours to reach the open sea.

In the early morning hours of the next day, we sighted Denmark and soon passed Grosser Belt. We arrived at the city of Kiel in the afternoon for passage through the one-hundred-kilometer-long Kiel Canal. It took from 1908 to 1914 to complete this waterway which saves seafarers hundreds of miles. The entire length of the canal was lighted. As we sailed through, we saw high bridges, goats and cattle grazing on the banks, and farmers working in the fields.

After having passed visa and customs inspection, we checked in at Hotel Kronprinsen in Hamburg. It was a pleasant surprise to meet a classmate, Charles D. Mattson, here. He, too, had spent the summer in Sweden and was traveling in Germany and France, with a return reservation on the same ship.

Sigurd Weichelt of Bennett's Travel Agency, whom we had met aboard the *Kong Ring,* became our guide for a trip to Carl Hagenbeck's Tierpark at Stellingen. This park had been built with an unusual architecture. The animals on display appeared to be in their natural habitat. It was a wonderful zoo with a large and varied collection of animals from all parts of the world.

Mr. Weichelt remained with us as we boarded an afternoon train on September 29 for Berlin. The ride took us through forests and well cultivated farm land, generously stocked with domestic animals. We stayed at the Hotel Excelsior in Berlin.

Mr. Weichelt promised to take us to Potsdam. He advised, however, that we should pack a lunch in order to save time. I offered to buy bread, meat, and cheese. Signe and Ellen were to make sandwiches. At the store when I paid for the items, I received some change including a currency bill for *fünfzig milliarden* mark. I did not examine the bill until I had returned to the hotel. I could not interpret the amount—whether it was fifty million or fifty billion marks. I showed the bill to the hotel cashier as I thought the grocery clerk had made an error. If so, I wanted to return any overpayment. He took a pencil and spent several minutes figuring the value of the bill in American money and then he said, "The clerk did not make a mistake. The bill is worth 4½ cents." I had another experience with the same kind of money the next day. I paid 300,000 marks for a cigar. Germany had gone through a financial crisis after World War I, and the printed money became practically worthless. Now new money had been issued, but there was still some old money in circulation. I still have some of these worthless bills.

Fortified with lunch and with Mr. Weichelt as our guide, we journeyed to Potsdam. There we visited the famous Sans Souci Palace, a beautiful building surrounded by formal gardens and a lake. We ate our lunch in an area reserved for tourists. Upon our return to Berlin, we made a circle tour of the city and visited Hofkirche, museums, Tiergarten, and Lupzinger Strasse, the principal street. The Swedish Travel Agency was located on Unter den Linden.

On October 2, we were on our way to Wittenberg. There we saw Lutherhaus, Luther's grave, Lutherstube, and Schlosskirche, on the doors of which Martin Luther so boldly nailed his ninety-five theses. This day meant much to me as I had studied Luther and was familiar with his life and work.

Our next stop was Leipzig, where we hired an auto to take us to the battlefield of Lützen. Here King Gustavus Adolphus of Sweden was killed in 1632 in the Thirty Years' War. We visited the memorial chapel which had been built in his honor. We also had time for a short sightseeing tour of the city of Leipzig before boarding a night train for Frankfurt. From there we continued our journey to France, traveling through such well-known places as Metz and Chateau Thierry. We arrived in Paris the morning of October 4 and found lodging at Hotel De Malte.

Checking on the return sailing schedule at the steamship office, we learned that the ship on which we were to sail had lost its rudder and was in a drydock in Boston. We were further informed that we were now booked on the *S. S. Leviathan*, which was not to sail until October 16. In view of the delay, we were promised thirty-five francs per day for board and room while waiting. This amount did not fully cover expenses, but we had twelve extra days which we planned to use to the utmost.

On the next day, Sunday, we attended services at the Swedish church at 9 Rue Guyat. It was a beautiful building with extra rooms for library, gymnasium, and offices. We had an enjoyable visit with the pastor, Birger Bjurstrom. At the Louvre Museum that afternoon we met the Stenlunds of Chicago, who had come over with us on the *R. M. S. Andania.* We enjoyed *Parsifal* together that evening.

An auto excursion took us to the west side of Paris where we visited many historical places such as the Tomb of Napoleon, the statue of Washington, the Arch of Triumph, and the Tomb of the Unknown Soldier. On the east side of the city, we found additional historical sites, such as the Pantheon, Notre Dame Cathedral, the Palace of Justice, and the school of the Latin Quarter. A visit to the top of the Eiffel Tower with its magnificent view was a memorable experience. The tower was built in 1889 and is 984 feet in height. We made an all-day tour of the Chateau Malmaison, home of Napoleon I.

I traveled to Angoulême with the hope of seeing some French friends whom I had met during my stay in that city as a member of the 54th Ammunition Train during World War I, but I had no luck.

We decided to take a two-day excursion through the battle-fields, sponsored by the American Express. We visited such places as Chateau Thierry, Belleau Woods, Quentin Roosevelt's grave, and Rheims. Rheims Cathedral was partly in ruins but was being rebuilt. While in Rheims, we were fortunate in being conducted through underground tunnels extending many blocks in all directions, where wine was being stored for aging. From Rheims we continued to Berry-au-Boc and the Hindenburg Line. Often we left the bus to walk over fields into trenches and caves. In the afternoon we came to Vic-sur-Aisne and Rethondes (Armistice monument), and the Compiègne Castle, where Joan of Arc was arrested. We returned to Paris in the late evening.

We left Paris October 15 by train for Cherbourg, where we found lodging at the Anglo-American Hotel. It was in this city that the members of the 54th Ammunition Train had landed. I tried to locate the rest camp where we had been quartered a couple of days, but it had been demolished. Cherbourg was a quaint old city with cobblestone streets, stone houses and no modern improvements. The evening was spent observing street life.

October 16 was our departure day. The morning was given to writing letters to relatives in Sweden. We boarded the *S. S. Leviathan* in mid-afternoon and sailed at 6:00 p.m. We had calm, clear weather the first three days during which the passengers became accustomed to the motion of the ship. Few, if any, became ill. Everybody enjoyed the various activities on board. We found a most entertaining movie, Buster Keaton in "The Navigator." We made good use of the ship's library, where the sea edition of the *Chicago Tribune* was most welcome reading. Miss Marcel Spring, who was going to America for the first time, joined Charles, Ellen, Signe, and me in a variety of games. We reached New York on October 21. Our extended summer holiday was at an end.

Just before leaving Sweden for the return trip, I had received a call from Ansgarius Lutheran Church, Manistee, Michigan, to serve that parish during a vacancy at a salary of $150.00 a month. For many days I considered this call. I needed work and I was eager to repay the loan to my friend, Eugene Lothgren. I wrote an acceptance of the call while we were in Germany and mailed the letter in Paris. Now back in U.S.A., I was eager to go to work. After calling on relatives in Chicago, and a couple of days of visiting on the Augustana campus, I was on my way to my new responsibilities as a student pastor.

MY DAYS AS STUDENT PASTOR

I arrived in Manistee by train in the evening of November 1, 1924. A welcoming committee from the Ansgarius Lutheran Church was at the station. The group was headed by the chairman of the church council, John Nelson, and members John L. Anderson, Oscar Lundbom, Arvid Johnson, and their wives. A dinner had been arranged at a nearby restaurant. I was grateful for this thoughtfulness. This get-together helped me become acquainted. Then I was taken to the home of a widow where lodging had been arranged for me. A young man, operator of a men's store and a member of the congregation, Harry Thompson, had a room at the same place. A downtown restaurant had been recommended for my meals. I was assigned to a table for six men who were either in business or professions. We always had good discussions which sometimes became quite lively.

Manistee was not a large town but is beautifully located on Lake Michigan. Besides Ansgarius, there were three other Lutheran churches, a Danish, a Norwegian, and a Missouri Synod. The Danish church had no pastor, and the Norwegian church was served by an older pastor, both churches with a small membership. I had no contact with the pastor of the Missouri Lutheran Church, nor did the pastors of the other churches.

Ansgarius Lutheran Church was organized in 1884 and had at the time of my service 472 communicant members and 129 children. Since it had become vacant, five calls had been extended to pastors, four of whom had declined. Now the members were awaiting an answer from Rev. C. E. Holmer. Rev. J. A. S. Landin of Emanuel Lutheran Church, Ludington, was the vice pastor.

There were many active organizations in the Ansgarius Lutheran Church, such as Ladies' Aid, Women's Home and Foreign Missionary Society, Dorcas Society, Lutheran Brotherhood, Luther League, Junior Mission Band, and the choir. The Sunday School had a teaching staff of eighteen. The Swedish language was used in all meetings of the Ladies' Aid; English was used in all other organizations. Two worship services were held each Sunday, English in the morning and Swedish in the evening. Every other Sunday, the procedure was reversed. There was a different text and sermon for each morning and each evening service. A worship service was also held every other Tuesday evening at Eastlake Chapel, and a mid-week prayer service at the church every Wednesday evening.

The Sunday School, under the leadership of John L. Anderson as superintendent, had an excellent teaching staff, many of whom were public school teachers. I still remember the unique and inspiring Christmas program given by the children and the teachers. Besides regular graded classes in the Sunday School, there were three Bible classes: two in English, one for young women and another for young men; and a third in the Swedish language for older members. The Swedish class was my responsibility. I also taught the confirmation class of five. When the time came for these children to be confirmed, the vice pastor, J. A. S. Landin, had charge of both confirmation and Holy Communion. It was my responsibility to conduct worship service that Sunday in his church, the Emanuel Lutheran Church of Ludington.

It had been the custom that the pastor serve as president of the Ladies' Aid Society. I was asked to serve in that capacity during the vacancy and also as president of Luther League. These two organizations as well as the Lutheran Brotherhood were very active in the church. In all three organizations, topics for study were assigned, such as missions, homes for children and elderly, hospitals, and colleges. These programs did much to acquaint members with and enrich their knowledge of our beloved Augustana Church.

The members of the Luther League met twice each month. I remember the successful banquet held New Year's Eve in honor of out-of-town members home from colleges and universities. There was excellent publicity given the program entitled, "A Trip Around the World." The eighty-five leaguers as passengers on a ship (transported in seventeen automobiles) were bound for many places and countries of the world, such as China, India, France, Germany, and Scandinavia. At each stop, either at a home or at the church, a guide described the country, and tasty food typical of the country was served. As for the ship, the Rock of Gibraltar, and many other well-known tourist spots, all one needed was a good imagination.

I had prepared a stereopticon slide travelogue from pictures taken during my summer in Scandinavia. I titled the program, "A Trip to the Land of Sunlit Nights." The Luther Leaguers had charge of promotion and ticket sales. According to the *Manistee News-Advocate:* "Ansgarius Lutheran Church was filled to capacity." The money earned was used by the leaguers to redecorate Luther Hall. This travelogue was also given in Tustin, Cadillac, Traverse City, and Ludington.

During the winter and spring of 1925, I conducted eighteen funerals. Nine were for non-members, whose families wanted a Lutheran pastor and service. It was the custom to give a short sermon in both the Swedish and English languages, whether the services were in the church or in a funeral chapel.

Oscar F. Lundbom, a cashier in the Manistee County Savings Bank and treasurer of the local congregation, had just come from an appointment with his doctor when we first met. The doctor had informed him that he had symptoms of diabetes and had prescribed a strict diet for him. He said that he was not feeling quite right and that he perhaps needed exercise. "Join me in walking," I said. He accepted my suggestion and became very faithful in meeting me every day at 6:00 a.m. at the Catholic Church. We walked for two hours down to the First Street beach, along the shore of Lake

Michigan for a distance, and then cross country back to town.

After three weeks' walking for two hours each day, Oscar returned to the doctor for a check-up. The doctor said, "You are a perfect patient, one who adheres to the strict diet I prescribed. I now do not find any symptoms of diabetes."

"Doctor," said Oscar, "I have not even started the diet you prescribed." Then he told how he had joined me in a two-hour walk each morning. The doctor was pleased and told him to continue walking.

Oscar and I became good friends. We had time to discuss many topics during our daily walks. However, each Sunday morning he let me walk in silence. I then had time to review my sermons for the day.

When the Oriole Chorus of Augustana College, during its 1925 spring concert tour, appeared in our church in Manistee on April 16, the members were lodged in homes. I suggested to Oscar that we entertain the twenty choristers and their officials at a breakfast. He agreed that we do this on their last morning and that it be held at the First Street beach. The girls were delighted with the Michigan scenery as well as our cooking. We served them fruit, bacon, eggs, sweet rolls, and coffee. When the Augustana *Observer* reported their spring tour, it was mentioned that their visit in Manistee and especially their breakfast on the beach was one of the highlights on the tour.

Another close friend was Harry Thompson, who lodged at the same place as I. One day he said that he and his friend, Teckla, had decided to marry. He had arranged that the pastor of the Norwegian Lutheran Church should perform the ceremony and asked me to be the only attendant. Harry was happily married, prospered in business, and reared a family. We kept in touch with one another throughout the years until his death in 1975.

I have many pleasant memories from my months in Manistee. I had become well acquainted with many men and women in the Ansgarius Lutheran Church whom I admired for their willingness to work and for their faithfulness. My visits in various homes and invitations to dinners were always a pleasure, and my calls on the sick and the elderly were very much appreciated. The enthusiasm of the young people made working with them a joy. My experience as a student pastor had been most satisfying.

I also had pleasant relations with the protestant pastors in Manistee. We shared in programs such as memorial services for war veterans, Thanksgiving services, and community observances. When these pastors heard about my approaching departure, they arranged a farewell party for me. I quote from the *Manistee News-Advocate:* "Seven Protestant pastors gave a farewell to Student Pastor Birger Swenson of Ansgarius Lutheran Church Monday afternoon. It was in the form of a fishing trip and picnic at which the guest had all the luck and cooked the supper."

Good news reached the members of Ansgarius Lutheran Church. Rev. C. E. Holmer had accepted the call to be pastor of the congregation. He and his family would arrive the first week of July 1925. I had been called by the Illinois Conference to serve the Oak Park Lutheran Church at Traverse City for the remainder of the summer. As soon as Pastor Holmer arrived in Manistee, I moved on to my new assignment. Here I was given both lodging and board with Mr. and Mrs. John Winnell at 855 Wester Street.

I arrived in Traverse City on the morning of July 4. The Winnells were ready to leave for the peninsula north of the city where special Fourth of July activities were scheduled for the afternoon. They invited me to accompany them. The country was beautiful. The land in all directions was covered with cherry trees. One could not help but speculate that this peninsula would some day become one of America's great summer resorts.

Traverse City was a popular tourist resort. The Oak Park Lutheran Church, where I would be working, was organized in 1892. It had in 1925 only twenty-seven communicant members and eleven children. The church property consisted of a chapel and a parsonage which was occupied by a family named Johnson. Mr. Johnson operated a grocery store.

The executive board of the Illinois Conference asked me to canvass the west side of the city. For this project, I enlisted the help of the women of the congregation. Five hundred families were visited. The members of Oak Park Lutheran Church became enthusiastically convinced that there was a promising field for an English Lutheran church on the west side. I notified Dr. Peter Peterson, president of the conference, of the result of the canvass. He arrived

Thursday, September 10, to conduct a service and a congregational meeting. In the evening at an informal meeting, the twenty-seven communicant members expressed their confidence that they could raise seven hundred dollars toward a pastor's salary. Their enthusiasm impressed Dr. Peterson, who later placed a pastor on the field. The name of the congregation was changed from Oak Park to Bethlehem Lutheran Church. Eventually the congregation grew and became self-supporting.

My work as a student pastor had come to an end. I appreciated my experiences in Manistee and Traverse City. I enjoyed working with young people and liked pastoral duties, but I was not sure that I should enter the ministry; hence I had no definite plans to return to Rock Island to enroll in the seminary.

My brother, Ragnar, had married in 1925. He and his wife, Frida, had invited me to visit them at their south side apartment in Chicago. I had given Rev. Carl Bostrom, pastor of Tabor Lutheran Church, South Chicago, my brother's address. He called me upon my arrival and asked me to preach in his church on the following Sunday. I promised to do so. After the service, I was invited to the parsonage for dinner. Then he handed me the following telegram.

WESTERN UNION TELEGRAM

Rock Island, Illinois
September 22, 1925

Birger Swenson
Care of Rev. C. D. Bostrom
7950 Escanaba Avenue
Chicago, Illinois

The church needs you and we believe God wants you in the ministry we bid you welcome and should rejoice to see you here tomorrow when matriculation committee meets again.

P. Peterson, G. A. Andreen

MY YEAR IN THE SEMINARY

As I was undecided about enrolling in the seminary, I waited two days before going to Rock Island. When I arrived, I discovered that the matriculation committee had disbanded. A special committee was called to interview me, consisting of the theological faculty, the president of the synod, Dr. G. A. Brandelle, and Dr. G. A. Andreen. A most friendly welcome was extended me. Although I was late, I was told that I could enroll. Dr. Conrad E. Lindberg, dean of the Seminary, asked me for my personal history, a prerequisite for each person entering the seminary. It was to include not only family, education, and religious background but also a statement as to my reasons for studying for the ministry. My answer was that I did not have a written personal history prepared. Instead I asked permission to enroll for a year. If, after a year, I felt I should continue and eventually enter the ministry, I would be happy to submit a personal history. Dr. Sven Youngert said, "I believe this fellow has a mind of his own. I think we should let him do what he wants." I was given permission to enroll and soon I was settled. I was assigned a room in the new seminary residence hall.

After consultation with Dean Lindberg, I decided to take courses for study that would lead to the degree of Bachelor of Divinity. My subjects and teachers were as follows: Hebrew with Dr. Carl A. Blomgren; church history, Dr. Adolf Hult; church polity, Dr. Conrad E. Lindberg; philosophy, Dr. Sven J. Youngert; and Bible and homiletics, Professor Sven J. Sebelius. I found that I needed a third year of Greek. Together with others, I enrolled in a special third year Greek class with Frank Bonander as teacher.

At the first meeting of the junior class (the first year), I was delighted to see so many Augustana graduates, whom I had known during my college days. In this class of twenty-three members, there were also alumni from other Augustana Synod colleges—Bethany, Upsala, and Gustavus Adolphus. The class elected the following officers: president, John Leaf; vice president, Eskil Englund; treasurer, Reuben Pearson; and secretary, Emil R. Carlson.

The year of 1925 was a significant year for Augustana College and Theological Seminary. Dr. G. A. Andreen reminded us time and again that it was fifty years since Augustana had come to Rock Island. A group of professors and students had come from Paxton, Illinois, in the fall of 1875 to a new home erected on the slope of Zion Hill. The new home, which later was used as a men's dormitory, housed Dr. T. N. Hasselquist, the president, and his family, Professor C. O. Granere, and students. There were classrooms, a chapel, a library, a museum, a dining room, and a kitchen—all under one roof.

Two students in 1875 were still in the service of Augustana in 1925; namely, Professor Carl L. E. Esbjörn and Dr. Gustav A. Andreen, beloved by both students and friends.

Dr. Andreen related that in 1875 when the building was dedicated, all guests were deeply impressed by the commodious building, the view over the cities, the Mississippi River, and the Arsenal Island. He further stated that all the hopes of the teachers, students, and friends for moving to Rock Island had certainly come true. The new location had brought many advantages as well as blessings to the institution which they so deeply cherished.

Homecoming was combined with the 50th anniversary of the location in Rock Island. The three-day program on October 22-24, 1925, was well-planned with divine services, concerts, lectures, culminating in an anniversary-homecoming banquet. It brought former students and visitors from all parts of the country for this happy occasion. The highlights for me were the pioneer programs, depicting the hardships, the struggle, and the success of the founders of Augustana. The combined anniversary-homecoming banquet was held in the gymnasium, Friday evening, October 23. Dr. Andreen was the toastmaster and music was furnished by the college band and the Wennerberg and Oriole choruses. Speeches were made by Mr. F. C. Denkmann, whose family gave the college library; the mayors of Rock Island and Moline; Dr. G. A. Brandelle; Mr. Wendell Lund, representing the homecoming committee; Mr. Carl Peterson, the athletes; and by Senator C. S. Deneen. This anniversary observance will never be forgotten by the faculty, the students, and visitors.

Rev. Carl J. Johnson had now been business manager of Augustana College and Theological Seminary for two years, succeeding Mr. David Beckstrom. While I was serving the congregation in Manistee, Michigan, Rev. Johnson wrote to me several times inquiring if I intended to return to Augustana to enter the seminary. He wanted me to resume my former position as manager of the cafeteria. This inquiry was rather amusing to me as I had understood that he had felt that I was overpaid for the job in my senior year. I had been paid forty dollars per month and board. Now he wrote that he was willing to pay more if I would accept the responsibility as manager. His complaint was that he had not received monthly financial reports from my successor, and the business of the cafeteria had fallen off. Two boarding houses were now operating in the neighborhood.

In taking over the work as manager, I did not want to hurt anyone. I shifted assignments, but no one was eliminated from the staff. I knew that the women on the regular staff were as efficient as ever and willing to cooperate. In order to create interest, I proposed a contest. Any student who could suggest a new dish for the menu—meat, vegetable, or dessert—should inform the manager. If the suggestion was popular with the students, reasonable in price, and acceptable to the management, the winner would be given a week's free board. We were pleasantly surprised at the response. We were also delighted to see business gradually returning to the cafeteria.

I remained active in some of the college organizations such as Olof Rudbeck Literary Society, the Student Council, and the Omicron Sigma Omicron fraternity, the members of which were referred to as the OSOs. This last named group had a sleigh ride party at the first snowfall on November 8. It was a happy occasion.

Being in the seminary, I joined the Concordia Society, founded in 1898, which included in its membership all seminary students. It held bi-weekly meetings with the following two goals: to invite lecturers on subjects helpful to pastors and to promote the seminary and its program among students in all colleges of the Augustana Lutheran Church.

Once a month the seminary students held an informal dinner and social hour, known as the seminary stag. A variety program followed the meal, such as talks and musical selections by the students. One of the features of each meeting was the reading of the *Semville Siren.* This monthly journal had not only news but also humor and happenings in the classroom. The December stag was known for its old-fashioned Christmas dinner and program. At this stag the theological faculty were guests of honor.

A pleasant surprise to all on the campus came as we returned from Thanksgiving vacation. We learned that Professor Esbjörn had answered the call of Cupid and was married on Thanksgiving day. He was serenaded and congratulated by students and friends.

The annual *Messiah* concert was held on December 11. We were approaching the end of the fall term and the beginning of Christmas vacation.

A letter from Dr. Peter Peterson, dated November 18, 1925, informed me that by unanimous decision of the Executive Board of the Illinois Conference, I was extended a call to serve the churches at Traverse City and Mancelona, Michigan, during the coming Christmas holidays. As remuneration the board pledged one hundred dollars together with my railroad fare. I received this call because of my experience in Traverse City the past summer. Mancelona was new to me. I was grateful for the call and accepted by return mail.

As soon as I could leave my duties in the cafeteria, I went by train to Traverse City. I was happy to renew acquaintances of the past summer. The people seemed pleased to see me and were grateful to the Illinois Conference for sending me. My host and hostess for board and room were the same friendly couple, the John Winnells. I decided to divide my time on the field. The first week was spent in Traverse City; the Christmas week in Mancelona; and the remainder of the holiday period back in Traverse City. We had busy days together with divine services, Sunday School, Ladies' Aid, and young people's meetings. I remember a most enjoyable occasion with the young people in a home. It turned out to be an unrehearsed song service. We all agreed that we should have a similar program on New Year's Eve. The young people promised to practice.

The Gustav Adolf congregation in Mancelona was organized in 1899. It had at the time of my visit twenty-six communicant members and twelve children. Lodging had been arranged for me in the home of a widow. She, however, together with her children, was leaving the day of my arrival to visit friends in Minnesota. She left their dog with me. I had no trouble with him except that he insisted on staying in my room at night.

Besides a divine service on Sunday, a Ladies' Aid meeting, and calling on members, the highlight of my stay was the *Julotta* (early morning service on Christmas Day). The service was announced for 5:00 a.m. I arrived at the church at 4:40 a.m. and found the door locked. There was more than a foot of snow on the ground and below zero weather. I waited until the janitor arrived just in time for the service. He had overslept and was very apologetic. The worshipers, still dressed in their heavy coats, arrived and filled the pews. I went before the altar and conducted the opening service wearing my overcoat; however, the big stove fired by wood soon became red hot. A candlelit Christmas tree also gave heat. By the time I was to enter the pulpit, I could remove my overcoat. In spite of the cold, the organ was working, and the congregation sang with gusto the familiar hymn "Var Hälsad Sköna Morgonstund" (All Hail to Thee, O Blessed Morn). We had in this isolated congregation a typical Swedish *Julotta,* which was very much appreciated. This was followed by another service at 11:00 a.m.

My short stay in Mancelona passed quickly. I had only my breakfast to prepare as I was invited out for the other meals.

I returned to Traverse City for another full week of activities. We had a large gathering of members and friends for the New Year's Eve program with music, reading, and talks followed by refreshments and good fellowship. It was a memorable evening for me and also for the members who as yet had no permanent pastor. I felt that my holiday visit to these two congregations was indeed worthwhile.

When we resumed our studies after the Christmas vacation, some of us questioned the value of Hebrew. It was a difficult language to learn as well as to write. One student asked our teacher, "Do you think we will have to know Hebrew in Heaven?"

He answered, "I would feel sorry for you if you don't."

One of the professors had a list of eight or ten names of men on the blackboard to whom he would often refer as ultra liberals. Among them were Archbishop Nathan Söderblom and Dr. Harry Emerson Fosdick. The professor always opened our class with prayer. One day after concluding this prayer, he pointed to the list of names on the blackboard and said,

"These men use the same words and phrases when they pray, but they mean different." I immediately objected and said,

"You have just prayed. I cannot judge your sincerity; neither can you judge these men whose names are listed on the blackboard. Only God can be the judge." He looked at me and turned to the lesson of the day. The next time we met, the professor said,

"I apologize to all of you. I had no right to judge the spirit and sincerity of anyone offering a prayer, including those whose names are listed on the blackboard." I admired him and thanked him for acknowledging his misjudgment. The list, however, remained on the board.

A teacher I liked very much was Dr. Sven G. Youngert, professor of New Testament and philosophy. He was scholarly, respected, and warmhearted, but often was confused in his expressions. One time, to illustrate a point, he said with great emphasis, "I tell you, theological students, it was like a pistol out of a shot."

Dr. Youngert had a dog named Mickey. He would sometimes refer to his dog and tell us how smart he was. Lunch time came at 12:20 p.m., but Mickey would come and bark outside the classroom door at 12:00 noon. When Dr. Youngert heard the dog, he would say, "I don't know what time it is, but I hear Mickey. Class dismissed."

The big event during the spring term was the second Christian Conference held at Augustana February 11-14, 1926, with the challenging theme, "The Master is here and calleth thee." The conference, which proved to be the largest of its kind ever held in the synod, was sponsored by the Christian Brotherhood at Augustana and by the synodical Luther League. It was headed by a committee of twelve with Cecil G. Johnson, chairman, and Rev. Conrad Bergendoff, program chairman. Dr. Ralph H. Long was one of the many speakers, and music was furnished by local and visiting groups. The conference left memories which lingered long afterward.

Professor Sebelius was our class guardian and counselor. I had talked with him about my future as I was undecided as to whether or not I should continue my theological studies and eventually apply for ordination. I loved my church and wanted to serve. Could I better serve my Lord and my church as a layman? This was a question I would soon have to answer.

During this school year, besides my work as manager of the cafeteria, I had been quite successful taking orders for sets of books offered by the Augustana Book Concern. Mr. A. G. Anderson, the manager, and Rev. Emil F. Bergren, circulation manager, offered me a job to travel in New England during the summer of 1926 in the interest of the Book Concern, especially the church papers, *Augustana* and the *Lutheran Companion*. The remuneration was a commission or a percentage allowed on each sale. I was accustomed to such an arrangement and I accepted hoping that by fall I could come to a full decision about my future.

When my first year in the seminary came to an end, I also finished my work as manager of the cafeteria. Students whose help was needed came and went. The mainstay, however, was the regular crew of six or more women. Mrs. Ida Anderson, who for some time had been in charge, had replaced Mrs. Watson. Mrs. Nelson, the cook, was still with us. I marveled at her strength and steadfastness. I owed a heartfelt thanks to these women. Their cooperation and loyalty had made my work as manager much easier.

The annual meeting of the Augustana Synod was scheduled to be held in Philadelphia the second week in June. I suggested to Mr. Anderson, the manager of the Augustana Book Concern, that I attend this synodical meeting in order that I might meet many of the pastors of the New England Conference. He concurred that becoming acquainted with these pastors would be a help to me.

Dr. George A. Fahlund, Sunday School secretary of the synod, in whose home I had had lodging for a couple of years, was also traveling east. Arriving in Chicago, we learned that the John Ericsson League of Illinois had arranged for a special train on the Baltimore and Ohio Railroad to take the Illinois members to Washington, D.C., to attend the unveiling of the John Ericsson monument. We were invited to join them. Both of us enjoyed the accommodations assigned us. Neither of us had ever traveled so luxuriously before. We were also informed that we could stay at the Hotel Willard, where the league had reservations for the entire group. As we felt that it was an advantage to stay with the group, we accepted.

Upon our arrival in Washington in the early morning, we were told that our baggage would be taken directly to the hotel and placed in the assigned rooms. The group was taken by sightseeing buses to Mount Vernon and other places of interest during the forenoon. We arrived at the Hotel Willard about noon and had lunch there.

The big event was scheduled for the afternoon. Buses took us to Potomac Park for the unveiling of the John Ericsson monument. We were favored with reserved seats in a special section from which I could take close-up pictures of President Coolidge, Crown Prince Gustavus Adolphus and Crown Princess Louise of Sweden. The principal addresses were made by the President and the Crown Prince. I felt fortunate to be present at this august occasion when a son of my home province, Värmland, namely, John Ericsson, was honored.

In the evening, the John Ericsson League banquet was held at the Hotel Willard, with the Honorable Herbert C. Hoover, Secretary of Commerce, as speaker. Carl R. Chindblom, a Republican member of the United States Congress from Illinois, also had a part in the program. Music was furnished by the U.S. Marine Band. It was a black-tie affair. Dr. Fahlund could dress as a clergyman; I had only a business suit, which upon inquiry was acceptable. I had another reason for hesitating to attend when I learned the price of the ticket was ten dollars. I was not accustomed to paying $10.00 for a meal. This occasion, however, was something special. We attended and felt that the experience was well worth the price.

The Illinois group moved on to Philadelphia the next morning. Dr. Fahlund and I wanted to stay a couple of days longer for more sightseeing. When I asked for the bill at the hotel, I was told that it was paid in full. Three weeks later I received a statement from the office of the John Ericsson League of Illinois. Dr. Fahlund and I agreed that we should find less expensive lodging, as the hotel charged $10.00 per day. We soon found a room at the nearby YMCA for $1.50 per day per person.

During the next two days we visited many places of interest, such as Arlington National Cemetery, the Lincoln Memorial, the Smithsonian Institute, the Library of Congress, and the Capitol. As Congress was in session, we had the privilege of seeing the young Senator LaFollette of Wisconsin on the floor and hearing him speak. We wanted to take a ride to the top of the Washington Monument, 555 feet high, but we found the elevator out of order. We decided to walk up. We were quite proud of ourselves when we reached the top, until we saw a young woman with a babe in her arms who had also walked to the top. There we had a thrilling view of the city of Washington.

Our next stop was New York City. We checked in at the Swedish Lutheran Immigrant Home, of which Rev. Axel C. Helander was superintendent. This institution had given wonderful service to seamen and immigrants over a long period of years. Shortly after our arrival, we had a visit from Dr. Mauritz Stolpe, pastor of Gustavus Adolphus Lutheran Church. This church was organized in 1865. Now the congregation was to be honored by a visit from Crown Prince Gustavus Adolphus and Crown Princess Louise on Sunday. The service was to be a *Högmässa* (high mass). Dr. Stolpe wanted his sermon translated for the daily press. He offered Dr. Fahlund two tickets if he would do the translation. Dr. Fahlund accepted and invited me to accompany him. We were asked to attend an orientation meeting an hour before the service where we were instructed how to bow and curtsey before royalty. It was really amusing. The women were dressed in their finery; the men, in tail coats and high hats. As a student I got by in my business suit. We met the royalty without mishap. In church they were seated in large chairs on the right side of the pulpit near the altar rail. We were seated directly behind them. Both choir and pastor did well at this festive occasion.

Following the service, Dr. Fahlund and I were luncheon guests of Mr. Carl Bohman, former manager of the Augustana Book Concern branch store in New York City. Then he took us on a double decker sightseeing bus. We covered most of Manhattan Island, thereby getting good views of various historic buildings and places which he pointed out to us from the upper deck. After another day of sightseeing in New York City, it was time to move on to Philadelphia for the synodical convention.

The Augustana Lutheran Church had two small congregations in Philadelphia, neither large enough to host the synod; therefore, the convention was held in a German Lutheran church. I found lodging with a former college roommate, Enoch Sandeen, in the home of an Augustana church member. It took us more than an hour to travel each way, but we did not mind the distance and appreciated the kind hospitality.

At this annual convention, the Augustana Book Concern had a sales display in charge of the book store manager, D. W. Dahlsten. I decided that the best place to meet the pastors from the New England Conference was at the book display. I was fortunate in meeting most of them in less than two days. They welcomed me to visit their congregations. The annual convention of the Augustana Lutheran Church generally lasted a week, but as my mission here was accomplished, I was eager to leave for New England to begin my summer's work.

My first stop was at St. John's Lutheran Church, Stamford, Connecticut, with Nore G. Gustafson as pastor. This church is in the Hartford District in which there were twenty-six congregations, most of which were organized before 1900. As the Augustana Book Concern had no branch stores in New England, I found people eager to listen to what I had to offer in the way of devotional books, hymnals, and church papers. I was encouraged by the orders that came to me for books and subscriptions to church papers. I also found that the Swedish language was more common in the East than in the Midwest; therefore, the Swedish weekly, *Augustana,* attracted as much interest as the English paper, the *Lutheran Companion.* As I was ready to move on to Salem Lutheran Church, Bridgeport, Connecticut, Pastor Gustafson asked me to come back to speak at the midsummer festival on June 24, which invitation I accepted.

Upon arrival in a new place, my first call was on the pastor. When I met A. J. Okerblom, pastor of Salem Lutheran Church, he invited me to preach at the morning service on the following day. He thought that in this way the people would learn to know me. Similar invitations became a regular procedure during the whole summer. Besides sermons in either English or Swedish, I was asked to give talks to Ladies' Aids, the Luther Leagues, and men's groups. The text for this first sermon was on the prodigal son. My title was "Lost and Found."

While I was in New Britain, I had the pleasure of spending a day with my friend, Andrew Larson, one of my traveling companions from my home parish in Sweden when we emigrated to America in 1912. When my brother, Ragnar, and I moved to Chicago, after a short stay in Proctor, Vermont, Andrew stayed on in New England.

Some congregations in New England had large memberships. The First Lutheran Church in New Britain, with Abel Ahlquist, pastor, had 1656 members; the Emanuel Lutheran Church, Hartford, with Julius Hulteen, pastor, had 1296 members; and Gloria Dei Lutheran, Providence, with Karl Johanson, pastor, had 912 members. The total number of congregations in the Hartford and Providence districts was forty. I did not have time to visit all of them, but I hoped to return.

During the summer I gradually realized that I could perhaps serve my church better as a layman than as a pastor. In looking back on my experience as a student pastor, I found that the work with the people, both young and old, appealed to me. I had felt satisfaction in teaching, preaching, calling on the sick and visiting the members in their homes. I failed, however, to have the same enthusiasm and interest in my work at the seminary. It appeared to me that I was being cast into a mold which I did not fit; therefore, when a letter came to me from the manager of the Augustana Book Concern offering me a job as a field representative, I decided to accept. My remuneration was to be a $160.00 per month plus traveling expenses. Upon my return to Rock Island, I spent one day at the seminary visiting professors and classmates and informing them of my decision. During the next four days, I conferred with the manager and the circulation manager of the Augustana Book Concern regarding my work as a field representative.

Birger's parents, Sven and Johanna Spetz Svensson

Signe and Birger, age 4;
Rickard, age 2

Birger, age 14

Birger's birthplace, Averstad, Skattkärr.
Left: Sister Annie, brother Sven, Mother, and brother Rickard.

Brothers and sisters who emigrated to the United States.
Robert, Signe, Birger, Ragnar, and Hilma. Another brother, Rickard, spent 5 years in
the United States, 1925-1930.

Corporal Birger Swenson, 1918-1919

Birger at Augustana Academy 1917

Birger, Augustana College graduate, 1924

Lyal

At time of marriage,
August 14, 1943

Birger

V

A CAREER IN CHURCH PUBLICATIONS

I spent many hours in order to become familiar with the products and services that the Augustana Book Concern had to offer. I also wanted to know more about the church at large. By chance I found a large box of pictures in a storeroom on the top floor of the Book Concern. Here were pictures depicting various operations within the publishing house, such as typesetting, printing, and binding of the church papers and books. Here also was a large assortment of pictures of the 1300 churches which comprised our synod, of the colleges, and of the forty or more charitable institutions throughout the United States which were owned and operated by the church. I decided to make up a stereopticon lecture with the title, "Augustana Today." My friend, Ernest Schroder, of the Victor Animatograph Corporation, Davenport, promised prompt service. His company made slides which were hand colored. This lecture proved popular and was a great help to me.

I began my field work in the La Porte District of the Illinois Conference. The first congregation I visited was Bethlehem at Gary, where many of the members were employed in the steel mills. I spent several days in South Bend, where the Studebaker Automobile Company was located, employing many of our church members. The pastor of Gloria Dei Lutheran Church was E. H. Carlson.

When I arrived in La Porte, the pastor of the Bethany Lutheran Church, M. W. Gustafson, was waiting for me and offered to take me to the homes of the many members living on farms. We spent two days in the country and added many subscribers to our church papers, *Augustana* and *Lutheran Companion,* as well as orders for hymnals and devotional books.

The Augustana Synod had two conferences east of Chicago, New England, which included the six New England states, and New York with the states of Ohio, Pennsylvania, New York, New Jersey, Maryland, and the District of Columbia. I had visited part of New England in the summer of 1926 and now I was to travel for a year in these two conferences.

My first visit was in the Cleveland District of the New York Conference. I was fortunate in arriving in time to attend a mission meeting held at the Bethlehem Lutheran Church in Cleveland. Here I had the opportunity of meeting all the pastors of the district. With their cooperation, I had no trouble in arranging a schedule for my illustrated talk, "Augustana Today," and a plan for visiting their parishes in the interest of our church publications. The pastor of Bethlehem Lutheran Church, Rev. J. A. Lundgren, had arranged an interesting program for this mission meeting. Among the speakers was Dr. Julius Lincoln, field secretary of the Augustana Synod. Another speaker was a young attorney, A. Robert Johnson, a member of Bethlehem Lutheran Church and president of the Lutheran Brotherhood of the New York Conference.

Pastor Otto O. Oleen of the Messiah Lutheran Church, Ashtabula, Ohio, asked me to give my program at noon on Thanksgiving Day, when a potluck dinner had been planned at the church. This affair proved to be a successful occasion.

Rev. Göran E. Forsberg, pastor of Bethlehem Lutheran Church, Erie, Pennsylvania, asked me to come on a Friday to give the "Augustana Today" lecture that evening and to preach for him at both the Swedish and the English services on Sunday. He said he would meet me in his "trollhoppa" (Model T Ford), but since I was uncertain as to the time of my arrival, I did not notify him. As it turned out, I arrived in a snowstorm. After checking in at the YMCA, I went directly to the church for the program. The attendance was good in spite of the stormy evening.

Pastor Forsberg invited me to come for breakfast the following morning and to spend the day in his study to prepare the two sermons for Sunday. After breakfast he took me to a barn back of the parsonage, inside of which stood his "trollhoppa." After inviting me for a ride, he drove around the block and back into the barn and said, "You did not believe I could drive, did you?" This was his way of telling me that he was displeased that I had not informed him of the time of my arrival.

After lunch Pastor Forsberg lay down on a sofa for his afternoon nap. His heavy breathing interfered with my study. When his daughter, Signe, looked in and said she was going uptown, I was ready to join her.

Sunday came when I was to preach in the English language in the morning and in Swedish in the evening. At lunch Pastor Forsberg said, "You were not orthodox in your sermon this morning." I was taken aback and asked, "Where and how did I make a mistake?" He did not tell me but suggested that I should apologize to the congregation in the evening before my Swedish sermon. After I had finished my sermon that evening and Pastor Forsberg was to make announcements, I was not sure what to expect. He surprised me with very friendly and appreciative remarks about my visit and wished me success in calling on his members during the following days.

I learned that Rev. Forsberg was a stone cutter before he studied for the ministry. He was rough and outspoken in his manner and yet kind. He was an able pastor of a congregation of more than 600, including children. He had a lovely family. His daughter, Signe, married Rev. Frank Bonander, and his son, Theodore, became an Augustana pastor.

I spent December 1926, and part of January 1927, in the Jamestown District. I found the city of Jamestown a Lutheran stronghold. The First Lutheran Church had 1744 communicant members and 986 children; the Immanuel Lutheran Church, 967 communicant members and 700 children. There were two other Augustana churches, namely Holy Trinity and Bethel. It was fun and very encouraging to work in this district. The pastors were friendly and most helpful; the people were interested in the church and eager to learn about our church papers, hymnals, and devotional books. I was often invited to homes of both pastors and members. I was a guest of Dr. and Mrs. Felix V. Hanson for Christmas Eve and of Rev. and Mrs. Daniel Nystrom on Christmas Day.

On New Year's Eve I had a rather unique experience. The pastors of Holy Trinity, Immanuel, and First Lutheran, all had asked me to give my lecture "Augustana Today" that evening. Luckily the churches were located only a block or two apart and able to agree on a time, Holy Trinity at 9:00 p.m., Immanuel at 10:00 p.m., and First at 11:00 p.m. We had a large gathering in each church.

At a pastors' meeting in Jamestown, I met Rev. C. O. Bomgren of Bethlehem Lutheran Church, Falconer. He invited me to visit his church the following Sunday and promised that I could bring a greeting. In this way he felt that his members would know me when I called on them. Since I had difficulty with transportation, I arrived at the church just as Pastor Bomgren entered the pulpit. During his announcements, he greeted me. Then to my surprise he stated that I was to preach at the Swedish service which was to follow. At the close of the English service, I approached him and said, "Pastor Bomgren, you never asked me and I have not promised to preach." He said, "I know, but my people will be very disappointed if you don't." I did preach but not on the text for the day. I had a few familiar texts that I could use in an emergency.

After a delightful luncheon at the parsonage, Pastor Bomgren took me to Zion Lutheran Church, Frewsburg, of which he was also pastor. Here I spoke at an afternoon service.

I did not hesitate to accept requests for preaching or speaking as I found these opportunities a great help to me in my work. I was asked to fill the pulpit a number of times for Dr. Felix V. Hanson when he was away on duties as president of the New York Conference.

During the winter months of 1927, I traveled in the Pittsburgh, Warren, Wilcox, and Williamsport districts. I met many interesting people, both pastors and lay members. I especially remember Pastor Carl A. Rask of Tabor Lutheran Church, Kane, Pennsylvania. He was short and stocky and liked his food, and his wife was an excellent cook. During my visit in Kane, many of the church organizations held meetings. After each one, day or evening, Pastor Rask invited me to the parsonage for a meal or a snack. He was a most genial fellow and a good promoter of our church papers.

Pastor Clarence H. Anderzon, Lebanon Lutheran Church of Du Bois, and his wife, Rosa, were friends of Augustana days. I was their house guest during my visit at this congregation. While there, I wrote an application for the position of circulation manager of the Augustana Book Concern, a vacancy having occurred with the resignation of the Rev. Emil F. Bergren.

While working in Gustavus Adolphus Lutheran Church, Pittsburgh, I had the pleasure and unique experience of attending my first sound motion picture. The star was Al Jolson, singing "Mammy."

The annual meeting of the New York Conference was scheduled for April 27–May 1, 1927, at the St. Paul Lutheran Church, Brooklyn. Rev. John Eastlund was the host pastor. I was asked to take charge of a book display shipped from Rock Island. This convention proved to be very pleasant for me as I had met most of the pastors and many of the delegates during my months of travel in the conference.

The convention of the New England Conference followed and was held May 4-8 at Emanuel Lutheran Church, Hartford. The host pastor was Rev. Julius Hulteen. Under President S. G. Hagglund's leadership, the Swedish language was still very much in use although English seemed to be gradually becoming the official language. The official minutes, however, were still published in Swedish.

Following this convention, I decided to stay in New England to visit Worcester, Providence, and Boston districts, which time had not permitted me to cover the previous year. Many congregations in these districts had large communicant memberships and were a good field for my work. In the city of Worcester with five Augustana churches, one of them, Calvary Lutheran, was an English congregation organized in 1921. The pastor, A. O. Hjelm, told me he had about fifteen different nationalities in his church. The daily papers gave good coverage on church news. One such news item appeared in the *Worcester Telegram* on June 25: "A midsummer festival was held at the Greendale Lutheran Church on June 24. Birger Swenson, a student from Rock Island, gave an address entitled, 'Midsummer in Sweden.' "

While I was in Worcester, an event took place that stirred the world. I was at a movie on May 27, 1927, when suddenly the news was flashed on the screen that Charles A. Lindbergh had completed his solo, nonstop, transatlantic flight and had landed in Paris in his small plane, the Spirit of St. Louis. This news electrified the world and made him a universal hero overnight, and justly so.

During the summer of 1927, I also attended two Luther League events. One was an overnight boat trip from Boston to Portland, Maine. Upon our arrival we were taken in a smaller vessel to an island for an all-day outing which included hikes, swimming, a ball game, and a clam bake. In the evening an interesting program was given by Luther Leaguers at Immanuel Lutheran Church, Portland. I had the opportunity of bringing a greeting from the Book Concern. The other event was the annual meeting of the New York Conference Luther League held at Eagle's Mere, Pennsylvania, July 9-16. We had lodging at a beautiful hotel, The Raymond, on the Lake of the Eagle. This tourist center is located in the mountains, twenty-four miles from Muncy, the closest railroad station. I had ordered a shipment of books from Rock Island. Business was good as the attendance was large and made up of older leaguers. The week's program was excellent. The Bible teacher was Dr. Samuel Miller; the speakers were pastors and lay people including the president of the New York Conference.

I was working in Gethsemane Lutheran Church, Manchester, New Hampshire, when I was recalled to Rock Island to take charge of a campaign for our church papers which had been initiated by the board of directors of the Augustana Book Concern.

On the train back to Rock Island, I had time to think about my year's work as a field representative. It had been a good year. The experience gained would be a help to me in my future work with the Augustana Book Concern.

I was fortunate on my return to Rock Island to obtain lodging and board with my former hosts of college days, Dr. and Mrs. George Fahlund.

During my year of travel, new leadership had come to the Augustana Book Concern. A. G. Anderson had held the position of general manager from 1889 to 1926. He died July 9, 1927. Otto Leonardson, manager of the Minneapolis branch of the Book Concern, had been called as interim manager and was succeeded by J. G. Youngquist at the meeting of the board of directors on October 12, 1927. Mr. Youngquist came from the Great West Printing Company of Minneapolis. Others with whom I would be working were Clarke L. Swanson, office manager and cashier; D. W. Dahlsten, book store manager; and Oscar G. Ericson, production manager of the manufacturing department.

My new assignment was also a new experience. For years I had been promoting and selling subscriptions by word of mouth; now I would be using direct mail and advertising. Besides *Augustana* and the *Lutheran Companion*, the circulation of the following periodicals was also my responsibility: *Augustana Quarterly*, a theological journal; *Bible Study Quarterly*, with a student and teacher edition; and the Sunday school papers, *The Young People,* the *Olive Leaf, Little Folks,* and *Barnens Tidning.*

I had six willing workers in the circulation department, all women, two of whom could take dictation. I found that I could keep them busy as the correspondence related to the promotion of the church paper campaign was heavy. I was surprised to discover that a considerable correspondence required an answer in Swedish. As none of these women could take dictation in Swedish, I had to write letters in longhand to be typed. The campaign carried the motto, "A church paper in every home." Each participating congregation had organized a committee with a chairman. With pleasure I often found that the chairman was one whom I had met while I was a field representative. The result of the campaign was most encouraging; consequently, I recommended to the board of directors that a week be designated each fall as Church Paper Week. This recommendation was adopted.

It was a happy day for me when I learned that the board of directors of the Augustana Book Concern had accepted my application and had named me circulation manager as of March 1, 1928, at a salary of $2,500.00 per year. I succeeded the Rev. E. F. Bergren, who had resigned the previous spring to accept a call to become pastor of the First Lutheran Church, Des Moines. Rev. Bergren had taken up his work as circulation manager after Grant Hultberg had moved to Philadelphia to become general manager of the United Lutheran Publication House.

In the spring of 1928, I joined a group of about twenty men who were designated as "Ready to hit the line for a greater Augustana." We were asked to give four or more weeks of our time to do advanced canvassing among the alumni and former students of Augustana College. With the permission of the management of the

Book Concern, I spent about six weeks traveling in Illinois, Iowa, and Nebraska, and calling on prospective donors. I would return to Rock Island each Friday evening and work all day Saturday to clear my desk. Mrs. Olga Quist, former secretary of Professor Andrew Kempe, treasurer of Augustana College, helped with correspondence. I would leave again on Sunday afternoon. Although Dr. O. H. Pannkoke was the director of the campaign, we worked directly under Rev. Knut Erickson, who was in charge of the campaign office. This effort for a greater Augustana College with a goal of $1,500,000 was successful; however, the great depression that followed made payment of pledges difficult. It became necessary to make adjustments on some pledges.

During summers I was asked to take book displays to Luther League camps, such as at Ogden, Iowa, Crystal Falls, Michigan, Long Lake, Illinois, Round Rock, Texas, Eagle's Mere, Pennsylvania, and later, Camp Augustana, Lake Geneva, Wisconsin. I took the display as I drove my car to all camps, except in Texas, at a car allowance of two cents a mile. The friendships made with young people that I met have lasted a lifetime. After forty or fifty years, I still correspond with some of them.

Annual meetings of the thirteen conferences of the Augustana Synod were held during April and May. The synodical meeting came in June and was held in a different section of the country each year. Augustana College and Theological Seminary was the host in 1930. Book displays were sent to all meetings except in Canada, where there was only an occasional display. These displays were staffed by people from Rock Island and from the two branches, Chicago and Minneapolis. I often spent several weeks on the road, traveling from conference to conference. I appreciated the contacts I made and enjoyed meeting pastors and lay delegates. Our manager, J. G. Youngquist, would often join me at larger meetings, such as the Minnesota Conference and the Synod. We worked well as a team, both at home and on the road, and became good friends. Mr. Youngquist was tall in stature and was often asked, "How tall?"

He would reply, "Five feet, eighteen."

The stock market crash of 1929 grew into a world-wide depression, the low point of which came in 1932 and 1933. The effect of the market crash and the slackening of business activity was soon felt in all departments of the Augustana Book Concern—manufacturing, mail orders, and subscriptions. Some of us on a salary basis informed the board of directors that we were willing to take a five percent cut. The outcome was that the board made a ten percent cut in all salaries and wages. Fortunately the Book Concern fared better than many other business establishments. Few employees were laid off, in fact only six, and they were called back after a few weeks.

In 1930 Dr. George A. Fahlund resigned his position as Sunday School secretary of the Synod to accept a call to Bethlehem Lutheran Church, Grand Rapids, Michigan. He was succeeded in 1931 by Dr. J. Vincent Nordgren. When the Fahlunds left Rock Island, I lost a good home. I had become fond of this family including Moster, an older woman who lived with them. They had two sons. Luther, the older son, became a veterinarian. He worked for a while for the U. S. government in the Virgin Islands and Nigeria. At present he resides in Knoxville, Tennessee. The younger son, George, Jr., became a physician and surgeon. I helped him through the University of Chicago Medical School. With pride I add that years later I was reimbursed in full. George and his wife, Angie, reared a family of four children. They have now retired and live in Grand Rapids, Michigan. We have kept in touch through the years.

The Rock Island YMCA became my new home. Here I met Philemon Martin, a teacher in Rock Island Senior High School. We became good friends and often had dinner together in Johnson's Cafeteria, Rock Island, or at Bishop's Cafeteria, Davenport.

Although I lost a home at Dr. Fahlund's departure, I gained a secretary. Eva Alvine had served as Dr. Fahlund's secretary and had also given me part-time secretarial help. She served me and the Augustana Book Concern loyally and efficiently during my entire thirty-seven years at the Book Concern.

I soon found that another person depended on my secretary for help, Dr. G. A. Brandelle, president of the Augustana Synod, who had his office in his home with no secretary. Often he would come to the Book Concern, walk up to Eva's desk and ask, "Do you have anything on today?" This question meant, "Do you have time to take some dictation today?"

I did not object, nor did Eva, for we were glad to give assistance to the president of the church.

From Dr. Fahlund I also inherited the editorship of the *Almanac,* which was published in both English and Swedish. Astronomical calculations for the calendar were made by P. W. Benzon. It was also my duty to solicit advertising for the *Almanac,* the income of which helped to defray printing and mailing costs since the *Almanac* was sent free to all subscribers of our two official papers. The *Almanac* in English was sent to subscribers of the *Lutheran Companion* and the *Almanack* in Swedish, to the subscribers of *Augustana.*

The series of pericope texts and festival dates for the church year was listed in the *Almanac,* which information helped to make it a useful book. Each year in May, I received the following inquiry from the president of the Mission Covenant Church of America: "How soon will the series of texts and festival days be ready for next year?" The Mission Covenant Church had its own yearbook but wanted to use our texts. Thus the pastors of both churches generally preached each Sunday on the same text. I continued as editor of the *Almanac* from 1930 to 1947. This publication was followed in 1948 by the *Augustana Annual.*

The new publication, the *Augustana Annual,* was in a sense, a continuation of the *Almanac* and the older annuals, *Korsbaneret* and *My Church.* Sigfrid Engstrom served with me as co-editor from 1948 to 1955. He was followed by E. E. Ryden, who was responsible until 1962. Since the first issue of the *Augustana Annual* was published for the centennial year, 1948, it was dedicated to the congregations of the Augustana Synod. The *Augustana Annual* became a valued resource book for pastors and lay workers. In it they found besides the series of texts and festival dates for the church year, a clerical and church register, and much useful and informative material about the church, its institutions, and its activities.

In my annual report to the board of directors for 1933, I called attention to the very difficult conditions under which we had to operate. The severest of these was, of course, the bank moratorium; the second, perhaps just as severe, was reduced income. The factors affected the circulation of *Augustana* and the *Lutheran Companion* more than the Sunday School papers; however, it looked as if we had reached the low point and that we could now look forward to a gradual increase in circulation.

A series of graded lessons from the beginners' department to that of pupils of high school age had been worked out under the direction of Dr. J. Vincent Nordgren. These courses were known as the "Word of Life Series." The circulation department had charge of promotion and distribution.

During the days of depression we received many kinds of letters from subscribers. Here is one I would like to share:

Minneapolis, Minnesota
October the Tenth, 1933

Augustana Book Concern
Rock Island, Illinois

Friend Birger:

It is now two and a half years since I received a copy of the *Augustana Quarterly*.

Or maybe one and a half.

Or half a year—I dunno.

Anyhow, I have certainly seen four full moons bewitch the world with silver since I looked a *Quarterly* in the face.

Has my subscription expired? My credit too?

(Between you and me, my credit isn't worth much. For the crash ruined me, the NRA is killing me, and who will be generous enough to bury me when that time comes? If I were you I'd go slow on the credit business.)

But couldn't you get the janitor to snoop around in the basement and try to find an old copy that looks as if it had come this side of the Apple Harvest? He might succeed. And if his breakfast pancakes were good he might be kind enough to kick it off in this direction, and thus I'd get it—maybe.

My name is C. A. Wendell, my husnummer is 52 Saymour Avenue, my telephone number is G1 1221, and my wife—bless her heart!—has the old friendly name of Anna.

P.S.—This is good paper. The last left over from good times.

Another P.S.—The belated *Quarterly* just came. Thanks.

Dr. C. J. Bengston, who had served as editor of the *Lutheran Companion* for nineteen years, was succeeded by Dr. E. E. Ryden in February 1934, with C. E. Nelson as assistant. Mr. Nelson served in this position until he became assistant editor of *Augustana* in February 1941. Dr. Ryden had been pastor of Gloria Dei Lutheran

Church, St. Paul. He continued to serve his parish for many months, commuting between Rock Island and St. Paul each weekend. Dr. Ryden was an experienced newspaper man and gifted writer as well as a hymn writer and translator. In 1946 Miss Charlotte Odman became his assistant and served sixteen years. She was an able writer and made many worthy contributions to the *Lutheran Companion.*

A noteworthy birthday party in honor of *Augustana's* editor took place at the Harper House, Rock Island, March 2, 1936. Dr. L. G. Abrahamson, who had filled the editorial chair of *Augustana* for twenty-eight years, became an octogenarian on this date. He continued to fill this important post with undiminished vigor. More than 200 persons had gathered this evening to celebrate with Dr. Abrahamson and his family. It was not an ordinary banquet. The speakers had serious reflections but also much humor. Dr. E. E. Ryden was the toastmaster. I quote from the *Lutheran Companion* of March 14, 1936:

> Dr. Abrahamson's varied activities as a synodical leader were reflected in the tribute given by the several speakers; Dr. Peter Peterson, president of the Illinois Conference, spoke for the subscribers of *Augustana;* Dr. Conrad Bergendoff, president of Augustana College and Theological Seminary, told of Dr. Abrahamson's contributions to that institution; Dr. O. N. Olson, a member of the board of directors of the Augustana Book Concern, spoke of the part he had in the development of the synod's publishing work; and Mr. E. I. Erickson, superintendent of Augustana Hospital, Chicago, Illinois, told of the veteran editor's leadership in the growth of the synod's largest hospital.
>
> The employees of the Augustana Book Concern then stood while Mr. Eric Liljegren read a tribute to Dr. Abrahamson on their behalf.
>
> A pleasing incident in the program was a tribute to Mrs. Abrahamson by Mrs. J. G. Youngquist, who also presented the wife of the guest of honor with a beautiful bouquet of roses.
>
> More than a thousand greetings from readers of *Augustana* had been received by letter and telegram. Selections from these were read by Mr. Birger Swenson, circulation manager of Augustana Book Concern, after which he presented all of them to Dr. Abrahamson in a large box. The greetings reflected not only the deep affection with which the editor of *Augustana* is regarded by the membership of the synod, but also the tremendous influence he has wielded in countless lives.

One of the letters, written in Swedish, described Dr. Abraham-son as he appeared in the pulpit:

> Tall and impressive as he looked out over his audience and stretched out his long arms, one felt as he sat in the pew that Dr. Abrahamson could embrace the entire congregation.

The writer ended his letter with these words, "Dr. Abrahamson var en baddare till präst." I consulted a couple of seminary professors as to the English equivalent of *baddare* who agreed with me that a good translation was "humdinger." We agreed with the writer that Dr. Abrahamson was a "humdinger" of a preacher.

I have translated another letter, written in Swedish. This one came from Rev. Carl A. B. Swanson, who in his unique letter also remembered Dr. Abrahamson's birthday.

Savonburg, Kansas
February 9, 1936

Birger Swenson

Dear Brother:—

Listen, you old boy, Birger. I am now enclosing a bank note in the amount of five dollars and twelve cents which I figure is all I owe A. B. C. Three and twelve for a Christmas gift and two dollars for the best small magazine which is printed in America. Out with the other which now tries to come to life within the Augustana Synod. You know what I mean.

How are you these days? Here it is so cold, so cold. One day I went out to milk, but I could not do it. The milk froze as fast as it came and punched holes in the milk pail. Now I measure the milk in two foot lengths and sell it at four feet to the gallon. Ya—it is better to be without bread than not to know what to do, as they say.

Will you be along in St. Peter next June? What did you say? That is good. I shall also be along this time. I must help with the meeting. The little fellow who is now in charge of the synod needs help, and I shall advise him. Here in Kansas one finds many who give advice.

Perhaps you do not know that the next President of the United States will come from this region. His name is Alf M. Landon. What a man he is! The best there is.

You sent me a letter the other day and informed me that our esteemed Dr. Abrahamson is to become 80 years old. You suggested that a two-dollar subscription to *Augustana* would please him. I am one of those who receive his paper for nothing. I am on the free list. Tell him I wish him the best. I have always loved him. His good humor is like cotton wool around the heart. Greet him from me and hand him a cigar—a ten cent cigar. I will reimburse you when we meet in St. Peter—I mean St. Peter here on earth. Now I must say farewell for this time. My Swedish is not very good. Besides it is so cold here that even one's thoughts freeze.

Greet everyone in Rock Island, especially the police.

Brotherly, etc.

Carl A. B.

Years ago Dr. Abrahamson rode with me to an Iowa Conference convention in Sioux City. It was a long drive from Rock Island. We had time to discuss national and church politics, finance, investments and other subjects.

Dr. Abrahamson said, "I tell you, Birger, that I have invested in many things. I invested in silver and gold mines and lost. Then I bought a farm in South Dakota, and that was not good either. But when I was pastor of Salem Lutheran Church in Chicago, a few of us got together and organized a cemetery. Of course, I had to buy a few shares. I tell you, Birger, that investment in the cemetery, that's dead sure."

On the retirement of Dr. Abrahamson, Dr. A. T. Lundholm took over the editorship at the beginning of 1940 with Mr. C. E. Nelson as assistant editor. Dr. Lundholm had a good understanding of *Augustana's* circle of readers and continued as the editor until the decision was made to cease publication at the end of 1956. There was a natural decline in the number of subscribers because of death. Then, too, the English publication, *Lutheran Companion*, took its place as the official publication of the church.

Dr. L. G. Abrahamson had distinguished himself not only as the editor of *Augustana* but also as one who held positions of trust and honor of the Synod for a period of sixty years. In view of these facts, the board of directors of Augustana Book Concern decided to commemorate his service by a portrait painted by a recognized artist. The man selected was Carl A. E. Tolpo, a Chicago artist. I was asked to serve on a committee to invite friends of Dr. Abrahamson to send their gifts of gratitude. I contacted all subscribers of *Augustana* by letter. We had no difficulty in raising the funds for the portrait.

Even after his retirement Dr. Abrahamson continued to attend the annual meeting of the Synod. At one meeting, he was introduced by the president, Dr. P. O. Bersell, who mentioned that Dr. Abrahamson had reached a venerable old age. In reply Dr. Abrahamson said, "Yes, yes, I am old, much too old, but I am on my way home. After each time of travel, the day came to return to Rock Island, my home. It was a pleasant feeling. Now I am looking forward to going to my heavenly home. It is a glorious feeling. Soon I will be with my Lord."

The fiftieth anniversary of the Augustana Book Concern was a festive event, recorded in the *Lutheran Companion* of November 2, 1939. I quote the editor, Dr. E. E. Ryden:

"Augustana Book Concern, as the official publication house of the Augustana Synod, is fifty years old this year. In commemoration of the event, Book Concern employees, members of the Book Concern board, and the Board of Christian Education and Literature, representatives of Augustana College and Theological Seminary, and synodical officials—numbering in all some 116 persons—sat down at a banquet in the parish house of St. John's Lutheran Church, Rock Island, Wednesday noon, October 18.

"Among the guests of honor at the banquet were three aged women, all of them widows of men who had made important contributions to the publishing work of the Synod. They were Mrs. Uma Bersell, whose husband, Prof. A. O. Bersell, was one of the incorporators of the private stock company which for five years carried on the publication business until the Synod took it over in 1889; Mrs. C. W. Foss, whose husband was a board member for many years; and Mrs. A. G. Anderson, whose husband was manager of the Book Concern from 1889 to 1926, a period of thirty-seven years.

"Presiding at the banquet was Mr. J. G. Youngquist, manager of the Book Concern since 1927. Dr. S. J. Sebelius, dean of the seminary, offered prayer. An historical sketch was given by Dr. E. W. Olson, who previous to his coming to the Book Concern in 1911 was connected with the Engberg-Holmberg Publication House in Chicago.

"Dr. Olson pointed out that the Book Concern is more than fifty years old. Its real beginnings must be traced back to the Hasselquist Printery in Galesburg, which was established in 1854.

" 'Dr. Hasselquist, the father of our publication enterprise,' said the speaker, 'edited *Augustana* and its precursors for no less than thirty-seven years from 1854 to 1891.'

"Dr. Olson noted that the development of the synod's publication business falls into periods that are peculiarly symmetrical. The various steps are as follows:

1854 - 1859	Hasselquist Printery in Galesburg
1859 - 1874	Lutheran Publication Society in Chicago
1874 - 1879	Engberg-Holmberg Publishing Company in Chicago
1879 - 1884	Ungdomens Vänner at Augustana College and Moline
1884 - 1889	Privately owned Augustana Book Concern in Rock Island
1889 - 1939	Augustana Book Concern as the official publication house of the Synod

"The speaker reviewed the rapid development of the Book Concern after the Synod took it over in 1889. In 1899 a new brick building was erected at a cost of $23,000, and in 1911 another building was added at a cost of $35,000, more than doubling the size of the structural unit. The warehouse just completed is the third permanent structure to be erected.

"Brief addresses were also given at the banquet by Dr. O. N. Olson, chairman of the Book Concern board, and Dr. P. O. Bersell, president of the synod.

"During the course of the dinner, Manager Youngquist called attention to the fact that eight men have served the Book Concern for periods between forty and fifty years. They are Hjalmar Nyquist, Arthur Lincke, Rudolph Lindstrom, William Bohman, Swan Nyquist, Arthur Oberlander, John Gilbert, and W. A. Bjorkman. Each one was asked to relate some incident from the early history of the institution.

"The eight men were presented by Mr. Youngquist with gilded nails from the old warehouse as mementos of the fiftieth anniversary. Dr. O. N. Olson, as chairman of the Book Concern board, received a gavel made of wood from the old structure.

"After President Conrad Bergendoff of Augustana College had

concluded the function at St. John's Church with a prayer, the entire assembly repaired to the site of the new warehouse, where eight sturdy Moline elms had been planted to set off the structure. In the tree planting ceremony which followed, Dr. Bersell placed the final shovel of dirt around one of the trees and then delivered a beautiful address, taking as his theme 'The Trees of the Bible.' This ceremony climaxed the anniversary celebration.

"The new warehouse is 50 by 108 feet in dimensions and is constructed of Galesburg red brick at a cost of approximately $14,000. It is divided into twelve rooms which are equipped with steel shelves."

The anniversary received much favorable publicity in the church press and also in the Rock Island *Argus*.

LUTHERAN COMPANION VACATION TOURS

One of my delightful memories of my association with Dr. E. E. Ryden, editor of the *Lutheran Companion*, was our annual *Lutheran Companion* tour, which we sponsored in cooperation with the Great Northern Railway. The participants, who came from many states, generally met in St. Paul. The group numbered about fifty each year. We were assigned two private Pullman cars, named LC -1 and LC -2. Our goal was the great and glorious West. I would like to share a brief account of three of these trips.

The 1939 tour was named, "America the Beautiful." It included the Montana Rockies, Mt. Rainier National Park, the Pacific Northwest, Seattle, Victoria, B. C., San Francisco and the Golden Gate International Exposition on Treasure Island, Los Angeles, and the Grand Canyon. I was so fascinated by the sunset on the Grand Canyon that I lingered too long with my camera to try to record the grandeur and I missed my dinner. I was richly rewarded.

"America's Northern Wonderland" was the name of the 1940 *Lutheran Companion* tour. After reaching Seattle, we boarded the ocean liner *S. S. Yukon* and sailed north through the Inside Passage to Alaska. Majestic scenery greeted us all the way. At Ketchikan, our first stop, I sat for two hours in the rain at a river watching salmon fighting their way up a waterfall, a fascinating experience. Fishing in 1940 was a $50,000 annual business in Alaska. Our next stop was

Petersburg, sometimes referred to as Little Norway, because of the large number of Norwegians who settled there. It is sometimes called the "shrimp capital" of Alaska. Next we came to Juneau, which is remembered for its Mendenhall Glacier just thirteen miles from downtown. Juneau is the state's capital and the first city established following the purchase of Alaska from Imperial Russia in 1867. Skagway, the gateway to the Klondike, was once a boom gold rush town of 8,000. It now had only 500 inhabitants. The last town visited, Sitka, was once the Russian capital of Alaska. It is famous for its historic churches, the Block House, Totem Park, and the wishing stone. In and around these picturesque towns we met native born Alaskans—Indians. We saw small farms and beautiful flower and vegetable gardens in this land of the midnight sun. After returning to Seattle, we transferred to the Canadian Pacific for a steamship trip to Victoria and Vancouver, B.C. From there we continued to Jasper National Park, returning home via Winnipeg.

We entitled our 1941 tour, "From Sea to Shining Sea." We assembled in Chicago and traveled on the Rock Island Lines to El Paso, Texas. There we boarded buses for the Carlsbad National Park. After we had descended to the depths of this famous cavern, the entire group gathered and with the lights turned off sang the old familiar hymn, "Rock of Ages." We continued west to Los Angeles, Santa Catalina Island, San Francisco, and Portland. After a drive on the Columbia River Highway, we were guests at a reception arranged for us by the Emanuel Hospital in Portland. Both Seattle and Victoria, B.C., were visited for the third time. Homeward bound, we had five very interesting days in Glacier National Park. Another memorable *Lutheran Companion* tour had come to an end. Besides the pleasure enjoyed by the participants, valuable good will was also created through these annual tours.

APPOINTMENT AS SALES MANAGER

In 1942 I was appointed sales manager, as well as continuing to have charge of the circulation department. In addition I was to direct both the sales work in the book store and in the manufacturing department. I was also to have charge of the branches in Chicago and Minneapolis.

Mr. D. W. Dahlsten was the faithful manager of the book store and the mail-order division. Miss Edith Kjellberg was his loyal assistant. I was to direct advertising and assist in promotion and mail-order sales.

Mr. Oscar G. Ericson was in charge of the manufacturing department. He was an efficient and well-trained production manager who took pride in first-class products. I was to work with him in the promotion and solicitation of printing orders from various boards, institutions, and conferences of the Synod. We had the advantage of having proof readers who became familiar with names of officials and leaders in the church; therefore, accurate work was appreciated. We were proud of the fact that over the years practically all printing needs of various boards and conferences were met in our manufacturing plant.

It was a pleasure to work with Mr. Dahlsten, Miss Kjellberg, and Mr. Ericson, from whom I received good cooperation. We worked well as a team. Unfortunately one of our team, Mr. Dahlsten, became ill and died in December 1942. He had been in continuous charge of the book store and mail-order department since 1900. He was a conscientious and hard worker who lived to see the steady growth and increased sales of his department. He will long be remembered for his valuable service and good will. A committee consisting of J. G. Youngquist, Edith Kjellberg, and myself took temporary charge of the book store and mail-order department. The retail store was managed for brief periods by Frank Lunn and James Holliday. They were followed by Mrs. Allen H. Johnson.

DEATH OF MR. J. G. YOUNGQUIST

At the beginning of 1944, Mr. J. G. Youngquist, who had been in failing health for some time, was given a three-month leave of absence. He and Mrs. Youngquist went to Minneapolis with the hope of his recuperating. However, after several months, with no sign of improvement, his physician advised him to relinquish his responsibility as head of the Augustana Book Concern. The board of directors accepted his resignation with regret. Mr. Youngquist had been general manager of the Synod's publishing house since 1928. He remained in Minneapolis until his death in 1952.

Mr. Youngquist will be remembered for successfully guiding the Synod's publishing house through the depth of the depression in the thirties. The much-needed warehouse was erected during his term as manager. Another worthwhile project was the remodeling of the first floor of the main building into modern offices and the renovation of the book store to one of the finest in the midwest. The new shelves, counters, and display racks were finished during the war by means of portable woodworking machinery, giving architectural unity to the store. The store was completed in 1944.

I have fond memories of Mr. Youngquist as a co-worker, travel companion, and friend. He and Mrs. Youngquist were genial hosts in whose home I had many delightful hours. Sometimes we vacationed together on the north shore of Lake Superior in Minnesota.

VI
BIRGER TAKES A WIFE

After Dr. A. T. Lundholm left his position at the Augustana Theological Seminary to accept a call to a congregation in Minnesota, he wanted to sell his home which he had built on 34th Street in Rock Island. He interested me and I bought it as an investment. When he returned in 1940 as editor of *Augustana,* he wanted to buy his former home. I was happy to accomodate him, but neither of us made any money on the deal.

As news spread that I had bought a house, rumors started to circulate that I was to marry. My first answer to these rumors was that I had a job at the Augustana Book Concern as circulation manager. My job was to circulate.

In the Kiwanis Club of which I was a member, there were only two single men—a Catholic priest and I. I was always teased. I readily agreed that marriage was a wonderful institution, but as for me, I was not ready for an institution. I also used to say that it is better "'to have loved and lost' than to be wedded and forever bossed."

But it did happen in 1943. Certainly it took me a long time. On August 14, I married Lyal Westerlund, an English teacher in Rock Island High School. The ceremony took place in St. Paul Lutheran Church, Orion, with Rev. Martin S. Lingwall, the pastor, officiating. The only attendants were Lyal's mother, Mrs. Perry Westerlund, and her brother, Mahlon Westerlund. Being an avid camera man, I wanted a picture of the small wedding party as it came out of the church.

Along came Rev. Robert A. Hull of Andover. He asked, "Who is getting married?"

Rev. Lingwall answered, "Birger."

Pastor Hull, quickly responded, "I don't believe it. You will have to show me the license."

He was not the only one who was doubtful of my ever marrying. Mr. Cain, executive director of the Rock Island Welfare Association, had this to say:

"It took the power of the press to convince us that it has really happened."

Judge Eskil Carlson of Des Moines, wrote:

"Well, well, well, so you, too, are a benedict! I thought you were as much opposed to union as the Missouri Synod."

President of the Augustana Synod, Dr. P. O. Bersell, had this to say in a letter:

"One of the biggest pieces of news, ranking next to the unconditional surrender of Italy in importance, was the announcement of a wedding in Orion, Illinois, August 14. I am sure that the whole Augustana Synod received the news with bated breath.

"I am just wondering what effect this is going to have on the Augustana Synod. What stories will Birger Swenson think up to tell at the conference meetings? He will have to get a whole new stock in trade or perhaps he will not be permitted to travel anymore."

At this writing we have been happily married thirty-five years. As my dear Lyal and I look back, as well as to the future, we both say that we are mighty glad it did happen.

Lyal received her early education in the Orion schools, attended Augustana College three years, and received her A.B. degree from the University of Illinois in 1925. Later through additional study, she obtained her M.A. degree from Northwestern University in 1939.

Her first teaching experience was in Lovington Township High School, Lovington, Illinois, where she taught English and Latin. She taught one year at Farmer City, Illinois, before joining the teaching staff in the English department of Rock Island High School in 1929. She remained in this position until our marriage in 1943. Later, in 1958, she was asked to return to her former position in high school as there was a need for additional teachers. She continued until June 1963, the year I retired from the Board of Publication.

Lyal is active in her church, especially in Lutheran Church Women, both on the local and synodical levels. The YWCA has been her favorite community service in which she is still active. She has served as president and was the chairman of the building committee when the present YWCA quarters were erected. She is also active in the Lutheran Hospital Auxiliary, the P.E.O. Sisterhood, and King's Daughters.

At present she is serving on the board of directors of the Rock Island Historical Society. Both of us have been interested in this organization for a number of years. Other historical associations in which both of us have membership are the Augustana Historical Society, Andover Historical Society, and Swedish Pioneer Historical Society. I have also been a member of long standing of the American-Swedish Historical Foundation and the Illinois State Historical Society.

THE WESTERLUND FAMILY

My wife, Lyal, is a descendant of a pioneer family. Her grandfather, Peter Westerlund, at the age of eleven, came from Hassela Parish, Hälsingland, Sweden, to Andover, in 1850, together with his father, Eric Abraham Westerlund, one sister and three brothers. His mother and a younger sister had died on the voyage and were buried at sea. For a time the family lived next door to Rev. Lars Paul Esbjörn in Andover. Peter, having begun his education in Sweden, later attended schools in Andover and Lynn townships.

In 1863, Peter married Eleonora Christina Hultman from Skepperstad, Småland, Sweden, from where she had emigrated in 1861. To this union were born six children. The youngest, Perry, was the father of my wife, Lyal.

Lyal's mother, Selma Edmund, also was the daughter of Swedish pioneers, Anders Johan Adman and Johanna Elisabet Carlson of Småland, Sweden. They had emigrated to the U.S. in the 1860s and settled in Henry County, Illinois.

Peter, after farming the original homestead for a brief period, bought in 1865 a tract of wild prairie land near Orion, where he lived until 1897.

Perry inherited 160 acres from his father, which he farmed until his death in 1934. Then his younger son, Mahlon, assumed the responsibility. Now Mahlon's son, Marcus, is the operator.

I did not have the privilege of knowing Lyal's father. Her mother, Selma, lived with us for a number of years, and I became very fond of her. She died in 1962.

We delight in visiting the family farm, Cloverdale, where Mahlon, his wife, Ruth, and their two sons, Marcus and David, reside. Another son, Thomas, was tragically killed in an auto accident in 1973.

Lyal had an older brother, Forrest. He and his wife, Rosa, and their two children, Phyllis and Perry, made their home in Oxnard, California, where Forrest was principal of the high school. He died in 1948.

The Westerlund family has grown through the years. Their descendants are found in many states. Lyal and her cousin, Leona Sundeen, are working on updating the genealogical record of the Westerlund family. They have previously published two booklets in 1947 and in 1960 on the various branches and their descendants. This interest is kept alive by biennial reunions which are attended by members from far and near.

VII

GENERAL MANAGER ABC

After having served as acting manager during 1944, I was appointed general manager and treasurer of the Augustana Book Concern at the board meeting held March 5, 1945. Officers at this time were Dr. A. D. Mattson, president, Rev. O. V. Anderson, vice president, and Ivar E. Johnson, secretary.

I accepted the appointment with gratitude, and I appreciated the confidence and good will of the board. I was also grateful to the staff, editors, and employees for their acceptance of me as head of the institution. We had worked well together in the past, especially in 1944. With their cooperation, I looked forward with confidence to the days and years ahead.

In preparing my annual report to the board of directors, I as manager wanted at the same time to brief our employees on the result of the past year's operation. This communication, which I mailed to each of my co-workers, was very much appreciated.

Many problems due to the war were still with us. The war years had been abnormal years. Besides the shortage of paper, ink and other materials, it had been practically impossible to secure enough help. Both men and women were drawn to the war industries on account of higher pay. Yet while struggling with shortages in personnel and material, we were able to produce and fill orders with a high degree of speed and efficiency. My co-workers in all departments demonstrated splendid loyalty and the best of cooperation. A word of gratitude was due all members of the ABC family.

Another problem was our relations with labor unions. The pressmen, typesetters, and compositors were organized. Every so often I had to meet with their representatives to renegotiate new contracts. The difficulty was that I was not allowed to meet with my own men. The union secretary, and the union negotiators were strangers as far as the operation of the Augustana Book Concern was concerned and had little sympathy for the work of a church institution. Then, too, I had a board member who was very friendly to labor, thus causing much frustration, especially to me.

I asked the board for permission to obtain help from Graphic Arts Industry, a management consulting firm. We were indeed glad to receive this assistance.

Wages should be a high reward to the workman. I tried to be fair to all members of our ABC family. A new contract with the Typographical Union was negotiated in November 1945. A voluntary wage adjustment was made for the members of the Tri-City Pressmen's Union as well as the employees in the bindery, shipping room, and office. It was interesting to note and study the upward trend in wages granted in our plant during the last ten years. The largest increases, of course, came after 1941. The average increase in wages in the manufacturing department during a ten-year period, 1939-1949, was more than sixty percent, and in the office 57.77 percent. The three highest paid groups—press feeders, compositors and linotype operators—had increases of sixty-nine percent, while editors and administrators had twenty-eight percent. The adjustment for editors and executives came later.

RETIREMENT PLAN AND GROUP INSURANCE

It was with a sense of deep gratitude to the board of directors that I could report to my co-workers that the long-considered employer-employee sponsored retirement and group insurance plan was adopted during 1946. The group insurance plan was with the Travelers' Insurance Company while the group retirement plan was with the Aetna Insurance Company. Both were contributary plans. Approximately thirty-seven percent of the premium was paid by the employees and sixty-three percent by the Book Concern.

The older employees were not forgotten. A special reserve fund of $90,000 was authorized by the board to take care of those already retired and those over sixty-five who were not eligible for the benefits of the existing retirement plan. We were happy to report that the money had already been set aside and that the fund was in operation. All present pensioners became beneficiaries of the new plan on January 1, 1946. One well-known pensioner, Dr. L. G. Abrahamson, died during 1946.

As soon as the employees of the Augustana Book Concern became eligible for Social Security, the board of directors took prompt action. All employees became enrolled under United States Social Security as of January 1, 1951.

OPEN HOUSE BRINGS WONDERMENT

The celebration of the Augustana Centennial in June of 1948 is recorded elsewhere, but I would like to share with you my account in the *Augustana Annual* of 1949 of an open house held during the convention:

> They—more than two thousand of them, delegates and visitors—came, saw, and concluded that the Augustana Book Concern is indeed an institution unique in the church. Most of the visitors, customers for years, were in Rock Island for the first time. As they lined up two-deep for nearly a city block on some of the tours, they at first saw only a five-story brick structure with an adjacent warehouse, covering half a city block. Not bad for a church publishing house.
>
> But what will it look like inside? "Amazing," said a California delegate when he entered and saw the streamlined and attractive book store. The entire store is furnished in natural finish, quartered gumwood, with a light acoustical ceiling and indirect fluorescent lighting. Large flat-top floor display cases and four semicircular book sections, finished in the same wood, offer feature sales space for books, Sunday School and church office supplies, altar ware and ecclesiastical appointments. Equally imposing are the business offices on the same floor, housing the mail-order, circulation and accounting departments.
>
> Once inside the plant they found that the story of book and magazine manufacturing began to unfold and what a story it was and

is. They saw for the first time how their own church papers, the *Lutheran Companion* and *Augustana,* as well as textbooks for the Sunday School, fit into the smooth but complicated system of production. Many expressed wonderment over the linotypes and monotypes which operate with the precision of a fine watch. The making of forms and the actual running job, offset, and cylinder presses were of great interest, especially the large two-color press on which lesson material of the Christian Growth Series was being printed. Delegates often lingered to watch the intricate bindery machinery in operation, as well as the gold edging and stamping of books.

The visitor was also given an eight-page illustrative folder with information that the Book Concern has been serving the Augustana Lutheran Church as the official publication house since 1889. Through its mail-order department and main store in Rock Island, together with the branches in Minneapolis and Chicago, it reaches out into local congregations, schools, and homes in every part of our nation and many foreign countries.

With an up-to-date printing plant and complete bindery, the Augustana Book Concern has produced hundreds of book titles and each year turns out six million copies of periodicals and lesson materials, and other millions of folders, pamphlets, and tracts.

The 130 or more employees—the ABC Family—were exceedingly happy to receive these visitors. Come again and bring others with you. The Book Concern is your institution. We are here to serve you and the Church. We want you to know that we not only take pride in our work, but also are convinced that next to the ministry itself the church papers, lesson materials, tracts, religious books, and hymnals are the best and most effective messengers of the church. We are eager to have a part in their production and distribution.

The following statement of purpose was proposed by me and adopted by the board of directors in 1945—*The printed word also proclaims the Gospel.*

Two social events were held each year for the employees and their families—a picnic in the summer and a dinner in December. These were enjoyable gatherings at which we had the opportunity to honor employees for long service. At the dinner in December 1948, there were four who had given fifty years of service each. They were Rudolph E. Lindstrom, Hjalmer E. Nyquist, Swan J. Nyquist, and Arthur E. Oberlander. Each was given a gold watch. At this time the

Book Concern had six employees with fifty or more years of service and twenty-five with twenty-five or more years of service. These on the honor roll had given an aggregate total of 996 years in service.

I recall with pleasure our golf foursome during my years at the Book Concern. Dr. E. E. Ryden and Dr. Victor Pearson, an Augustana College professor, were always partners. Dr. Knut Erickson, business manager of the college, and I were the other twosome. We chose to play at Saukie golf course in Rock Island whenever we could after work and sometimes on Saturday afternoons. It was a competitive foursome. We were very good friends, but if anyone had heard us discussing the game, he might have had a different opinion. All arguments ended at the eighteenth hole. We had time to discuss church news and politics. Golf was good therapy for us after hours of work and tension. We also learned to know each other better. Our togetherness strengthened our friendship.

I remember one occasion when Dr. Conrad Bergendoff had joined us as a substitute. We were playing at Indian Bluff golf course. On the third tee we had to drive over a wild gully. Conrad's drive went to the right with his ball disappearing in the rough. We all went to look for it on a very hot sultry day. Picnickers had left food in this rough patch, which by this time had become very, very foul-smelling. As Conrad with the help of an iron club sought the ball, we heard him say,

"I can readily understand why some men are apt to swear on the golf course." Then we knew that the dignified college president had a common touch. Interesting as well as pleasant memories linger from these activities with friends.

SCANDINAVIAN TOUR, 1949

Our two-month tour to Scandinavia in June and July 1949, was made for business and pleasure. The Book Concern had not been able to communicate regularly with overseas publishers and manufacturers during World War II. The board of directors, therefore, wanted me to call on many of these firms to renegotiate contracts, settle accounts, and look for new items for our book store. Lyal's cousin, Leona Westerlund, accompanied us.

We sailed on the *M/S Gripsholm* of the Swedish American Line from New York on June 7 and returned on the same ship on August 6. My older brother, Sven, met us upon our arrival in Gothenburg. We stayed from time to time at his home, Averstad, in Östra Fågelvik parish, Värmland, which was the old family home. Sven's wife, Esther, had died six months earlier. His daughters, Ulla and Rachel, were at home, and my oldest sister, Amanda, kept the house. Sister Annie and her family lived at Björka nearby. My younger brother, Rickard, had married. He and his wife, Greta, and two children, Lars and Margaretha, lived in Karlstad.

Among the publishers, I called on Rickard Runmark, director of Svenska Kyrkans Diakonistyrelses Bokförlag, Stockholm. Although it was a private firm, it was in a sense the official publishing house of the Lutheran Church in Sweden. We had been doing considerable business with this firm over the years. Mr. Runmark invited us for lunch and took us to a roof-top restaurant in AB Nordiska Kompaniet, Sweden's largest department store. For dessert we had *lilleput filbunke* with *pepparkakor.*

On another day I called on Carl Wiberg, president of Herzogs AB. We owed this firm considerable money as we had bought a large number of Swedish Bibles and *psalmböcker.* Now I was there to settle the account. He was very pleased and invited us to dinner. He called for us at the hotel and first took us to Millesgården. This was of interest to us as we had met Carl Milles, the sculptor, aboard ship. Then we proceeded to Soliden Restaurant in Skansen. Dinner was followed by an open-air performance of Shakespeare's *As You Like It* in Swedish—*Som Ni Behagar.* This evening was unusual and most enjoyable.

Midsummer week was spent at Siljansborg Hotel at Rättvik in Dalarna. We attended festivals at the hotel and at Gammalgård and watched the church boats come in from Lake Siljan for Sunday morning services. It was a unique experience for us to see the local people raising ·Maypoles and dancing around them in colorful provincial costumes.

In far north Kiruna, we were entertained by Lyal's and Leona's relatives—the Liljas. We visited the famous iron ore mine, saw and took motion pictures of the midnight sun from Mt. Luossavaara. We visited the so-called king of the Laplanders, Nils Nilsson Skum, who was a well-known artist and author. He and his wife invited us to have lunch, which was a typical Lapp lunch—hardboiled eggs in the shell, potatoes with the jackets on, boiled salmon, sun-dried deer meat, which we chewed and chewed. It was like chewing gum. *Filbunke* was served in a large wooden bowl. We still cherish the memory of our visit with the hospitable and friendly Laplanders.

An electric train took us to Narvik, Norway, where we saw several wrecked German warships in the fjords. We traveled south by bus, ferries, and train over Salt Mountain to Mo i Rana, Trondheim, and Oslo. Returning to Sweden we visited Britta Newman and her mother at Växjö. Britta had graduated from Augustana College in the spring of 1949. During our last days in Sweden, we were royally entertained by relatives and friends in my home parish and in Karlstad. One day we were luncheon guests of Bishop Arvid Runestam, Karlstad. The bishop had visited Rock Island in 1948 and had received an honorary doctor's degree from Augustana College.

Time came for our return. The trip had given us two months of business and pleasure.

VISITORS FROM SWEDEN IN 1950

Brother Sven, his daughter, Ulla, and her friend, Ingegard, came to visit us in early spring of 1950. They joined Lyal and me on a trip to Miami, Florida, to attend the annual meeting of the New York Conference. We also visited interesting places along the way, such as New Orleans, Jacksonville, Daytona Beach, and Cypress Gardens.

The annual meeting of the Augustana Lutheran Church was held in Washington, D. C., in June of 1950. Sven accompanied us once more and saw much of Washington. Lyal was his guide while Dan Nystrom and I tended the book display. One day we had the honor of having President Harry Truman visit and address the convention—a unique experience for all of us.

During Sven's six months' stay in the United States, we took him to many places of interest. In Iron Mountain, Michigan, we attended the wedding of a niece, Anita Swanson, daughter of brother Ragnar and Frida. We visited the north shore of Lake Superior and the iron range in Minnesota.

When Sven returned to his home in Sweden, his daughter, Ulla, and her friend, Ingegard, decided to remain in this country, having obtained favorable employment here.

EMPLOYEE RELATIONS

Daniel Nystrom, Jr., after having served his country as a gunnery officer during World War II, specifically in the Pacific, returned in 1946. Before enlisting in the Navy, he had been manager of the Chicago branch. I was happy to see him appointed promotion manager. I continued to have charge of the circulation department until 1953, when Leonard Lilyers took charge.

A year after I was appointed treasurer, I suggested to the board that I relinquish that position in favor of Clarke L. Swanson, who had supervised the general office and had held the position of cashier since 1908. My recommendation was accepted. Mr. Swanson was made treasurer and office manager and served faithfully until his retirement in 1952.

Our production manager, Oscar G. Ericson, completed twenty-five years of service in 1949. During these years he had been in charge of the manufacturing department to which he had given excellent service.

Our assistant production manager, Gustav Magnusson, now serving as foreman of the composing room, completed twenty-five years of service in 1950. He had learned his trade as a compositor and linotype operator in our plant and had become a most valuable employee.

The Korean crisis and the intensified national defense effort took four of our men, namely, Joseph Olson, bindery; Richard Anderson, press room; James Holliday, retail store; and Daniel Nystrom, Jr., our promotion manager. We could ill afford to lose any one of these men. Our hope was that there would not be any more who would have to go into service.

Frank Beranek, who had bound books for half a century at the publishing house of the Augustana Lutheran Church, was honored by the board and the employees of the Augustana Book Concern at the annual Christmas dinner, held in the First Lutheran Church, Moline, on December 28, 1951. He received a fifty-year lapel pin and a wrist watch. Four others were honored for having served twenty-five years. They were Oscar Larson, Harold Swanson, John G. Nelson, and Birger Swenson. Each received a twenty-five year lapel pin.

EMPLOYEE RETIREMENTS

Rudolph E. Lindstrom, foreman of the bindery for thirty-five years, retired in March 1948, after fifty years of service. Department heads and editors of the Augustana Book Concern held a luncheon in his honor at the Fort Armstrong Hotel. Mr. Lindstrom recalled some of the changes that had taken place. He began at the age of twelve as a bindery apprentice on May 6, 1898. He worked ten hours a day for two dollars a week. He recalled that men drew wages of nine to twelve dollars a week.

The Book Concern then had about twenty-five employees compared to 131 in 1948. It was housed in a small wooden building on its present site. The bindery was across the street in the building which later was occupied by the College Pharmacy. In those days all religious pamphlets, periodicals, and books printed there were sewed and bound by hand. Presently machines did the work.

In my remarks on this occasion, I concluded, "We are going to miss Rudy. We never had any worries about the bindery when he was in charge."

Members of the board and staff of the Augustana Book Concern gathered for another retirement luncheon on August 14, 1949, at this time to honor Dr. E. W. Olson who had served the Book Concern as an efficient office editor for thirty-eight years. Although he planned to move to Chicago, he had promised to continue on a part-time basis. He was formerly editor of *Svenska Tribunen,* Chicago, and had served as literary editor of the Engberg-Holmberg Publishing Company, Chicago. Dr. Olson was well known in literary circles and was considered as having one of the finest minds in Swedish America. He was the author of several historical books, such as *The Swedish Element in Illinois* and *Olof Olsson,* a biography of a former president of Augustana College. His last work, *Selected Poems, English and Swedish,* was published in Stockholm in 1947.

Dr. Daniel Nystrom, who had served so ably as secretary of literature since 1930, completed twenty-five years of service in 1955. Although the Nystroms had moved to Chicago in 1954 on account of Mrs. Nystrom's failing health, Dr. Nystrom had continued as a part-time employee and wanted to remain as such.

Many manuscripts were examined and edited during his years at the Book Concern. In 1940 he became editor of a new devotional quarterly for family and individual use, entitled, *The Home Altar,* which periodical achieved by 1960, a circulation of 200,000. He was also responsible for a newsletter, *What's New in Books.* Dr. Nystrom was the author of three devotional books: *Today with God, God in our Home,* and *When We Pray.* He also translated Dr. O. Olsson's *Vid Korset* with the title, *Salvation in Christ.*

Dr. Victor A. Beck accepted the position of secretary of literature in 1954 and served until the merger in 1963.

Due to the fact that a number of our employees had become eligible for Social Security in 1952, eight of them found it desirable to retire after long years of faithful service to the Augustana Book Concern. Among them was John Gilbert, pressroom foreman, after sixty years of service! He was succeeded by John Gordon. Another was Clarke L. Swanson, treasurer and office manager, after forty-four years of service. He was succeeded by Harold A. Swanson. Allen H. Johnson was serving as cashier.

In September 1950, Maurice Anderson, who had been in the employ of the Book Concern for twenty-four years, resigned from his position as foreman of the composing room. Gustav Magnusson, assistant production manager, took his place.

SEMINARY RELATIONSHIP

I was grateful for the permission of the board to establish an Augustana Book Concern lectureship at the seminary. A yearly contribution of three hundred dollars made possible a lectureship for the midwinter convocation and homecoming. The first lecture was held February 1-2, 1950. A yearly scholarship of fifty dollars was also granted to a worthy seminary student selected by the faculty.

Members of the seminary graduating class were dinner or luncheon guests of the Book Concern each year. We were always happy to have the president, Dr. Karl E. Mattson, join us when he could. I recall one such occasion when Dr. E. E. Ryden spoke on "Our Church Papers," and Dr. Conrad Bergendoff's topic was "Reminiscences of Twenty-five Years in the Ministry." Dr. Bergendoff was president of the senior class in 1921. He stressed how twenty-five years of service in the church had broadened his outlook regarding the problems of church and society. Each seminary graduate received a gift of a church service book, in leather, stamped with his name.

INCOME AND REAL ESTATE TAXES

A serious problem confronted us. The Revenue Act passed by Congress in 1950 held that non-profit institutions, such as church-owned publication houses might be subject to tax on "unrelated business." The Revenue Act of 1951 made further amendments, one specifically applicable to publishing. Although we had sought legal advice and had also conferred with our auditor, we were not able to determine what was meant by "unrelated business."

I learned from my friend, Dr. O. A. Dorn, manager of Concordia Publishing House, St. Louis, that a young lawyer, Mr. Fred L. Kuhlmann, had successfully handled a similar case for them. We engaged Mr. Kuhlmann to prepare a brief for a ruling and file it with the Commissioner of Internal Revenue. The brief was filed January 28, 1953, and a ruling was made in less than two weeks. A letter from the United States Treasury Department, dated February 11, stated that on the basis of the evidence furnished we were entitled to exemption, as it was shown that we were organized and operated exclusively for religious purposes.

We asked a local lawyer friend, Mr. Lloyd Schwiebert, to use the same brief and submit it for a ruling relative to our real estate taxes. We had to appear in court, sit in the witness chair for three hours, and answer many questions. Again it was ruled that the Book Concern was entitled to exemption. Taxes in the amount of more than $9,000, paid under protest, were refunded. We were also exempt from paying sales taxes.

CHURCH PAPER CHANGES

During the year 1949, in view of recommendations made by the *Lutheran Companion* committee and of action by the church, our official church papers, *Augustana* and *Lutheran Companion,* came in for more attention than other publications. On January 1, 1950, the name *Augustana* was changed to *Augustana Lutheranen* and the name *Lutheran Companion* to *Augustana Lutheran*. With many new features inaugurated in the first issue of each paper under the new name, it was thought that the changes would be readily acceptable to the readers. The name changes, however, lasted only a year.

A new life, so to speak, was experienced in our Sunday School story papers when Delores Kanten took over the editorship of all three papers in 1954. Names were changed as follows: *The Young People* to *Teen Talk, The Olive Leaf* to *Junior Life,* and *Little Folks* to *'Til 8 Stories.* All three papers were published in a new format. These changes met with ready acceptance by pupils and teachers alike. We were most grateful to Miss Kanten and the Board of Parish Education for their help and cooperation in achieving these much needed changes. Dr. Lael Westberg, director of the Board of Parish Education, continued as editor of the *Church School Teacher.*

A TRIP TO THE WEST COAST

Lyal and I decided to drive to California to attend the annual meeting of the Augustana Lutheran Church, which was held in Angelica Lutheran Church, Los Angeles, in June 1954. On the way we visited Mesa Verde National Park in Colorado, the Petrified Forest and the north rim of the Grand Canyon in Arizona, Bryce Canyon and Zion National Park in Utah, Hoover Dam and Las Vegas in Nevada. Arriving in California, we visited my brother, Ragnar, and his family near Los Angeles. He was employed by a construction company erecting a large military hospital. We also visited Lyal's sister-in-law, Rosa Westerlund, at Oxnard.

The convention had a large attendance, perhaps because it was held in California. The program was excellent. The Augustana Book Concern had been given space in the parish house for its display. Here I would like to quote Dr. Ryden from the *Lutheran Companion* of August 4, 1954:

> The parish and patio of Angelica Church presented a bustling scene throughout the Los Angeles synod. From nine in the morning until late at night, delegates and visitors milled about the spacious church property. A favorite rendezvous that intrigued pastors and book-lovers was the display conducted in the parish house by the

> Augustana Book Concern. Here Manager Birger Swenson and Promotional Manager Daniel Nystrom sold tons of books with a smile. Not content with this prosperity, however, Birger conceived the idea of opening a "branch store" on the patio, where sales also zoomed.

After the convention, we headed north and visited Yosemite, my cousin, Adolph Swenson and his family in Modesto, and many cousins of the family of Gustaf Spetz, my uncle, living in Palo Alto, Oakland, and Arcata. Then we continued into Oregon, where we visited Lyal's Aunt Ella Westerlund and her cousin, Mrs. Lillian Salade, in Medford. While there we had a day trip to Crater Lake, where we found snow many feet deep in midsummer. On our homeward journey, we stopped at Boise, the capital of Idaho, and also the state's new recreational resort, Sun Valley, where we spent two happy days.

GRATIFYING PROGRESS REPORT

By the end of 1954, I had completed ten years of service as general manager. In my report to the board of directors, I wrote:

> In reviewing the past decade, it is interesting to note that the volume of business has increased by 137 percent. The total net profit for this period exceeds that of the first fifty-five years of the Book Concern. About one quarter million dollars of new printing, building, and office equipment has been installed. Three properties north of and adjacent to the present building have been acquired for use in possible expansion. The fund for building and equipment has now reached the sum of $251,000. A fund of $100,000 has been set aside for superannuated employees. The active employees have two retirement plans, namely, Aetna and Social Security, plus group insurance. Wages and salaries have almost doubled in the ten-year period. Paid holidays have been granted, and a more liberal vacation program allowed. In addition to the above achievements, Augustana Book Concern has during this decade contributed $86,690 to the Board of Parish Education and three other agencies of the church.

Although grateful for progress, we wanted to emphasize that the main objective of the Augustana Book Concern was the distribution of the printed page. The promotion of the printed page comes in the distribution of Bibles, gift books, lesson materials, church papers, story papers, tracts, devotional guides, and hymnals. Next are new books and supplies, such as weekly bulletins, offering envelopes, and the like. Our publications made a constant impact upon our people in the fields of evangelism, missions, Christian teaching and Christian social action. Further, our literature was the means whereby members of our church might study and train themselves to communicate more adequately the gospel in every area of their lives and in their particular community. No one can measure the great value for good and for witness to God in the literature of the church. We of the Augustana Book Concern rejoiced in the opportunity to serve. We appreciated the fine cooperation of our pastors, teachers, lay administrators, and all our church members in our endeavor to proclaim the gospel through the printed page. Personally I was also grateful to the members of the board of directors and to co-workers for their loyal support. The outstanding result of the Augustana Book Concern during the past decade could not have been accomplished without this splendid support from all.

We had two very attractive and effective promotional items— one a house organ, "A Drop of Ink," printed and edited by Gustav Magnusson, our assistant production manager. It was mailed to our pastors and printing customers. The other, a film-strip, "A Drop of Ink Will Make a Million Think," was produced for loan to congregations. The title was taken from a Church Paper Week slogan of a few years before. It was a twenty-five minute colored film strip with recordings which portrayed in an interesting manner the story of the Augustana Book Concern and the contribution it had made and was making to the church.

ILLNESS AND HOSPITAL CONFINEMENT

In early February 1955, while Lyal and I were attending an All-America City celebration at the Rock Island High School auditorium, I became ill and was taken by ambulance to the Lutheran Hospital, Moline, where I remained three weeks under treatment for a duodenal ulcer. My doctor, John Souders, successfully brought me back to health without surgery. For months I had to be careful in the selection of food, especially during my travels. I had a good recovery and have not had a recurrence of this illness.

Because of my illness, I missed the annual meeting of the Protestant Church-Owned Publishers Association held at Williamsburg, Virginia, in February. I was very sorry to miss this meeting although the Book Concern was represented by our promotion manager, Daniel Nystrom, Jr. I was generously remembered by my friends in the association with cards, letters and flowers.

APPOINTMENTS AND RETIREMENTS

In the fall of 1956, Don Wallerstedt, a graduate of the University of Nebraska and the Kansas City Art Institute, became our artist and art director. Mrs. Ruby Dick was later engaged as his assistant. Mr. Wallerstedt replaced Edwin Holmer, who had resigned to study for the ministry.

Just before Christmas 1956, a testimonial dinner was held in the Fort Armstrong Hotel, Rock Island. The honored guest was Dr. A. T. Lundholm, who was retiring from active service at the age of eighty-one. He had had fifty-four years in the ministry, seventeen years of which had been spent as editor of the church's official Swedish organ, *Augustana.* His retirement at the end of 1956 also marked the end of *Augustana,* after serving the church for nearly a century. Among those present were the members of the board of directors of the Augustana Book Concern, publication house personnel, members of the executive committee of the church, and representatives of the seminary and the college. Brief words of commendation were spoken by Dr. Oscar A. Benson, president of the church; Dr. Clifford A. Nelson, of the Book Concern board of directors; Dr. E. E. Ryden and Birger Swenson.

Oscar G. Ericson, who for thirty-four years had been in charge of the manufacturing department of the Augustana Book Concern, retired in March 1958. He was honored at a recognition dinner, sponsored by the board of directors, on March 4. Mr. Ericson was succeeded as production manager by Gustav A. Magnusson, whom he had hired as a boy apprentice thirty-two years before. Mr. and Mrs. Ericson maintained their home in Rock Island but looked forward to doing some traveling; however, illness came and death claimed Mr. Ericson on August 5, 1963.

SERVICE BOOK AND HYMNAL

The publishers of the *Service Book and Hymnal,* authorized by the eight Lutheran bodies cooperating on the hymnal, were the Augsburg Publishing House, Minneapolis; Augustana Book Concern, Rock Island; the Finnish Lutheran Book Concern, Hancock, Michigan; Lutheran Publishing House, Blair, Nebraska; United Lutheran Publication House, Philadelphia; and the Wartburg Press, Columbus, Ohio. The first printing came off the press in March 1958, and was the largest cooperative effort ever undertaken by the member Lutheran churches and their publishing houses. The wide acceptance of this new hymnal did much to establish Lutheran unity. In 1960 the American Lutheran Church, the Lutheran Free Church, the Evangelical Lutheran Church, and the United Evangelical Lutheran Church merged to form the new American Lutheran Church. The other large merger became effective July 1, 1962, when the Augustana Lutheran Church, the Finnish Lutheran Church, United Lutheran Church, and the American Evangelical Lutheran Church united to form the largest Lutheran Church body in the United States under the name of the Lutheran Church in America.

The publication of the *Service Book and Hymnal* became one of the most significant projects of the year 1958 in the book store and the mail-order division of the Book Concern. Accumulated orders for the new *Service Book and Hymnal* called for more than 165,000 copies which were delivered to about 850 Augustana Lutheran congregations before the end of 1958. Before the year closed, we had also sold and delivered 10,000 copies of the liturgical music of the *Service Book and Hymnal.*

For several years we had been able to plan for and to publish twelve new titles a year. We were also encouraged by the substantial increase in circulation each year of our official church papers, story papers, and the devotional guide, *The Home Altar.*

In view of this increase in business, the Augustana Book Concern had become and remained the biggest customer of the Rock Island Post Office. Each day many truck loads of mail and packages left the Augustana Book Concern plant for the post office.

We might well call 1958 an abnormal year on account of the large volume of sales of the new *Service Book and Hymnal.* Total sales amounted to $2,191,446.58, a 44.5 percent increase over the previous year and a net profit of twenty-two percent.

When news of our large profit reached the Executive Council of our Augustana Lutheran Church, I was asked to appear before this august body at the 1959 annual meeting. The president wanted to know why I had not recommended to my board to share $100,000 of the profit with the Augustana Lutheran Church. I told the members of the council that it was true that we had been very fortunate, but that we had no money in the bank. I reminded the council that the estimated building cost of the addition and the remodeling recently completed was $1,250,000; therefore, we needed the larger than usual profit on our operation.

The result of my appearance before the council was that instead of being reprimanded the Book Concern was commended.

BUILDING AND REMODELING

At the meeting on March 19, 1957, of the board of directors, I reported that our dream for additional space and the remodeling of present quarters in order to serve our pastors, congregations, and church more efficiently would soon be realized. We had acquired several properties north of and adjacent to our present building which would give us ample building site as well as much needed parking space. The architectural firm of Swanson and Maiwald had promised working plans for this meeting and stated that plans should be ready to submit to contractors for bids within a few weeks. The work was to be done in two stages; first, the new addition and then the remodeling of the present building.

The three-floor addition was to be constructed of reinforced concrete, brick, and stone. The structure would give the plant about 50,000 square feet of additional space. The entire building was to be air-conditioned.

Ground was broken for the new addition in August 1957. The general contractors were Semate and Waters. Good progress was made, and the addition was completed in October 1958. We immediately began to move various departments. We were fortunate in that we were able to move heavy machinery, such as linotype machines, printing presses, cutting machines, and other equipment without outside help. The employees under the capable direction of Gustav Magnusson and Carl Anderson saved thousands of dollars in expense. Harold Swanson, Ernest Swanson, Daniel Nystrom, Jr., and Leonard Lilyers were in charge of moving stock and office equipment. Moving meant much overtime work. All employees had worked under a handicap during the year on account of the construction project and would continue to do so until the entire job was completed. Their cooperation and interest meant much to me.

The second stage, the remodeling of the original building, was next on the schedule. We had asked the architects to complete the plans so that all outside work could proceed. This work would mean rebuilding of the front, new windows to conform with those in the addition, and brick veneering of the entire structure.

In the original planning, we had suggested that a light-colored brick similar to that in Centennial Hall across the street on the Augustana campus be used for the new addition and the remodeling project. The architect pointed out that that kind of brick would be too brittle. The new addition was built to withstand considerable vibration caused by the operation of many heavy machines. A stronger kind of brick similar in color, but at a higher price, was selected.

The building project took two years and three months to complete. The total cost of the new addition was $843,910.66, and the total cost of the remodeling was $372,939.99, making a total for the entire project of $1,216,850.65.

We rejoiced that we now had a greatly enlarged and modernized facility. The new addition of three floors, the remodeling of the existing building, and the purchase of new equipment made ours one of the most modern and best equipped church publishing houses in the country. We were fortunate, too, in being able to meet all obligations, including payments to contractors and for new equipment and end with a mortgage indebtedness not exceeding $300,000.

The dedication of the new addition and remodeling was held Wednesday, November 4, 1959, at which time our board was host to the board and staff of the United Lutheran Publication House. A number of representatives from other Lutheran publication houses as well as from the Protestant Church-Owned Publishers Association attended. The dedication service included songs by a chorus of Book

Concern employees under the direction of Leonard Lilyers, prayer by Dr. E. E. Ryden, the story of the building project and the description of our new facilities by Birger Swenson, the dedicatory address by Dr. Malvin Lundeen, and the rite of dedication by Pastor Russell W. Johnson, chairman of the board of directors. In his address, Dr. Lundeen said in part: "We of the Augustana Church thank God for those whose foresight and planning have made possible these new and renovated facilities, knowing that, under God, they will make possible an ever more effective ministry for Him among us. For it is true, as the inscription on the placque at the entrance to this building puts it, 'The Printed Word also Proclaims the Gospel.' "

The dedication was followed by three days of open house during which thousands of people were conducted through the plant. Much favorable publicity was given the Augustana Book Concern in news stories, editorials, and pictures both in the local press, church papers, and in religious trade journals throughout the country.

CENTENNIAL PUBLICATIONS

The key event of 1960 was the Centennial Synod held in Rock Island in June. The Augustana Book Concern was co-sponsor with Augustana College and Augustana Theological Seminary. The preparation for this centennial year of our church greatly affected many of our operations. It was our privilege to cooperate with the centennial planning committee in planning, printing, and promoting two publications, namely, *This Is My Church* and *Centennial Essays.* More than thirty thousand copies of *This Is My Church* were sold within weeks. This book was also singled out for special attention. Both the publication committee and the Augustana Book Concern received the Mead Award of Merit. The publication committee was commended for its capable presentation of subject matter and the Augustana Book Concern for fine craftsmanship and outstanding skill in graphic art.

Other centennial publications, for which the Book Concern was responsible for both printing and sales, were *Foundation for Tomorrow* by the Board of World Missions and *The School of the Prophets,* by G. Everett Arden. It should be mentioned here that the

1948 centennial book, *A Century of Life and Growth,* also sold more than 30,000 copies.

We asked the committee in charge of the publication of the centennial book of 1960, *This Is My Church,* for permission to place copies in selected institutions and libraries in the United States and Sweden. We felt that this book was most worthy and merited a place not only in church libraries but in other educational institutions as well.

DR. E. E. RYDEN RETIRES

Dr. Ryden's twenty-seven years of distinguished service to the *Lutheran Companion,* to the publication house, and to the church will long be cherished by associates and readers everywhere. The ready acceptance of Dr. Ryden's editorship of the *Lutheran Companion* was singularly manifested at the end of 1959, when circulation reached 96,888 subscribers. A year after the Church Paper Week was introduced in 1927, a budget plan for our church papers was offered congregations. Eight hundred fifty congregations had adopted this plan by 1959.

At a recognition luncheon in Dr. Ryden's honor much humor came to light as readers' requests and comments were quoted. A man had been placed in an old people's home. He was required to take a bath once a week. He did not like this rule. "Could you as editor do something about it?"

A woman wrote the editor, "Five years ago you buried my husband. I certainly appreciated it."

A man from Buffalo wrote, "Can the editor find me a good, strong wife?"

A certain congregation that was preparing to adorn its altar wrote the Book Concern inquiring about prices of acolytes. Luckily, they did not ask for samples. In telling this story, I am reminded of a Chicago pastor who told of a mother who called him on a Sunday morning with this disturbing information: "Our Henry came down with the mumps this morning and will not be able to acolyte in church today."

A highlight in 1961 was the call extended to and accepted by Mr. Paul E. Gustafson, religion editor of the *Milwaukee Sentinel,* to succeed Dr. E. E. Ryden as editor of the *Lutheran Companion.* Dr. Ryden completed his service as editor with the last issue of February in 1961. Mr. Gustafson began his duties with the first issue of March 1961. Charlotte Odman remained as assistant editor.

JOURNEY TO THE NORTHWEST AND CANADA

One of the rewards in our work was the privilege of attending conference meetings and annual conventions of the church. At these meetings we had the pleasure of seeing friends and making new acquaintances. The 1961 annual convention of the Augustana Lutheran Church was scheduled for June 12-17 at the Gethsemane Lutheran Church, Seattle. Many arranged to combine the convention with vacation. Lyal and I decided to do just that. We left by bus for Savanna, where we boarded the Great Northern Empire Builder. We found many friends on board both from the East and the Middle West. Among these friends were Rev. and Mrs. John Breck and Rev. and Mrs. David Ekstrom. We also found upon arrival in Seattle that many friends had been assigned to the same hotel as we, namely, the Benjamin Franklin.

After setting up the Book Concern display at the church, we had time for a couple of days of sightseeing before the convention. Together with Jean and Leonard Lilyers we toured the city of Seattle and the university and ended the day with a dinner at a Japanese restaurant, the Bush Garden, with the Daniel Nystroms and Eloise's mother, Mrs. Nelson. We also visited Pacific Lutheran University in Tacoma and Paradise Lodge on Mt. Rainier.

The convention itself was unique in that this was the last time that a local church was the host. The last annual meeting of the Augustana Lutheran Church before the merger would be held in a convention hall in downtown Detroit; therefore, we made the most of sociability while in Seattle. It was fun to meet friends at such restaurants as the Hofbrau, the Camlin Hotel Sky Room, Trader Vic's and Iver's Acres of Clams on the waterfront, pier 54. We will not soon forget the boat trip to Blake Island on the steamer, *Virginia,* where a salmon barbecue had been arranged for the delegates and visitors. Indian dancers were present to entertain us.

Leaving Seattle on June 18, Lyal and I traveled on the Great

Northern Railway along the Pacific coast to Vancouver, B.C., where we had two days of sightseeing and shopping. We continued eastward on the Canadian Pacific through the beautiful Fraser River Canyon to Chateau Lake Louise, Alberta, a place of spectacular beauty and charm. During our two-day visit here, we had many scenic walks, one of which was a climb to the Teahouse of Many Glaciers. On our way to Jasper National Park, we stopped for a ride by snowmobile over the glacier at the Columbia Ice Field, the largest body of ice south of the Arctic Circle. (The ice was 1,000 feet deep.) Near Jasper Park Lodge, we visited Mt. Edith Cavell and the Glacier of the Angel. We returned to Banff for two days, another scenic spot with a castle-like hotel.

Time came for our homeward journey. We traveled by train to Winnipeg, where we had a day for sightseeing and a visit to the capitol. In the evening we boarded the Great Northern for Minneapolis. Traveling with us were Rev. and Mrs. Daniel Martin. The next morning we had breakfast with them before we boarded the Burlington Zephyr for Savanna. We arrived at noon and were met by Harold and Martha Swanson.

Harold dropped some disturbing news. He informed us that the Augustana Book Concern was subject to the Illinois State Unemployment Compensation Act as well as sales tax. We had been charged fifty thousand dollars which Harold had paid with a loan from the First National Bank of Rock Island. As soon as I could, I contacted members of the board for permission to engage legal assistance as I firmly believed we were entitled to exemption. Isador Katz of the firm Reidy, Katz, McAndrews, Durkee and Telleen, was engaged and promptly asked for a hearing. After several hearings at which I had to answer a multitude of questions, we were told to wait for a ruling. Word came to us in November 1962, that the Department of Labor of the State of Illinois had determined that the Augustana Book Concern was exclusively a religious corporation and therefore exempt from any liability under the Illinois Unemployment Compensation Act as well as sales tax. We, therefore, applied for a refund of $61,486.62, paid during the last year-and-a-half. A refund came promptly but no interest for the time the money was held.

MERGER OF PUBLICATION WORK

The Joint Commission on Lutheran Unity appointed a committee in 1957 to prepare for the merger of the boards of publication of the four Lutheran bodies, namely, American Evangelical Lutheran Church, Augustana Lutheran Church, Finnish Lutheran Church, and United Lutheran Church. I was designated as chairman of this committee, and Dr. H. Torrey Walker, secretary. Our first meeting was held in Chicago, October 29, 1957. In attendance were Dr. Walker and Frank G. Rhody of the United Lutheran Publication House, E. M. Laitala of the Finnish Lutheran Book Concern, and I represented the Augustana Book Concern. The American Evangelical Lutheran Church did not have a publishing house, but a publication committee. Occasionally this committee was represented.

We had many meetings over a period of nearly five years. Various staff members attended and gave us valuable help. In 1959 we began to issue cooperative catalogs, such as, *Christmas, Vacation Bible School, Fall Supply, Lenten* and *General.*

The year 1961 was a busy one for the sub-committee on merging the publication work. A constitution and by-laws were prepared as well as policies on procedure so that when the actual merger came, we would have a smoothly working organization. A joint meeting of the boards of publication of the four church bodies in the merger was held in Chicago July 12, at which time the by-laws and policy matters relative to the plan of operation were discussed and approved. At this meeting we had the opportunity to meet and learn to know the members representing the other Lutheran groups.

The Board of Publication of the new Lutheran Church in America was formally organized at a meeting held July 2, 1962, a day after the close of the constituting convention in Detroit. Dr. Franklin Clark Fry, president of the new church, convened the twenty-one member board. Bertram Wilde, Philadelphia, formerly president of the United Lutheran Church Board of Publication, was chosen president; Dr. Reuben K. Youngdahl, Minneapolis, former chairman of the board of Augustana Book Concern, was elected vice president. Dr. H. Torrey Walker, former executive secretary of the United Lutheran Publication House, became executive secretary of the new board. Frank G. Rhody, associate executive secretary of the

United Lutheran Publication House, and I became associate executive secretaries of the new board. E. M. Laitala, manager of the Finnish Lutheran Book Concern, was chosen as the director of printing of the new board; Harold A. Swanson, treasurer of Augustana Book Concern, was named assistant treasurer, and Daniel Nystrom, Jr., promotion manager of Augustana Book Concern, was named assistant secretary. In addition to Dr. Youngdahl, other former Augustana Book Concern board members elected to the new board of publication were Rev. G. Erik Hagg, Leonard Olson, and Harold A. Schwanbeck.

The board authorized signing of the contract with Cuneo Eastern Press of Philadelphia for printing *The Lutheran,* the biweekly magazine of the new church, the first issue of which was scheduled for January 1, 1963.

A MINISTRY OF PRINTING AND *AUGUSTANA HERITAGE*

In the account of my years at the Augustana Book Concern, I have tried to tell the story as a year to year experience, which may be somewhat incomplete. Therefore, I am happy to call attention to the history of our publishing house, *A Ministry of Printing,* by Daniel Nystrom. It came off the press just before the close of 1962. It tells the story quite fully of what the Augustana Lutheran Church undertook and accomplished in the publishing field during the years of its existence as an individual church body. More specifically the book brings the history of the Augustana Book Concern up-to-date, from its beginning in 1889 through 1962.

Augustana Heritage, a new history of the Augustana Lutheran Church, by Dr. G. Everett Arden, was also in preparation during 1962 and published in early 1963. It was being published jointly by the Augustana Lutheran Church and the Augustana Book Concern. *Augustana Heritage* was the last book to be copyrighted by and to carry the imprint of the Augustana Book Concern.

MY LAST ANNUAL REPORT, DECEMBER 1962

On January 1, 1963, the Augustana Book Concern became a part of the new publication house of the merged church, the

Lutheran Church in America. The three publication houses in the merger then made an institution with assets of more than six million dollars and a personnel of more than 600. Much preparatory work had been done prior to the merger, and Augustana Book Concern had the privilege of being a vital part of these surroundings.

In my last report, I included a short review of the accomplishments of the Book Concern during its seventy-three years of existence. It read as follows:

> From a small beginning in 1889, it has become an outstanding publishing house, not only among Lutherans but also among other Protestant denominations in America. Its buildings and machinery are up-to-date and efficient. With a loyal and experienced force of 154 employees, we have been able to render valuable service to the church, its various departments, its institutions, congregations, pastors and members. It is readily recognized that the printed word has been a significant factor in the growth of the Augustana Lutheran Church. Besides the various services rendered, the Book Concern has also been able to give financial grants to institutions and causes which over the years have amounted to more than half a million dollars. During the last several years, the Board of Parish Education has been the principal recipient.

As the Augustana Book Concern became history at the end of 1962, we fondly remember the men and women who through the years had been associated with us, whose labors had helped make Augustana Book Concern. They represented a diversity of gifts and skills all of which went into the making of the institution called Augustana Book Concern, the official publication house of the church.

My most cherished memory will be the Augustana Book Concern Board and family during my years as manager. It was a joy to work with them. I acknowledge in this way the service and friendship of all of them and say a heartfelt thanks. My sentiments for the future of the merger appear in Appendix C.

THE MERGED PUBLICATION HOUSE, 1963

We knew that the merger would bring many adjustments before we would have a smoothly working organization in the new merged publication house. Adjustments came as early as 1961. Many of the boards and departments of the Augustana Lutheran Church found it necessary to curtail printing of promotional and other material. Some discontinued printing altogether.

The big change came with January 1, 1963, the first year of the new merged publication house, especially in the Rock Island plant, which was referred to as the Board of Publication-West. The *Lutheran Companion,* formerly printed by the Augustana Book Concern, had been discontinued. The editorial, composing, press, and mailing rooms were now comparatively quiet. The big press, used to print the *Lutheran Companion,* had been in constant operation for sixteen hours a day for the last decade. This press was now used to print *The Home Altar* and *Light for Today.* Other presses were used to print the church story papers. The men on the night shift on the *Lutheran Companion* press were retired. Some employees in the mailing room were laid off.

The employees in the business office had adjustments too, such as becoming familiar with a new system of handling customer orders, invoices and other forms.

We were promised work from Philadelphia, but did not receive enough to take care of the loss of the *Lutheran Companion* and the twelve or fifteen new titles that we used to print annually at the Book Concern.

In the former Augustana Lutheran Church, leaders of various institutions and departments, were encouraged to have their printing needs done by Augustana Book Concern. The constitution of the new Board of Publication stated that except for certain items, "boards, commissions and the auxiliaries shall be free to decide whether to utilize the services and facilities of the Board of Publication for the publication of their periodicals and other printed material." In the Augustana Lutheran Church, all conferences had had their minutes printed by the Augustana Book Concern. I spent a good deal of time during 1963 soliciting the printing needs of various synods. Gustav Magnusson was very helpful in giving information of various kinds. We were encouraged with the response.

I was asked to participate in an interesting and informative five-day meeting of branch managers and sales executives held at Cherry Hill Inn, New Jersey, March 25-29, 1963.

During 1963 I had the privilege of attending quarterly meetings of the Board of Publication in Philadelphia. I learned to know the board members and appreciated their friendship. Even now after fifteen years I still keep in touch with some of them. The Philadelphia board meetings were, however, more formal than those of the Augustana Book Concern. I soon learned that one was not to participate in discussion unless he was asked. At the Book Concern, meetings were more open and free. Everyone was entitled to offer opinions and to participate in discussion. There was always a spirit of comradeship and humor. The board members always liked to have fun with the manager. For instance, when he recommended a piece of new equipment, someone would ask, "How is it working, Birger?" They did not accuse me of exceeding authority, for such a question was stated in fun. I have deep and lasting pleasant memories of the men who served on our board during the years of my administration.

The following served as presidents of the Augustana Book Concern board during my years of service—1926-1962:

Dr. C. W. Foss, 1926-1928
Dr. A. T. Lundholm, 1929-1938
Dr. Oscar N. Olson, 1938-1941
Dr. H. E. Sandstedt, 1942-1943
Dr. A. D. Mattson, 1944-1947
Dr. O. V. Anderson, 1948-1951
Dr. Clifford Nelson, 1952-1957
Rev. Russel W. Johnson, 1958-1959
Dr. Reuben K. Youngdahl, 1960-1962

RETIREMENT

Friends came from near and far to join the publication house employees at my retirement party. It was quite an affair. Let the *Inklings* tell the story:

> "Technically this is a Christmas party for the employees of the Augustana Book Concern, but it really was intended to be a surprise party for Birger Swenson. However, it didn't work out that way," said Dr. H. Torrey Walker, executive secretary of the Board of Publication, as he welcomed nearly 300 guests attending the annual Christmas dinner of the Augustana Book Concern. It was held on Wednesday evening, December 11, 1963, in Westerlin Hall, the girls'

dorm of Augustana College.

"Have you ever tried to keep a secret from Birger? Well, you can't," explained Dr. Walker.

Even though it turned out to be a non-surprise party for Birger, everyone enjoyed the occasion, most of all the guest of honor. Braving ice and snow to attend the event were Dr. Walker, Frank Rhody, A. Leonard Lilyers, William Pepper of the Board of Publication staff in Philadelphia; Bertram Wilde, also of Philadelphia and president of the Board of Publication; Harold Schwanbeck of Old Saybrook, Connecticut, Leonard Olson of Chicago, and Dr. Paul T. Warfield of Trenton, New Jersey—all members of the board; Dr. Malvin H. Lundeen, secretary of the Lutheran Church in America, who brought greetings from Dr. Franklin Clark Fry, and other friends of the Swensons from Minneapolis, Chicago, and the Quad-City area.

"This is an historic occasion," Dr. P. O. Bersell, former president of the Augustana Lutheran Church, interjected during the introduction of out-of-town guests.

"This is the first time Dr. Reuben Youngdahl wasn't able to take off!" Dr. Youngdahl, vice president of the board, was to have made one of the presentations to Birger, but weather kept him grounded in Minneapolis.

Birger Swenson is retiring as associate executive secretary of the Board of Publication at the end of this year. Since 1926 he has been with the Augustana Book Concern, the publishing house of the former Augustana Lutheran Church. He served as a field representative, circulation manager, and in 1942 became its sales manager. In 1944 he became acting manager and in 1945, general manager.

Gifts of money, luggage, a citation and a leather-bound book containing 400 personal letters from friends and associates here and abroad were presented to Birger from the employees, board, staff members, and friends by Mr. Rhody, Mr. Wilde, and Daniel Nystrom, Jr., western regional manager, Rock Island.

The Augustana College trio sang old ballads.

In his response, Swenson reminisced about his more than thirty-seven years at Augustana Book Concern, as the Rock Island branch of the Board of Publication has been known in this part of the country and by members of the former Augustana Lutheran Church. He also paid tribute to the loyalty and cooperation of the Book Concern employees, especially to those who have a service record of more than twenty-five and fifty years, and to Mrs. Eva

> Swanson, who has served him as secretary for more than three decades.
>
> Birger has made six trips to Europe, and the first of the year, he and Mrs. Swenson are embarking on a three-months' tour around the world, going by boat, train, plane, car, elephant and camel back.

Following the testimonial dinner, news of the event appeared in the press and radio, also editorials. We quote:

—Rock Island *Argus,* December 14, 1963:

> Birger Swenson brought to the Book Concern a combination of talents—energy, honesty, good judgment and good humor, sometimes at the expense of himself. In fact, he elevated good humor to the status of a dignified corporation asset.
>
> It would be difficult to imagine him spending the rest of his life in a rocking chair. We are happy to learn that he will continue to give some of his time to the church, college and community.

—Dr. H. T. Walker in *Inklings,* December, 1963:

> *Determination* is the word I want to use here, because that is Birger. He 'determined' that he would go to college. Without funds but with determination he worked his way through Augustana College. He is proud to relate that his principal job at college was running the college "beanery." He aimed at the ministry after graduating from college and spent a year at the theological seminary, but when an opportunity came to serve the church as layman with the Augustana Book Concern, he changed course.

—WHBF Radio, Rock Island, December 30, 1963:

> Tomorrow we lose one of our hard-working partners of many years standing in this community. Birger Swenson retires! To us who have known and worked with Birger in sundry community endeavors—enjoying to the utmost his humor and unending fund of jokes and stories—it just seems impossible that Birger has reached mandatory retirement age!

Honors have come to me far beyond what I ever had a right to expect. I had thirty-seven wonderful years at the Augustana Book Concern.

The King of Sweden in 1951 honored me by dubbing me a Knight of the Order of Vasa, First Class. In 1958, my Alma Mater, Augustana College, conferred on me the degree of Doctor of Laws.

In 1962 the historical society of my home province of

Värmland, Sweden, *(Hembygdsförbundet)* presented me with an honorary membership in the society. I also appreciate the life membership bestowed upon me by the Rock Island Chamber of Commerce.

Shortly after my official retirement, I was asked to write an article on how to enjoy retirement. It was published in *The Round Table,* the official publication of the Protestant Church-Owned Publishers Association. I would like to share my thoughts here on this subject:

HOW TO ENJOY RETIREMENT

Mandatory retirement means that one has to relinquish his job to someone else, but it does not mean that he has to give up all his other interests and retire to a rocking chair. My belief is that as long as health permits, one should remain active and never really retire. I am happiest when busy.

One should not give up outside interests. He should give service to others through voluntary community agencies and social service organizations. He should continue community activities, such as the Chamber of Commerce, city government, Community Chest, service clubs, YMCA, and many others.

One can work in his church on the local, regional, and national levels. A man who has time and interest is always wanted on boards and committees.

Many staff employees of various religious publication houses have opportunities to travel, but mostly in the United States and Canada. Retirement has given me the time to fulfill dreams of seeing far distant lands and to learn more about our neighbors. I have found that reading beforehand about countries to be visited pays good dividends. My picture-taking hobby has also been put to good use. Later at home I have had opportunities to share my experiences by giving travelogues to service clubs, church organizations, and schools.

I have more time for reading. My library has grown over the years, but I have never had time to become fully familiar with it. Now I am eager to learn to know the contents of books of which my knowledge has been only the title. Reading brings me not only excitement but also relaxation.

Keep in touch; write regularly to relatives and friends.

Hobbies are important, but a hobby cannot be picked up overnight. It should be a logical outcome of a developing interest which may be expanded when there is leisure time during vacations or retirement.

A sense of humor will prevent one's taking himself too seriously. My wife can testify.

Memories bring happiness. Present day activities stimulate and help one to look to the future, rather than the past. My advice—never fully retire.

THE AUGUSTANA BOOK CONCERN CLOSES

As the last manager of the Augustana Book Concern, I was very much saddened by the decision of the Board of Publication to close the plant in Rock Island in the spring of 1967, less than four years after the merger. This action was not even conceivable during the months and years of merger negotiations. There are, of course, casualties in mergers; in this one it was the Book Concern. It hurt me very much to learn that all the employees, who had spent many years in publication work, had to lose their jobs.

I had always looked upon the former Augustana Book Concern building as an historic shrine. In a sense it is a monument to all who have labored there and the many who have spent as many as fifty and sixty years in its fold—editors, printers, bookbinders, secretaries, stock and office staff—all members of the Book Concern family.

I was happy that Augustana College acquired the former Book Concern property. I was not pleased, however, in seeing the building renamed. I always felt that the Book Concern building belonged to all who had labored there a lifetime.

I was most grateful to the new president of Augustana College, Dr. Thomas Tredway, and Mr. Glen E. Brolander, vice president for financial affairs at Augustana College, who offered to place another plaque to commemorate the site of the original structure. This plaque would serve as a reminder to all who read it of the importance of the publication work of the Augustana Book Concern to the college and the church. This plaque was unveiled November 16.

1975, on the second floor of the former Book Concern building.

Speaking during the unveiling program, Dr. Conrad Bergendoff, president emeritus of Augustana College, paid homage to past editors and also expressed what the Book Concern had meant to the college and to the church. I spoke on behalf of the employees.

The ceremony was sponsored by the Augustana Historical Society. In charge of arrangements were Mrs. Dorothy E. Liljegren, president of the Society, Gustav Magnusson, former production manager of the Book Concern, and Mr. Glen E. Brolander.

A large number of former employees of the Book Concern, their families and friends attended the unveiling. A coffee hour followed at which time I heard many reminisce about former happy Augustana Book Concern days.

The text of the plaque is as follows:

On this site since 1889
THE AUGUSTANA BOOK CONCERN

served as the publication house of the Augustana Lutheran Church until 1962 when that Church merged to become a part of the Lutheran Church in America. The official church papers *Augustana* and the *Lutheran Companion* were issued under such renowned editors as S. P. A. Lindahl, L. G. Abrahamson, and E. E. Ryden.

The original structure, enlarged several times, was completely modernized and doubled in size in 1959 during the administration of Birger Swenson.

This complex was acquired by Augustana College in 1967.

I appreciated the letter that Dr. Thomas Tredway sent me following the unveiling:

OFFICE OF THE PRESIDENT

November 20, 1975

Dear Birger,

I was very happy Sunday at the unveiling of the plaque and the ceremony recognizing the great role which the Augustana Book Concern has played in the life of our church & our college. You must be very proud of the part which the many employees, present and past, played in that history, and especially of your own role. The college is very fortunate to have the use of the building now, and we will try to be good stewards of the building, its history and the love of many for it.

Tom Tredway

Birger and secretary, Eva Swanson.
Augustana Book Concern, 1943

Augustana Book Concern, 1943

FIRST HOME OF
AUGUSTANA
BOOK CONCERN
Rock Island, Illinois

A. G. ANDERSON
Manager of
Augustana
Book Concern
1889-1927

J. G. YOUNGQUIST
Manager of Augustana
Book Concern, 1927-1944

BIRGER SWENSON
Manager of Augustana
Book Concern, 1944-1962

PRESENT HOME OF
AUGUSTANA BOOK CONCERN
Rock Island, Illinois

Publication Work of the Synod

Dr. Conrad Bergendoff and Birger at unveiling of Augustana Book Concern plaque,
November 16, 1975

Augustana Book Concern Board of Directors, 1961
Left to right: G. Erik Hagg, Maurice Moe, Arthur O. Arnold, Birger Swenson,
Ivar Johnson, Reuben K. Youngdahl, C. Don Fuelscher, H. A. Schwanbeck,
Malvin H. Lundeen, Luther R. Livingston.

Birger's retirement, December 11, 1963
Dr. H. T. Walker, Lyal and Birger, and Bertram Wilde

Gustav Magnusson, Birger, Dr. Everett Arden, and Carl Anderson
celebrate the publication of Arden's *Augustana Heritage*

VIII

PROFESSIONAL ORGANIZATIONS

The story of the National Lutheran Editors and Managers Association is recorded in a volume published in 1957, entitled *Pen and Printing Press.* I want to relate a few highlights of my varied experiences in this association. The meeting held at the Lutheran Book Concern in Columbus, Ohio, in 1928 with Manager A. H. Dornbirer as host, was my first. It was also the first meeting for Randolph E. Haugan, newly elected manager of the Augsburg Publishing House, Minneapolis. J. G. Youngquist, manager of the Augustana Book Concern, Rock Island, had affiliated with the association the year before. Among other managers present were Grant Hultberg of the United Lutheran Publication House, Philadelphia, and Edmund Seuel, Concordia Publishing House, St. Louis. Editors whom I especially remember were our own Dr. L. G. Abrahamson, editor of *Augustana;* Professor Theodore Graebner, editor of the *Lutheran Witness;* and Dr. N. R. Melhorn, editor of the *Lutheran.*

Through Mr. Youngquist, I was asked to report at this meeting the result of our first Church Paper Week held in the Augustana Lutheran Church in October 1927. I related that many new subscribers for the *Lutheran Companion* and *Augustana* had been obtained and that nearly two-thirds of former subscribers had renewed during the campaign. Encouraged by this report, the managers voted to designate the last week in October 1929 as

Church Paper Week. This practice was continued annually for many years.

In the years that followed, many cooperative projects proved both practical and successful. Perhaps the greatest contribution of the association, especially that of the editors' section, was the consistent interest and promotion of the cause of Lutheran unity.

Another meeting I well remember was held at the Lutheran Publishing House, Blair, Nebraska, on September 10-12, 1930. The hosts were Manager K. P. Hemdahl and the editor of the *Ansgar Lutheran,* Rev. John M. Jensen. At a luncheon where the managers and editors were guests of Dana College, the toastmaster asked those who had been in Nebraska previously to relate in their greetings some of their experiences. Dr. L. G. Abrahamson, in his Swedish dialect and occasional stammering, included the following experience in his greeting to the amusement of all present:

> As a student I traveled all over Nebraska. Late one evening, I entered a hotel in a small town to seek lodging. There was a bright young fellow behind the desk who assured me he had a nice room and brought me to it. As I was tired, it wasn't long before I was in bed. I soon discovered I was not alone in the bed. I got up and sat in a chair all night and tried to get some rest.
>
> Early the next morning, I was back in the lobby. Behind the desk was the same bright young fellow. He said, "Good morning." I nodded my head. He asked,
>
> "Did you have a good night's rest?" I shook my head. He said,
>
> "You had the best room and the best bed in the hotel. William Jennings Bryan and President Cleveland have slept in that bed." I looked the man straight in the face and said,
>
> "When I registered last night, I did not expect to sleep with the whole Democratic party." The bed was infested with bed bugs.

At the Chicago Century of Progress World's Fair in 1934, a cooperative display of Lutheran literature produced by all Lutheran publishers proved to be a real success. Encouraged by the interest shown, it was agreed to provide a display of Lutheran Sunday School lesson material and periodicals at the World Sunday School Convention to be held at Oslo, Norway, in 1936. I was chosen the representative of all Lutheran publishers and was present at the Norway convention.

Regarding this Lutheran exhibit, I quote from the *World Convention Daily* of July 10, 1936:

> When it had been decided that the World Convention was to come to Oslo, the capital of a land where the Lutheran Church is the predominant religious shepherd of the people, it seemed to the leaders of the World's Sunday School Association that Lutheran religious educational literature should have special prominence in the general display. Accordingly they invited the publication boards of the various portions of the Lutheran Church in the United States and Canada to arrange and place such a display and to send a representative who could explain such exhibits to all.
>
> Mr. Birger Swenson of the Augustana Book Concern of the Swedish section of the church there is in charge and has a command of the Norwegian language so that he can satisfy the inquiries of most of those who visit the exhibition hall.

The Lutheran exhibit of the United States was the largest ever sent to a world convention. Devotional books, hymnals, reference books for teachers, Sunday School textbooks and periodicals were included. The major portion of the Lutheran exhibit dealt with lesson material such as the graded courses of instruction, the "New Christian Life" and "Word of Life" courses. Courses of this kind were not generally used in Europe; therefore they created more than ordinary interest for teachers and leaders.

Comments on the Lutheran exhibit were many. I quote Mrs. Alexander Smellie, editor of English International Sunday School lessons:

"I marvel at the way you Americans do things. The lesson material is well-arranged, easy to grasp, and the printing and binding are very attractive."

I also quote an Orthodox theological professor from the University of Sofia, Bulgaria:

"You got the best bibliotek!"

Dr. Allen Sutherland was in charge of the American exhibit; I was in charge of the United States Lutheran exhibit.

Even though we had long hours at the exhibit, Dr. Sutherland and I would take turns for time off so that we could attend some sessions. By so doing, I had the opportunity to meet and photograph some leaders such as Sir Harold Mackintosh, president of the World

Sunday School Convention; Dr. Robert M. Hopkins, general secretary of the World Sunday School Association; Bishop Lunde, primate of the Church of Norway; and Dr. Toyohiko Kagawa of Japan. Dr. J. Vincent Nordgren, director of Elementary Christian Education of the Augustana Synod and Mrs. Nordgren also were delegates to the convention.

Dr. Joshua Oden, pastor of Irving Park Lutheran Church, Chicago, and I were serving as officers of the Synodical Luther League Council of the Augustana Synod, he as president and I as treasurer. We had worked together on a number of projects for the Luther League. We had agreed on sponsoring a trip to Europe—a European pilgrimage including Lutherland and the World Sunday School Convention in Oslo, July 6-12, 1936. Forty-five enthusiastic pilgrims responded, and we were on our way.

We sailed on the *S. S. Berengaria* of the Cunard-White Star Line from New York on June 17, 1936. We visited historic places in Paris, Lutherland in Germany—Wittenberg, Eisenach, Lützen, Berlin, and Potsdam. In Scandinavia, we visited Copenhagen, Malmö, Gothenburg, Stockholm, Upsala, Karlstad, and lastly Oslo, where the World Sunday School Convention was held. After the convention, the group members sailed for England, where they visited London, Stratford on Avon, and Oxford before returning to New York August 3, on the *S. S. Georgic.*

Looking back, the group agreed that this forty-seven day pilgrimage had been a trip of a lifetime—at a cost of $472.50, round trip from New York. This amount included transportation, lodging, meals, entrance fees to museums and art galleries.

Some members of the group remained in Sweden to visit relatives and friends. After the convention, I traveled to my home at Averstad, Östra Fågelvik Parish in Värmland, where I met several group members whom my twin sister and I had invited to spend a few days with my family. My twin sister, Signe, was also a member of the group. Among our guests were Carl Lund-Quist, a newly ordained pastor, and Lyal Westerlund, my future wife. (She didn't know then, nor did I.) My family home had not changed except that I missed my mother, who had died in 1931. After additional sightseeing in Scandinavia, this smaller group met again in London. After a few days in England and Scotland, we sailed for New York on the *M. S. Britannic* on August 8, 1936.

Another highlight was being one of the nine Americans among twenty-four delegates to the First International Conference of Lutheran Publishers held at the University of Copenhagen, July 27-28, 1959. The meeting was sponsored by the Lutheran World Federation and presided over by its executive secretary, Dr. Carl Lund-Quist of Geneva, Switzerland.

American delegates were Albert E. Anderson, Augsburg Publishing House; Dr. Torrey Walker and Albert Lueders, United Lutheran Publication House; Birger Swenson, Augustana Book Concern; and Elmer Dornbirer, Wartburg Press.

The participants from America and Europe who met in the Danish capital agreed on the necessity of a greater exchange of information about new books they planned to publish or had under consideration. Their discussions dealt mainly with good Lutheran publications in the publishers' own languages, namely, English, Swedish, Norwegian, Danish, and German. They also gave attention to the religious literature needs of European minority Lutheran groups, such as those in France and Italy, and to those of the younger churches in Asia, Africa, and Latin America. A continuation committee was named to plan a second conference. The American delegation enjoyed having dinner each evening at Nimb's, Tivoli.

The Lutheran conference gave Lyal and me an opportunity to visit a number of countries in Western Europe. A friend, Lois Scheuerman, traveled with us. Our itinerary from June 29 to August 6 was as follows: Upon arrival in Rome, we met Florence and Torrey Walker at Hotel Flora, and traveled with them in Italy. Historical sights visited were the Trevi Fountain, the Colosseum, and the Sistine Chapel in the Vatican. The U.S. Ambassador and Mrs. James D. Zellerbach were our hosts on July 4th at the American Embassy. An auto trip took us to the Leaning Tower of Pisa and to Florence. The gondola ride in a regatta on the Grand Canal in Venice was a new experience. Carl Lund-Quist was our host at the Lutheran World Federation headquarters in Geneva, Switzerland. A trip to the Jungfrau from Lucerne and Interlaken was an unforgettable high point. We traveled by plane to Frankfurt, Germany, and by auto to Heidelberg. An SAS plane took us to Stockholm and Helsinki for a three-day stay. Our sightseeing after the publishers' conference at the

University of Copenhagen included Grundtvig Church, the Gefion Fountain, and the Mermaid. We returned to Sweden to visit relatives in Karlstad. My brother, Rickard, and his wife, Greta, had arranged a dinner for us with relatives and friends. At the John Ericsson day celebration at Filipstad, we were guests of the city for both lunch and dinner. On August 5 we returned to Copenhagen for an SAS flight home on August 6.

The Second International Conference of Lutheran Publishers took place at Loccum, Germany, on August 22-24, 1962. Sessions were held in the Evangelical Academy, located in Bishop Hans Lilje's diocese. Attending the conference were forty-three men and one woman, representing Lutheran publication houses from all parts of the world. The largest delegation came from Scandinavia and Germany, together with staff members from the Lutheran World Federation in Geneva, Switzerland. It was of special interest to have representatives of younger churches in India, Hong Kong, Madagascar, Taiwan, Japan, and Tanganyika. The United States Lutheran publishers and their wives were Dr. and Mrs. H. Torrey Walker, Mr. and Mrs. Frank Rhody, and Mr. Albert H. Lueders of the United Lutheran Publication House of Philadelphia; Dr. and Mrs. O. A. Dorn, Concordia Publishing House, St. Louis; and Lyal and myself representing the Augustana Book Concern. At the merger convention in June, 1962, I had been elected associate executive secretary of the Lutheran Church in America Board of Publication to take effect January 1, 1963. Bishop Hans Lilje was in regular attendance and addressed the conference.

These publishers came to discuss mutual problems on which they might help one another. It was reported that Lutheran books were reaching even East Germany, where they were carefully read, discussed, and passed around. It was an interesting and fruitful conference. Dr. Hans Bolewski, director of the academy, had done everything possible to make our visit comfortable and pleasant.

Our European itinerary was made more pleasant by the company of Dr. and Mrs. H. Torrey Walker. We sailed from New York on July 11, 1962, on the *S. S. Queen Mary*. After arriving in London, we had the pleasure of meeting Dr. and Mrs. Knut Erickson of Rock Island who were spending the summer with their daughter, Charlotte. The Ericksons were our guests for dinner.

A three-week sightseeing trip in England took us to Canterbury, Salisbury, Stonehenge, Bath, Glastonbury, Stratford on Avon, Coventry, Chester, North Wales, the Lake District, and Glasgow. Here we were guests of the Collins' Sons Publishing House for a delightful dinner at a lovely old castle on Loch Lomond. We traveled to Edinburgh by train and had a bus trip through the Trossachs.

After a few days of sightseeing in Holland, we traveled to Dusseldorf, West Germany, for a visit at the home of my niece, Rachel, and her husband, William Forsthoff, and children, Peter and Solveig. We continued by SAS airlines to Stockholm, where we conferred with Dr. Bo Runmark, director of Svenska Kyrkans Diakonistyrelsens Bokförlag, and other publishers. During our two days of sightseeing, we also enjoyed a visit with another niece, Ulla, and her husband, George Rastenberger. George is a member of the Stockholm Opera Orchestra. Their two children are Michael and Maria.

We traveled by train to Karlstad, my home city. My brother and his wife, Greta, had arranged a dinner party at their home to which relatives and friends had been invited. They have four children—Lars, Margaretha, Gunnar, and Marianne. One of the highlights of our visit in Karlstad was a dinner for thirty guests at the home of Bishop and Mrs. Gert Borgenstierna, given by the Society for the Promotion of Emigration Research (Värmlands Hembygdsförbund) in honor of C. F. Hellstrom, formerly Swedish consul-general in Minneapolis, and myself. (During a period of years I had sent over a thousand books to the library of Emigrantregistret, Karlstad.) Each of us was given an honorary membership in the society by the governor of the province, Gustaf Nilsson, who was also president of Värmlands Hembygdsför- bund. Among the guests at this dinner were Lyal and I and our traveling companions, Dr. and Mrs. H. Torrey Walker, my brother, Rickard, and his wife, Greta, Dr. Sigurd Gustavson, director of Emigrantregistret, and Mrs. Gustavson, Mr. Sture Stålfors, editor of *Nya Wermlands Tidningen,* and Mrs. Stålfors.

The next day, Sunday, we attended morning service in my home church in Östra Fågelvik, after which coffee was served in the parish house in honor of the visitors from America. Here I had the pleasure of meeting several of my confirmation class and school mates. From the church, we proceeded to Björka, where we were dinner guests at the home of my sister, Annie Johansson, and her family.

Annie's husband, Carl, and also my brother, Sven, had died since our last visit. Annie's two sons, Neon and Ingvar, were now operating the family farm in Averstad in addition to their home farm, Björka. Her daughter, Birgit, was in charge of a retirement home in Karlskoga.

Our return trip to the United States by SAS airlines from Copenhagen was on August 27, 1962. In Copenhagen we met my niece, Margaretha Svensson, who accompanied us to America to attend Augustana College for a year. After a year at Augustana, she met Brian Magnusson, son of Gustav and Thelma Magnusson. Gustav was the production manager of the Augustana Book Concern. A year later on May 16, 1964, Margaretha and Brian were married at Trinity Lutheran Church, Moline. Brian is employed by Deere and Company and has spent six years with its operation in Mannheim and Heidelberg, Germany. He is now at the headquarters in Moline. They have two children, Lars and Annika.

LUTHERAN EDITORS AND MANAGERS MEET

The annual meeting of the National Lutheran Editors and Managers Association was generally held in the city of the host publishing house. Separate sessions were held the first day and joint meetings on the second day. The sessions were both practical and inspirational. The managers had committees working during the year which reported at the annual meeting. Many mutual projects were completed and put into operation over the years, such as Lutheran highway markers, the joint Lutheran publication list, and the annual Church Paper Week. The managers take some credit for the publication of the *Service Book and Hymnal,* which came off the presses in 1958.

After the formation of the American Lutheran Church in 1960 and the Lutheran Church in America in 1962, the number of publication houses in our association was reduced to three. These houses with their general managers and editors were as follows: Augsburg Publishing House, Minneapolis, Dr. Randolph E. Haugen, general manager, and Rev. Edward W. Schramm, editor of the

Lutheran Standard; Concordia Publishing House, St. Louis, Dr. O. H. Dorn, general manager, and Prof. Theodore Graebner, editor of the *Lutheran Witness;* and the Board of Publication, Lutheran Church in America, Philadelphia, Dr. H. Torrey Walker, executive secretary, Frank G. Rhody and Birger Swenson, associate executive secretaries, and Dr. G. Elson Ruff, editor of the *Lutheran.*

The September 1963 meeting held in Minneapolis with the Augsburg Publishing House as host, was the fiftieth annual convention of the Lutheran Editors and Managers Association. It also happened to be my last meeting. as an active member as I was officially to retire at the end of the year. I had learned to appreciate the interest, cooperation, and friendship of these men representing various Lutheran groups.

At the final luncheon of this convention, Dr. Haugen presented me with an Atmos perpetual motion clock as a gift from the three member publication houses in recognition of my more than thirty years as treasurer of the association, as well as shorter terms as president and secretary.

INTERDENOMINATIONAL CO-OPERATION

Both my boss, J. G. Youngquist, and I became interested and decided to join the publishers' section of the International Council of Religious Education. This section was made up of protestant publishers of the United States and Canada with more than thirty different denominations represented. I served as president of this organization in 1950-1951.

Together with Dr. Clifford A. Nelson, president of the board of directors of the Augustana Book Concern, I attended the organizational meeting of the National Council of Churches in Christ in the U.S.A. held in Cleveland, in 1950. One of the divisions in this organization was the Board of Managers, Central Department of Publication and Distribution. I was elected a member of this board and served until 1954.

The Protestant Church-Owned Publishers Association (PCPA) had its beginning in Columbus, Ohio. Here in February 1949, twenty-four executive heads of church-owned publishing houses met to authorize the formation of a trade association. A committee of six was appointed to develop in detail the statement of purpose, function, and benefit for bringing such an organization into being.

Well do I remember when the call came to meet in Philadelphia in 1950 in order to adopt a constitution for PCPA. We met for several days. Pat Beard, Methodist Publishing House, Nashville, whose leadership we will always remember, was our first president. The Protestant Church-Owned Publishers Association was incorporated in Philadelphia in March 1951. Membership was limited to non-profit, protestant church-owned or church-controlled publishing institutions—one membership to each denomination operating such a publishing institution. The executive secretary, James H. Cooper, and his assistant, Mrs. Betty I. Loeb, comprised the paid staff of the association.

One of my first assignments was to head the exhibits and advertising committee of the new Revised Standard Version of the Bible, which came off the presses in 1952. This version of the Bible was published by Thomas Nelson and Sons and copyrighted by the National Council of the Churches of Christ in the U.S.A.

Annual meetings of four-day duration were held in February each year. The greater work of the association was carried out in committees in which a hundred or more members worked actively throughout the year. During my term as president, 1959-1960, a total of seventeen committees served the members under the PCPA banner outlining a practical program for present and future achievement. The annual meeting and workshops of PCPA at which I presided were held February 22-25, 1960, at the Homestead, Hot Springs, Virginia. About 300 delegates attended this meeting and workshops. The theme for discussion was "New Thinking for a New Decade." Other practical topics discussed were public relations, management, personnel, book editing, and merchandising. It was reported that publishing houses and book stores of the thirty-two denominations that were members of our association had gross sales of more than $100 million in 1959.

Each house brought many staff members as well as editors. I had three men with me for this meeting: Daniel Nystrom, Jr., promotion manager; Leonard A. Lilyers, circulation manager; and Victor E. Beck, secretary of literature.

As president, I had the duty of rendering a report of my

stewardship. I quote from the PCPA official publication, *The Round Table:*

> At the special luncheon on Wednesday, the outgoing president, Birger Swenson, pulled a surprise stunt. Instead of delivering his annual message orally, he had 'news boys' deliver it in the form of an *Extra Round Table* edition. This stunt brought delighted applause from the entire group. The president's only request was that each person read the paper entitled, "Your Association at Work," which outlined the work of the seventeen committees during the year.

My years in PCPA and my term as president were most rewarding. Although the membership represented many denominations, we were engaged in the same kind of business, we struggled with the same problems, and we strove for the same goal—to proclaim the gospel with the printed word. I am grateful for pleasant associations and good fellowship, and I cherish the many Christian friendships I made.

GRAPHIC ARTS INDUSTRY

Shortly after I became general manager, I asked the board for permission to have the Augustana Book Concern join Graphic Arts Industry, Inc., Minneapolis. This organization was a cooperatively owned non-profit management consulting and industrial engineering institution. It operated in the printing and publishing industry in the central part of the United States. The firm consisted not only of commercial printers but also of daily newspapers. Other Quad-City firms that joined the organization were Desaulniers and Company, Moline, James A. Martin, general manager; and Wagners Printers, Davenport, Karl H. Wagner, general manager. All of us received valuable service, especially in labor negotiation by Paul J. Ocken, general manager, and Peter F. King, assistant.

The Graphic Arts Industry, Inc., also gave specialized service in plant layout. This service was of great help to us in planning the new addition to the Augustana Book Concern. The architects commented that they had never had more efficient recommendations for the lighting system in all departments of the proposed printing plant.

At the annual meeting held November 22, 1963, Dr. Wilbur H. Cramblet, president of the Christian Board of Publication, St. Louis, and I retired as active members of the organization. I retired as a member of the board of directors and as an officer of the Graphic Arts Industry, Inc., and as a member of the board of directors of the Graphic Arts Technical School. Each of us was presented with binoculars and a Malacca walking stick with the best wishes of all our friends.

IX
CHURCH ACTIVITIES

Serving on the boards of deacons and of trustees, I had been active in my own congregation, Zion Lutheran Church, Rock Island, which through a merger in 1928, became St. John's Lutheran Church. Now with my work at the Augustana Book Concern, I became involved in the synod at large.

LUTHERAN BROTHERHOOD

Of more than usual importance was the annual meeting of the Lutheran Brotherhood of the Augustana Synod, held in June 1930, during the convention of the Synod at Augustana College. The brotherhood was granted one full day of the convention week. I served as general chairman of the committee on arrangements with Dr. G. A. Brandelle, ex officio, and Dr. F. O. Hanson of Augustana College, secretary-treasurer. We worked with several sub-committees.

The big event was the banquet held at the Rock Island Arsenal on the evening of June 9. I quote from the *Argus* of June 10, 1930:

> A crowd of 950 men enjoyed a banquet given by the Lutheran Brotherhood of the Augustana Synod in the dining hall of the Rock Island Arsenal last evening. The occasion brought together the largest group of men ever assembled at one time from all sections of the Synod.
>
> Dr. Frank Nelson, president of Minnesota College, Minneapolis;

> Dr. E. F. Pihlblad, president of Bethany College, Lindsborg, Kansas;
> Dr. John Christenson, Chicago, president of the American Federa-
> tion of Lutheran Brotherhoods; and Colonel D. M. King, comman-
> dant of Rock Island Arsenal, were the speakers. John A. Christian-
> son, retiring president of the synodical Brotherhood served brilliant-
> ly as toastmaster.
>
> In a short welcome, Colonel King gave some interesting informa-
> tion about Rock Island Arsenal for the benefit of the hundreds of
> visitors from distant points.
>
> This is the largest arsenal of the United States government, he
> said. It contains 900 acres which were bought from the Sac and Fox
> Indians in 1803 and a fort which was built on it during the War of
> 1812. Noted men who have been stationed here include Zachary
> Taylor, Abraham Lincoln, Robert E. Lee and Jefferson Davis.
>
> During the Civil War, 8,000 Confederate soldiers were imprisoned
> here and 1,186 died, mostly from smallpox. The island became an
> arsenal by an act of the Secretary of War in 1863. In 1898, the
> arsenal had 2,000 employees; in 1918, 19,000; and in the event of
> another great war, we would employ 30,000.

The Women's Missionary Society of the Augustana Synod held
a banquet of their own on the same evening, June 9, at the Fort
Armstrong Hotel.

Having been active in the brotherhood in St. John's Lutheran
Church, in the Rock Island District, and in the Illinois Conference, I
was elected president of the Illinois Conference Brotherhood at the
Rockford convention in October 1933. I served in that position for
two years. Other officers were Lawrence Dahlgren, Chicago, vice
president; Arvid V. Peterson, Rockford, secretary; and Tillman Palm,
La Porte, Indiana, treasurer.

The 1934 convention of the Illinois Conference Brotherhood
was held in Samuel Lutheran Church, Muskegon, Michigan, the last
week in August. A two-day concentrated program was presented to
the men who had assembled. Home mission had been and was the
objective of the conference brotherhood. To further this end, the
brotherhood pledged to raise fifteen thousand dollars for the church
extension fund which, in spite of the depression, was realized.

The brotherhood officers initiated and successfully conducted a
laymen's conference in connection with the annual convention of the
Illinois Conference. This get-together was held the day before the

opening of the convention at the same time as the pastors were meeting. The agenda for the convention was discussed. The lay delegates appreciated this opportunity to convene and to discuss matters to come before the meeting and urged the officers to continue the laymen's meeting to discuss Illinois Conference matters.

A fellowship dinner was served the delegates and guests by the women of Samuel Lutheran Church. Contributing to the success of the dinner was the Samuel Lutheran Male Chorus and Dr. E. E. Ryden, editor of the *Lutheran Companion,* who addressed the men on the theme, "The Upward Look." It was a happy assemblage of men who listened attentively to Dr. Ryden's challenging address.

We had a number of distinguished church leaders in attendance. We could dwell for some time on the greetings of Dr. G. A. Brandelle, president of the Augustana Synod, Dr. Peter Peterson, president of the Illinois Conference, and Dr. L. G. Abrahamson editor of *Augustana.* These leaders were with us throughout the convention.

The convention closed with an inspirational address by Rev. Clifford Nelson of Rock Island. His subject was "Building a Better World," based on the Book of Nehemiah.

The annual convention in 1935, my second year as president, was held in Nebo Lutheran Church, Chicago. Dr. P. O. Bersell, president-elect of the Augustana Synod, was the banquet speaker. His topic was "A Lutheran at Large." During my term of office, I found the men of the Brotherhood a mighty force in carrying out the great work of our Master. It had been an inspiration and a pleasure to work with them.

The members of the brotherhood were active in their local congregations, in their conferences, and in the Augustana Synod. They accepted and carried out the projects assigned to them. At annual conventions of the Augustana Synod, the brotherhood generally sponsored and promoted the banquet which men and women enjoyed as a social highlight of the convention.

In the 1940s Rev. C. Oscar Leonardson was elected executive director of the men's work of the Augustana Synod, with an office in Rock Island. The name of the organization was changed in 1956 from Augustana Brotherhood to Augustana Churchmen.

The men of the Augustana Synod were also active in the

American Federation of Lutheran Brotherhoods. Men of all the Lutheran Church groups were affiliated except those of the Lutheran Church-Missouri Synod.

I well remember the Eighth Biennial Convention of the American Federation of Lutheran Brotherhoods, held at the Stevens Hotel, Chicago, November 6 and 7, 1941. A large number of pastors and laymen were in attendance. Dr. Clarence M. Loesell, president of the federation, bade the group of men a hearty welcome.

Among the speakers were several Augustana men—Dr. Paul Andreen, Cokato, Minnesota; Dr. E. E. Ryden, Rock Island, president of the American Lutheran Conference; Harold LeVander, South St. Paul; Dr. Victor R. Pearson, Rock Island; and S. B. Wennerberg, Center City, Minnesota, who served as toastmaster at the banquet.

A session of more than ordinary interest was a panel discussion on the topic, "How can the layman help to promote Lutheran Church unity?" This discussion was conducted by Rev. F. A. Schiotz, following the address by Dr. Ryden. Augustana men who participated in the discussion were Judge Eskil Carlson, Des Moines, and Einar Carlson, Cleveland.

Among new officers elected for the biennium were J. Milton Deck, Philadelphia, president, and Einar Carlson, Cleveland, first vice president. I was re-elected treasurer. Following my four years as treasurer, I was elected to the Board of Governors.

J. G. Youngquist, Rock Island, was chairman of the resolutions committee. One of the resolutions submitted called on all Lutheran Church bodies to intensify their efforts to bring about unity and cooperation among Lutherans.

LUTHERAN MEN IN AMERICA

Lutheran Men in America was an organization in which I was interested for a number of years. It was a movement which began in Pittsburgh in July 1945. The membership was made up of twenty men from each of the following Lutheran groups: American Lutheran Conference, the United Lutheran Church, and the Missouri Synod. Most of the Missouri Synod men resided in Indiana. Our chaplain, Dr. O. P. Kretzmann, was the congenial president of

Valparaiso University.

Major aims of Lutheran Men were as follows: To develop better understanding and fellowship among all Lutherans; to help meet the great challenge which has come to all Christendom as the result of the world crises arising out of the war; and to encourage cooperation among all Lutherans.

Among those participating in the sessions from the Augustana Synod at the meeting of Lutheran Men in America held at Louisville, Kentucky, in the fall of 1948, were the following: Einar Carlson, Cleveland, convener and chairman, Harold LeVander, South St. Paul, and myself.

The aims as adopted at its first meeting were reaffirmed. From our friendly, lively, and provocative discussions, we gained a great deal. The spirit of the movement could be summed up in a statement by the assembly at the Louisville meeting:

"We can be very sure there is with us a majority of Lutherans who want unity and cooperation extended. We have that much to go on. But we must build on it—not tomorrow, not next week, not next year, but *now*."

I do not know what caused the breaking up of this group of men. Rumors circulated that the Missouri Church officials did not look with favor on the participation of their men in this organization—Lutheran Men in America.

LUTHER LEAGUE

The governing body of the Luther League was the Augustana Luther League Council, consisting of the elected executive committee and the presidents of the thirteen conference Luther Leagues.

During my years as treasurer, 1933-1937, Dr. Joshua Oden, Chicago, served as president, and Signe Anderson, Minneapolis, as secretary. The council also had a paid Luther League secretary.

The council met every two years. It also sponsored biennial youth conferences, which had no business meetings but had a program that was educational and inspirational. These biennial conferences were generally held at our colleges—Augustana, Bethany, Gustavus Adolphus, and Upsala. Young people in the hundreds and thousands attended. I have many fond memories of these large youth get-togethers. The Book Concern always had book displays, where we met many with whom we had previously become acquainted at Luther League summer camps or through correspondence during Church Paper Week. More than eighty percent of all organizations taking part in Church Paper Week were Luther Leagues. They served the church papers well. They also earned good money for the local league treasury in commissions on subscriptions. Another worthwhile Luther League endeavor was the Pocket Testament Movement sponsored in cooperation with the Book Concern.

The 1937 biennial youth assembly was held in Minneapolis at the same time as leagues of other member groups of the American Lutheran Conference were also meeting there. I remember accompanying Dr. Oden as we made courtesy calls on the other league groups.

At this meeting Rev. Wilton Bergstrand replaced Dr. Oden as president. Later he became director of youth work in the Augustana Lutheran Church with an office at church headquarters in Minneapolis. Through the years, Wilton became well-known not only among Augustana people but also throughout the Lutheran Church for his outstanding work and that of his staff. By 1954 Wilton and his staff had built an organization that numbered 1250 leagues with 40,000 leaguers.

OTHER CHURCH APPOINTMENTS

During my nine years as a member of the Board of American Missions, 1941-1950, my friend, Dr. S. E. Engstrom, was elected director. He brought enthusiasm and outstanding leadership to the department and served well until his untimely death in 1955.

I enjoyed very much my fourteen years of service on the Committee on Examination and Placement of Candidates for Ordination. On this committee were the president and secretary of the church, conference presidents, the theological faculty, and six members at large. Among the latter were two laymen—Dr. C. J. Lund and I. The laymen took their turns and were assigned candidates to be questioned on subjects ranging from doctrine to practical matters. Sometimes questioning seemed gruelling for the candidate, but the committee members tried to be fair and sympathetic.

In 1943 I was elected to the board of directors of the Lutheran Hospital, Moline, Illinois. I served for six years, including four as treasurer. I returned to this board in 1963 for another two years.

AUGUSTANA LUTHERAN FOUNDATION

The Augustana Lutheran Foundation was organized in 1931 as a synodical institution. Its main purpose was to provide a way for individuals to insure for themselves a retirement income for life and at the same time, while living, to make an exceptional gift to missions, church institutions, or the building fund of their own congregation. The buyer of an annuity could designate any cause within the Church or the foundation itself as a beneficiary.

The members of the board of directors were prominent men in business and professions who were willing to work for the foundation and to attend meetings at their own expense. Men who gave many years of service were Dr. Martin E. Carlson, Christopher Hoff, E. R. Jacobson, Arvid Lundell, Oscar A. Olson, Mauritz N. Ranseen, Carl H. Swanson, S. B. Wennerberg, and myself.

Otto Leonardson served as the executive secretary in charge of promotion. Substantial sums of money were raised for various causes through the work of the foundation and much good was accomplished. At the merger in 1962, the Augustana Lutheran Foundation became a part of the Lutheran Church in America Foundation.

AUGUSTANA ANNUITY TRUST

In 1918, after the close of World War I, the laymen of the Augustana Lutheran Church sponsored an ingathering of five hundred thousand dollars for the Augustana Pension and Aid Fund. The project was successful. Part of that money was invested in real estate loans in the state of Oklahoma. Then came the 1929 depression, which resulted in default of mortgages that led to foreclosures. The Augustana Pension and Aid Fund then became owner of a number of tracts of land in Oklahoma.

In order to comply with Oklahoma law, the Augustana Pension and Aid Fund formed the Augustana Annuity Trust with three trustees to manage the properties. Subsequently, gas and oil deposits were discovered. All money initially invested was recovered. A substantial profit resulted over the years from oil and gas royalties. The trust still holds mineral rights on ten units of land. Whenever land has been sold, half or more of the mineral rights have been retained for the trust.

Among former trustees are Dr. Hugo B. Haterius, Otto Leonardson, J. G. Youngquist, and Eskil Carlson as legal counsel. Present trustees are Walter G. Wendlandt, Austin, Texas; Charles E. Brownfield, Jr., Stamford, Texas; and myself. L. Edwing Wang, administrator of the Board of Pensions of the Lutheran Church in America (LCA), serves the trust as secretary; and Bernhard W. LeVander, Minneapolis, as legal counsel. The trust was not affected by the merger which formed the LCA except that the trust became a part of the Board of Pensions of the LCA. At this writing in March 1978, the trust is still in operation. I have been a member since the early 1950's and have continued as chairman for a number of years.

THE PRESIDENT'S CABINET

The President's Cabinet was organized at Augustana Lutheran Church headquarters, Minneapolis, October 9, 1950. The membership of the cabinet consisted of the president of the Church, the executive officer of each department of the Church, of its institutions and its auxiliaries. Meetings were held quarterly. Officers elected at this first meeting were Dr. P. O. Bersell, chairman; Dr. S. E. Engstrom, vice chairman; Dr. Martin E. Carlson, secretary; and Otto Leonardson, treasurer.

The cabinet's primary function was to advise the president and to make recommendations to the church through the executive council. It gave an opportunity for each department head to present his or her problems and plans in round-table discussions, to share future plans and programs, to avoid overlapping of activities, and to coordinate messages to pastors, combining communications in order to save mailing costs and duplicated efforts.

I represented Augustana Book Concern in the cabinet.

AUDIO-VISUAL SERVICE BOARD

Another board of which I became a member at the time of its organization was the Audio-Visual Service Board. This was an agency to promote the use of proper audio-visual aids within the work of the departments of the synod and within the congregations. It was also to produce motion pictures and other material and to assist in the general program of the Church.

A film strip, "A Drop of Ink Will Make a Million Think," was produced for Augustana Book Concern. It was a twenty-five minute colored filmstrip with recordings which portrayed in an interesting manner the story of the publishing house of the Church.

Bruce Sifford, an outstanding commercial photographer, became the full-time manager of the audio-visual service. Later his son, Roger, became his assistant.

CHURCH CONVENTIONS

I well remember the year of the 1935 convention for two important changes of leadership. Dr. P. O. Bersell followed Dr. G. A. Brandelle as president of the Augustana Lutheran Church, and Dr. Conrad Bergendoff succeeded Dr. Gustav Andreen as president of Augustana College. This annual convention of our church was held in June at Augustana College.

One day, weeks later, Dr. Brandelle came into the Book Concern on a stormy, rainy day. Always enjoying light talk with him, I said, "Are we to blame you for the stormy weather today?" Smiling, he quickly responded, "Who, me, Birger? Don't you know that I am not almighty any more?"

CENTENNIAL CELEBRATION, 1948

Already in the spring of 1941, Dr. P. O. Bersell, president of the Augustana Synod, appointed a centennial planning committee of which he himself was an ex officio member. Other members were Dr. Oscar O. Gustafson, Alexandria, Minnesota; Dr. Oscar A. Benson, Chicago; Judge Eskil C. Carlson, Des Moines; Einar G. Carlson, Cleveland, and myself. The Synod's mandate to the committee was to lay plans for the observance of the centennial anniversary and to initiate a synod-wide ingathering of funds.

The campaign for funds began in 1943 under the able leadership of Dr. Knut E. Erickson, Augustana College. After five years, the thank-offering "in gratitude to God for a century of blessings" had met with success. It had reached the sum of $2,181,000 in cash and additional funds to come. I was proud of the fact that the Rock Island District, in which I served as a co-chairman with Dr. Walter A. Tillberg and Dr. W. E. Berg, exceeded its quota and set a record in the amount of cash received.

A number of committees were appointed in 1948 to serve in various capacities to make the centennial a worthy observance in the history of the Augustana Synod. There was a committee for congregational observance and one for national celebrations. The members of the latter committee were Dr. P. O. Bersell, chairman, Mrs. Daniel Martin, secretary, Dr. Oscar A. Benson, Dr. Conrad Bergendoff, Dr. Knut E. Erickson, Dr. T. A. Gustafson, Dr. Malvin H. Lundeen, and myself.

Although the centennial was to be observed in a number of important centers throughout the U.S.A., the synodical centennial convention was scheduled for Rock Island in June 7-13, 1948. Here the highlight of the observance took place. The synod had invited each congregation to send its pastor and a lay delegate to the convention.

The program with the theme, "They came with the Bread of Life," featured historical addresses, greetings from the Church of Sweden, other Lutheran general bodies, the Lutheran World Federation, and the World Council of Churches.

There was the pilgrimage to the pioneer Augustana Church at New Sweden, Iowa. Delegates and visitors were transported by hundreds of autos and buses, escorted by state police. A huge tent had been erected on the pioneer church grounds to accommodate the large number in attendance.

The pilgrimage to Andover was scheduled for convention Sunday. The sermon was given by Bishop Arvid Runestam, Karlstad, Sweden. The large church was filled to overflowing, and hundreds were seated on the church lawn to listen to the bishop's message over the loud speaker. Visits were also made to nearby Jenny Lind Chapel and the cemetery where the two wives of Rev. Lars Paul Esbjörn, Rev. Jonas Swensson and other pioneers, lie at rest. An historical pageant that received much favorable comment was held at the Rock Island High School athletic field.

We were honored by six representatives from the Church of Sweden. The delegation was headed by Archbishop Erling Eidem, Uppsala. Others were Bishop Arvid Runestam, Karlstad; Professor Anders Nygren, Lund, president of the Lutheran World Federation; Dr. Hilding Pleijel, professor of church history, Lund; Rev. Fritz Holmgren, Bromma Parish, Stockholm; and Rev. S. A. Sigland, Norrköping.

In honor of contributions made by Swedish immigrants to U.S.A., a five-cent Swedish Pioneer Centennial stamp was issued by the U.S. Postal Department. My friend and neighbor, Postmaster John J. McCarthy, called and informed me that twenty-five thousand of these special stamps were available at the Rock Island Post Office and would be on sale that very day, June 5. "Will you be the first customer, Birger?" he asked. As some delegates had already arrived, I asked the following men to accompany me to the post office to buy some of these stamps: Dr. Arthur Wald, director of the Augustana Swedish Institute; Fritz A. Udden, president of the Augustana Brotherhood; and Dr. Thorsten A. Gustafson, director of stewardship of the Augustana Synod. The postmaster had an *Argus* photographer present to publicize our visit to purchase this special stamp.

LUTHERAN WORLD FEDERATION

The Third Assembly of the Lutheran World Federation held in Minneapolis, August 15-25, 1957, became known as the greatest gathering of Lutherans in history. Lyal and I had the good fortune of being present at this event. I had some duties at the exhibit hall, but time was given for the assembly sessions to see and hear world renowned church leaders.

Six major addresses were given at the plenary sessions on the assembly theme, "Christ Frees and Unites." The first was on the general theme itself by Bishop Hanns Lilje, the president of the Lutheran World Federation, and constituted his message to the Assembly. The other five addresses were as follows: "The Freedom

We Have in Christ," by Dr. Chitose Kishi, Japan; "The Unity of the Church in Christ," by Dr. Hans-Werner Genischen, Germany; "The Freedom to Reform the Church," by Bishop Bo Giertz, Sweden; "Free for Service in the World," by Dr. Edgar M. Carlson, president of Gustavus Adolphus College; "Free and United Hope," by Bishop Friedrich Wilhelm Krummacher, Germany.

Many prominent Augustana men were present and made important contributions. We were proud of our own Dr. Carl E. Lund-Quist, who was the moving spirit of this large gathering. He was serving as executive secretary of the fifty million-member Lutheran World Federation.

Highlights were many, such as special evening programs in the Minneapolis Auditorium and the First Lutheran Church, parades and picnics by youth organizations, the banquet at Hotel Leamington with Bishop Bo Giertz as speaker, the editors' and publishers' luncheon at the same hotel, the closing session on the last day when the incoming president, Dr. Franklin Clark Fry, spoke to thousands on the lawn in front of the state capitol in St. Paul.

One evening Lyal and I were asked by Dr. Clifford Nelson to escort Bishop Lajos Ordass, primate of the Lutheran Church of Hungary, to a dinner in St. Paul arranged by a layman of Gloria Dei Lutheran Church for foreign guests. We were grateful for the opportunity to become better acquainted with Bishop Ordass. He related among a number of things that Dr. Carl E. Lund-Quist had befriended him by bringing him a gift of a suit which Carl was wearing when he arrived in order to bring it into Hungary. During his student days, Bishop Ordass had spent some time in Sweden and spoke Swedish fluently. It was an experience to spend an evening with him.

Dr. Clifford A. Nelson, pastor of Gloria Dei Lutheran Church, St. Paul, had arranged a pilgrimage for the Swedish delegation to the historic Swedish communities of Chisago City, Lindstrom and Center City. After sight-seeing, all enjoyed boating, swimming, and a delicious dinner at the summer home of the Clifford Nelsons near Taylor's Falls, Wisconsin.

Among the hundreds of newsmen who attended the Third Assembly of the Lutheran World Federation were three Lutheran journalists from Europe. These editors sponsored by the Federation were Francois Rosenstiehl, Strasbourg, Aage Jensen, Copenhagen, and Lennart Edstrom, Stockholm. A visit to Rock Island had been arranged for them following the assembly. Here they were guests of the Book Concern for several days. They had come to America to study not only the Lutheran Church but also the home and business life of America.

They became much interested in the Augustana Book Concern, since in Europe a religious publishing house is generally privately owned. Visits were made to the daily newspapers in the Quad-Cities, where they learned how church news is handled. We remember a pleasant evening with these foreign guests and other friends at a barbecue in our yard.

I have another journalist friend, Sture Stålfors of Sweden, who has visited us a number of times. He is the editor-in-chief of a large daily newspaper, *Nya Wermlands Tidningen,* Karlstad. Sture has always been interested in the Augustana Lutheran Church and eager to report church news that I have sent from time to time. Lyal and I have had the pleasure of visiting Sture and his wife, Elsa, on travels in Sweden.

Whenever we are in Karlstad, we visit another good friend, Sigurd Gustavson, and his wife, Margit. Sigurd is one of the founders and the director of Emigrantregistret, a research institute for the large emigration of people from the province of Värmland to U.S.A. from 1840 to 1930. The institute has been very successful in locating both first generation emigrants and the descendants. He is also editor of the publication *Bryggan—The Bridge.*

CENTENNIAL SYNOD, 1960

Another memorable centennial synod was held in Rock Island, June 6-12, 1960, upon the invitation of three institutions: Augustana College, Augustana Theological Seminary, and the Augustana Book Concern. LeRoy Brissman, Augustana College, served as general chairman of the local committees. Many sub-committees worked long hours, such as registration, housing, and food service. Delegates and visitors numbered 2,700.

A number of inspiring festivities took place each day during the entire week. An historical service was held on Sunday, June 5, at

Jefferson Prairie, Wisconsin, on the site of the founding of the Augustana Lutheran Church on June 5, 1860. I value a picture I took of Dr. Malvin H. Lundeen, president of the Augustana Lutheran Church, and Dr. Fredrik Schiotz, president of the American Lutheran Church, at the historical monument.

Early in the celebration, we had the unique experience of having a rendition of the oratorio, "The Creation," given twice the same evening by the Augustana Oratorio Society. At both concerts the Centennial Hall was packed. The centennial drama, "Lift Up Your Eyes," was presented to audiences that filled Centennial Hall.

A number of services and programs took place during the week under the general theme, "His Kingdom is Forever." Outstanding was the centennial service one evening in the Rock Island High School field house, attended by several hundred pastors in clerical dress, delegates, and visitors. Greetings were brought by distinguished guests from Sweden, Hong Kong, France, Switzerland, and the United States. Some of these guests brought various gifts to the church. An appropriate climax to the week-long festivities was the ordination service in the Rock Island High School field house, when forty-two young men were ordained into the gospel ministry.

A delightful and cherished memory that Lyal and I have of the 1960 Centennial Synod was having friends and guests from Sweden at a buffet supper in our home following the ordination service. These guests were Archbishop Gunnar Hultgren, Professor and Mrs. Ragnar Bring, Bishop and Mrs. Gert Borgenstierna, Dr. and Mrs. Conrad Bergendoff, Dr. and Mrs. Karl E. Mattson, Dr. and Mrs. E. E. Ryden, and Carl E. Lund-Quist. The conversation was genial, lively, and humorous.

Someone asked for information as to the latest *Psalmbok* and Swedish Bible. I had just obtained a new Swedish Bible, which I asked our Swedish guests to autograph. Then I suggested that the Archbishop read a passage. Bishop Borgenstierna quickly responded,

"No, no, not yet!" He thought that I was asking for a devotional service which in Sweden customarily comes at the close of an evening get-to-gether. We had more time for good fellowship. The pleasant evening closed with a short devotional service by the Archbishop, based on Matthew 28: 18-20.

TWO MEANINGFUL CONVENTIONS

Delegates and visitors of the Augustana Lutheran Church gathered in Cobo Hall, Detroit, on June 25-27, 1962, for an abbreviated, but meaningful concluding convention.

In his report to the church, the president, Dr. Malvin H. Lundeen, called attention to the fact that across the years pastors and lay delegates had gathered in annual synod 103 times. Much could be said about important matters and festive celebrations that had taken place over the years, but there was not time for nostalgia; however, we were grateful for opportunities given to the Augustana Lutheran Church to proclaim the gospel and work for the extension of the Kingdom.

Much of the president's report was given to the merger convention which was to follow. Dr. Lundeen had served as chairman of the Joint Commission on Lutheran Unity. Now he was scheduled to function as chairman of the constituting convention.

Augustana pastors and delegates presented resolutions of appreciation and gifts to three Augustana presidents—Dr. P. O. Bersell, Dr. Oscar A. Benson, and Dr. Malvin H. Lundeen.

When the Augustana Lutheran Church was founded in Jefferson Prairie, Wisconsin, in 1860, a book was provided in which pastors attached their signatures to the church constitution, containing its confession of faith. The first signature was that of Lars Paul Esbjörn, Augustana Synod's first ordained pastor and the first president of Augustana College and Theological Seminary. The second was that of Tuve N. Hasselquist, who became the first president of the church.

Since that time every candidate for the ministry of the Augustana Lutheran Church has signed his name to the constitution as a requisite for ordination. At this final convention in Detroit, forty-five graduates of Augustana Seminary signed the 102 year-old book. The last candidate to sign was Gerald L. Youngquist, who became 2,514 on the Augustana Ministerium roll. The last ordination service of the Augustana Lutheran Church was held June 27, 1962, in the Ford Auditorium, Detroit, where these forty-five young men became pastors in the Lutheran Church in America.

The second gathering also took place in Cobo Hall. It was the constituting convention scheduled for June 28—July 1, 1962.

Here 7,000 persons were on hand to witness the largest Lutheran Church merger in history in the United States. The union brought together a total of 6,125 congregations, 6,499 ordained pastors, and a baptized membership of 3,200,000.

This meaningful constituting convention was called to order at 9:07 a.m. on June 28 by Dr. Malvin H. Lundeen, chairman of the Joint Commission on Lutheran Unity. The presidents of the four merging churches presented formal statements that the agreement of consolidation had been officially adopted by their churches. The Rev. A. E. Farstrup spoke for the American Evangelical Lutheran Church, Dr. Malvin H. Lundeen, for the Augustana Lutheran Church, Dr. Raymond W. Wargelin, for the Finnish Evangelical Lutheran Church, and Dr. Franklin Clark Fry, for The United Lutheran Church in America. These four church bodies formed the new Church—The Lutheran Church in America.

To us who were fortunate to be serving as delegates, the merger was an unforgettable event. Much has been written about it, even books, but here I will mention only a few highlights.

Dr. Franklin Clark Fry was chosen president, Dr. Malvin H. Lundeen, secretary, and Edmund F. Wagner, treasurer. A dramatic historical and prophetic feature, entitled, "That Men May Live," was presented in the form of a speech oratorio for voices and choir. The oratorio sketched the historical background of the four merging churches.

I quote from *The Story of the Founding of the Lutheran Church in America:* "The climactic moment came when four quarters of a massive white candle, each with a separate wick, were lighted by acolytes and then moved together to form a single light to symbolize the union of the four churches in one body.

"As the candle, three feet high and a foot in diameter, flickered and then burst into a bright flame on a pedestal inside the improvised chancel, it was encircled with a broad band of gold as a symbol of unity and eternity."

The entire floor of the convention arena of Cobo Hall had been transformed into a large sanctuary for the communion service, which was very impressive and in which 5,000 persons participated. There were six communion rails and forty administrants making it possible for the sacrament to be offered to 175 persons at one time. Dr. P. O.

Bersell, president emeritus of Augustana Lutheran Church, was the preacher.

Grateful for the merger, Dr. Bersell said, "We rejoice that at long last these four Lutheran bodies have come together, because they belong together; they have one Lord and one faith."

Mrs. Regina Fryxell, Rock Island, served as organist for both conventions.

The merging publication houses had a large display in Cobo Hall. Everything a congregation would need for its operation was on display, such as textbooks, Bibles, hymnals, story papers, communion ware, stoles, choir gowns, and visual aids.

Saturday, June 30, was the evening of the convention banquet with an attendance of 2,100 guests. The able toastmaster was the former governor of Minnesota, Judge Luther Youngdahl.

AN ILLINOIS SYNOD CONVENTION

I will let the news release by the editor of the *Illinois Lutheran,* Warren D. Nelson, tell this story:

> The Gold Room of the Blackhawk Hotel, Davenport, was literally wall to wall with clergy, delegates, guests and their wives, enjoying a fellowship dinner and an evening of entertainment, wit, and humor on the second evening of the third annual convention of the Illinois Synod of the Lutheran Church in America.
>
> Birger Swenson, local chairman for the convention, introduced the featured speaker for the evening, Dr. G. Elson Ruff, and humorously related the many different types of letters editors receive in the mail. He broke up his audience when he introduced Dr. Ruff as the editor of the *Lutheran Companion.* (The *Lutheran Companion* was the official publication of the former Augustana Lutheran Church, now extinct.) Dr. Ruff was the editor of the *Lutheran.*

At this 1965 convention of the Illinois Synod of the Lutheran Church in America, with Dr. Robert J. Marshall as president, I was elected a member of its executive board. I not only served six years on this board but also six years as a member of the synod's Committee on Examination and Ordination.

A WORTHY PROJECT

At the time of the centennial year, 1948, the Augustana Lutheran Church obtained ownership of the Jenny Lind Chapel, Andover, as a synodical shrine. After the merger, no one seemed responsible for the maintenance of the chapel and grounds. Seeing the need, interested persons formed a committee of ten in the fall of 1973. The officers were Dr. Conrad Bergendoff, chairman; Rev. Albert Lestor, secretary; Birger Swenson, treasurer; Kenneth Telleen, legal counsel; and Carl Swanson, building consultant.

The executive board of the Illinois Synod accepted the title for the chapel from the Lutheran Church in America and encouraged the formation of a Jenny Lind Chapel Association to solicit funds for the restoration and maintenance of the chapel. We were advised, however, that the solicitation of funds should be from individuals rather than from congregations. Through the cooperation of former Augustana Lutheran Church pastors and lay members, we compiled a good mailing list. We appealed for funds, and the response was most gratifying. In two-and-one-half years, we were able to restore the chapel, to make needed improvements and to safeguard it from future deterioration, at a total cost of $33,556.56.

A rededication of the Jenny Lind Chapel was held on June 13, 1976. The speaker of the day was Dr. Paul E. Erickson, president of the Illinois Synod. At this time the committee announced that an effort would be made to raise an endowment fund to meet the cost of maintenance of the chapel. Cooperation from committee members and friends was gratifying.

X

COLLEGE AND COMMUNITY AFFAIRS

I had been interested in Augustana College since my student days. Now with an office across the street, I became active in a number of organizations associated with the college, such as the Augustana Historical Society, the Augustana Chapter of the American Scandinavian Foundation, and the Augustana Swedish Institute. I held offices in these organizations from time to time.

The Augustana Swedish Institute, with Dr. Conrad Bergendoff as chairman and Dr. Arthur Wald as director, was an active organization. Dr. Wald directed a number of projects sponsored by the Institute, such as the Swedish Summer School, a yearbook as the official organ of the Institute, and the *American-Swedish Handbook,* which provided up-to-date information concerning Swedish-American activities. The handbook covered the religious, educational and charitable institutions founded by Swedish immigrants.

Dr. Wald introduced the Swedish Summer School at Augustana College. Later when Nils Hasselmo became a teacher in the Scandinavian department, he organized and promoted a Swedish Summer School in Sweden in order to study the language and history of the land. Sometimes he was assisted by Carl J. Engblom. Courses· were given at Dömle, Sigtuna, and Stockholm.

As treasurer of the institute, it was my duty to solicit funds from interested friends and organizations for scholarships. Having met with success, many ·students were assisted and thus were able to participate in this special summer school.

ALUMNI ASSOCIATION PRESIDENT, 1938-1939

At the annual meeting of the Augustana Alumni Association, held June 6, 1938, I was elected president for the year, 1938-1939, succeeding Rev. J. Vincent Nordgren. Professor O. L. Nordstrom was re-elected secretary-treasurer. Other members of the executive committee were Earl H. Hanson, Dr. V. R. Pearson, and Mrs. R. O. Sala. The immediate past president, Rev. J. Vincent Nordgren, Dr. Conrad Bergendoff, and Dr. C. A. Serenius, director of alumni work, attended our monthly meetings in an advisory capacity.

At the 1938 annual meeting, the committee was commissioned to carry out two projects—one to increase the Alumni Scholarship Fund from one thousand to three thousand dollars; the other, to have a portrait made of President Emeritus Dr. Gustav Andreen.

The committee was given four years to raise two thousand dollars for the scholarship fund. Although the depression was still with us, we were happy to report success. One thousand dollars was raised the first year. J. Iverne Dowie, class of '36, was awarded the 1938-1939 Alumni Association Scholarship so that he could continue his graduate work.

The Dr. Andreen portrait created a great deal of interest. Contributions came from near and far. Our goal was $630.00, which was reached before the completion of the portrait.

Our genial friend and former prexy, Dr. Andreen, came back to the campus each Monday from his congregation in Willmar, Minnesota. Each day during the week, he sat for the portrait. The artist was Christian Abrahamsen, a well-known portrait painter from Chicago.

After artist Abrahamsen had completed the portrait, I received the following letter from Dr. Andreen:

Moline, Illinois
November 30, 1939

Dear Friend Birger:

On this Thanksgiving day (old style) I desire to express the gratitude of my heart to you for making it possible for the artist, Mr. Christian Abrahamsen, to make a portrait of the president emeritus of Augustana. You could not have found a better place than you did for the studio; the Faculty Room of the Seminary was ideal for this purpose both as to size, location, and historical background. The artist could not adequately express his delight at the glorious view from Zion Hill. He felt at home in these surroundings and enjoyed to the utmost his association with you, the faculty, and the students.

He, and I also, thank you most heartily for your interest, your hospitality, and for your never-ceasing endeavors to bring about the consummation we have witnessed as you cheered him on in his work. He came to look upon you as the ideal Augustana alumnus.

Much success to you in all your various labors during days to come. Mrs. Andreen joins me in best wishes to you.

Cordially yours,
Gustav Andreen

At the 1939 meeting, a revised constitution of the association was submitted for adoption. One of the revisions was that the article on membership be changed to include not only graduates but also former students of the institution.

Christian Abrahamsen, the artist who had done a portrait of Dr. Andreen, completed a portrait of President Emeritus Conrad Bergendoff in the spring of 1965. Both portraits hang in the reading room of the Denkmann Memorial Library. At the unveiling ceremony of his portrait, Dr. Bergendoff spoke briefly of the many satisfying and rewarding years he had spent on the Augustana campus. He concluded his remarks with characteristic humor when he said, "I hope this picture reveals to you something of my gratitude for Augustana, and for Augustana I am willing to be 'hung.' "

Augustana College has many interests for us living in the Quad-Cities. I have already mentioned some organizations. Another, a rather unique one, is *Nytta och Nöje* (for fun and purpose). This organization, founded nearly eighty years ago, has no more than thirty members, as it meets monthly in homes. Membership in the past has been drawn from the college and the Book Concern. For many years Swedish only was used. The minutes are still written in Swedish. In earlier days proposed members were expected to give lectures in Swedish. That was true in my case when I joined in the early 1930s. The club is still active and very enjoyable.

Other interests at the college are athletics, lectures, and concerts. The most popular events are the concerts by the Augustana Choir and the oratorio, *The Messiah.* Henry Veld was the conductor of the choir and the Handel Oratorio Society for many years. He was succeeded by Donald E. Morrison, the present conductor.

Commencement in the spring and Homecoming in the fall bring back to the campus many alumni and former students. I will always cherish the memory of the golden anniversary celebration of my class of 1924. We were especially honored by Augustana College on Alumni Day, May 25, and Commencement, May 26, 1974. We were pleased to note that more than half the members were still living. Although we had not seen one another for a long time, in some cases not since graduation, we readily recognized each other. During the two days, we were guests of the college for meals and housing. Much credit for the excellent arrangements in honoring and entertaining our golden anniversary class of 1924 goes to Barbara LeVander, director of alumni relations. For the members of the class, this anniversary was an enjoyable and unforgettable experience.

AUGUSTANA COLLEGE FUND APPEALS

Augustana alumni were active in many fund appeals during the years. The Alumni Association, in 1944, sponsored an appeal to raise ten thousand dollars to be used for loans to returning service men who needed help in resuming their college studies.

An Augustana College development fund appeal was launched in April 1947, with a goal of $1,500,000. Dr. Conrad Bergendoff outlined the fund campaign, of which $750,000 was to be raised in the Quad-Cities, for construction of a community fine arts building and music hall on the campus. H. Parker Weeks served as Rock Island chairman, and Colonel C. A. Waldmann, Quad-City chairman of the appeal.

At the first report meeting, I was happy to announce a partial result of the solicitation at Augustana Book Concern. The board of directors had voted a gift by the Book Concern of five thousand dollars and contributions by the employees amounted to $3,831.50. Dr. Knut Erickson, vice president and treasurer of the college, announced that a section of 200 seats in the auditorium of the music hall was to be dedicated to the Book Concern and its employees in recognition of the gifts. Eventually these buildings were realized and named the Bergendoff Fine Arts Building and Centennial Hall.

A change in the presidency of Augustana College took place in 1962. Dr. Conrad Bergendoff retired after twenty-seven years of faithful and successful service. He was succeeded by an active layman, Dr. C. W. Sorensen, a professor and dean at Illinois State University, Normal, Illinois.

In February 1967, I participated in the leadership phase of the Augustana College Acceleration Program launched during the presidency of Dr. C. W. Sorensen. The Quad-City area goal was $1,500,000; the national appeal sought a sum of $3,500,000.

Frederic B. White served as area leadership chairman and Ellwood F. Curtis and LeRoy Liljedahl, as national co-chairmen. The success of the fund appeal helped to bring about many changes on the campus in the remodeling of old structures and the erection of new buildings. Many new walkways were laid, trees and shrubs planted, and lawns improved. A generous gift of $1,500,000 by Roy J. Carver, Muscatine, Iowa, member of the college board of directors, made it possible to complete the $3.5 million complex, known as the Carver Physical Education Center. All these changes did much to enhance the appearance of the campus.

The largest fund raising program in the history of Augustana College was launched in March 1977. It is a three-year project known as Agenda for Leadership with a goal of $11,700,000. The income from the fund is to improve academic facilities, student and community services, and long-term financial stability. The appeal is being conducted nation-wide among alumni and friends. The national co-chairmen are Robert A. Hanson, president of Deere and Company, Moline, and Donald B. Smiley, chairman of the board and chief executive officer of the R. H. Macy Co., New York. The college staff members for the leadership program besides the president, Dr. Thomas Tredway, are John L. Kindschuh, Robert E. Carlson, George Engdahl, and James J. Palincsar. The Agenda for Leadership met a ready response. At the end of the first year, 1977, more than half of the $11,700,000 goal had been pledged. I was honored to be asked to serve as a member of the National Executive Committee for the Augustana College Agenda for Leadership program.

AUGUSTANA FLOOD FIGHTERS

News of Augustana students' heroic actions in the great Mississippi River flood in the spring of 1965 spread as far as Europe. Newspapers in Chicago, New York, Los Angeles, and dozens of other cities carried wire-service pictures and stories of day-to-day happenings in Rock Island and other cities in the Quad-City area. I quote from the May 1965 issue of the *Lutheran:*

AUGUSTANA STUDENTS MAN DIKES TO FIGHT MISSISSIPPI FLOOD

"By the mighty Mississippi
on a rocky shore
Stands the school we love so dearly
Now and evermore."

So goes the opening verse of a school song at Augustana College in Rock Island, Illinois.

For more than a week, Augustana students learned the true meaning of these words as they worked on the rocky shore, helping to battle the greatest flood of all time on the mighty Mississippi.

Classes were dismissed for four days to permit students and faculty members to join the army of volunteers. They were successful in preventing millions of dollars of damage in the Quad-City area.

Dikes held firm for the most part in holding back a record-breaking crest of 22.5 feet, seven feet over flood stage. The College campus itself was not endangered.

Girls as well as boys pitched in to fill sandbags and pile them on hastily-erected dikes. Many coeds also worked at the Red Cross relief centers, helping to care for families forced out of their homes. Twelve students formed a show troupe and provided entertainment for evacuees at Red Cross relief centers.

Praise for the students' efforts came from many quarters. Dr. George B. Arbaugh, vice president and dean of the college, said in a letter to the student body:

"I want you to know that you have brought honor to the College, not only by your concern for the loss and danger experienced by our neighbors, but also by the fine spirit manifested. Augustana singing will be remembered for songs on the levee as well as in Centennial Hall."

Rock Island mayor, Morris E. Muhleman said: "Whenever they tell me that the youth are going to the dogs, the gripers ought to come down here and take a look." He thanked the students personally at a chapel assembly.

Dr. C. W. Sorensen, president of the College, also thanked the students and faculty for their "dramatic" demonstration of community cooperation.

TWO FRIENDS GONE BUT NOT FORGOTTEN

I miss two departed friends very much. One was Dr. Knut E. Erickson, retired vice president for financial affairs and treasurer of Augustana College. I worked under him in a number of fund-raising programs for Augustana. We were golf partners and good friends over many years. Knut died at the age of seventy-four on February 26, 1965.

The other friend was Earl H. Hanson, retired superintendent of schools in Rock Island. We were classmates at Augustana College, fellow Kiwanians, and teammates in many fund appeals. We served together on the YMCA, church, and Community Chest boards. Earl died on August 15, 1968.

OUR GIFT TO AUGUSTANA COLLEGE

While employed at the Augustana Book Concern, I established a scholarship at Augustana College, which I later renamed the Lyal and Birger Swenson Scholarship. The income from this endowed scholarship is awarded each year to worthy students who depend largely on their own resources to finance their education.

In later years, in gratitude to Augustana College for what it did for us during our college days and for what the institution means to us today, we established a permanent endowment fund to be known as the "Birger and Lyal Swenson Fund." Our aim was to encourage and help support contacts between Augustana College and the Scandinavian countries, especially Sweden. The fund will be maintained as an endowment with income used for instruction, guest lecturers, scholarships to Scandinavia, publications, exhibits, concerts, or other means of acquainting students and faculty with the cultural and religious life and the universities of the homeland of the founders of Augustana College.

As the first step in creation of the fund, Lyal and I on December 31, 1976, gave to the college our apartment building at 1536-21st Ave., Rock Island, which has been our home since 1943.

ROYAL VISITORS AT AUGUSTANA

I had the experience of meeting royalty for the first time in September 1924. It was at an Augustana Day of a church convocation held in Blaisleholm Church, Stockholm. Crown Prince Gustaf Adolf and Crown Princess Louise attended the session at which Dr. L. G. Abrahamson was the speaker. At the close of his address, the Crown Prince and the Crown Princess were introduced to the Augustana visitors by Archbishop Nathan Söderblom. I was fortunate to be one of these visitors.

In 1976, the bicentennial year of the United States, young King Carl XVI Gustaf of Sweden came for a visit. One of the many areas visited was the Quad-Cities. The King was welcomed on April 20 by an estimated host of 5,000 students, school children, and community residents at the Carver Physical Educational Center on the campus. Here the college president, Dr. Thomas Tredway, gave a speech of welcome and presented a gift of art to the royal visitor. The King responded and presented a gift of books to the college. Dr. Conrad Bergendoff, president emeritus, gave a brief address on the Swedish heritage of Augustana College. Both the Augustana Band and the Augustana Choir participated in the ceremony.

The next part of the program was a private visit to Denkmann Memorial Library, where the King met members of the local committee who had arranged his visit. Glen E. Brolander, vice president for financial affairs of the college and chairman of the committee, presented the King to the members of the committee and their spouses.

Then the King proceeded to the College Union for an informal gathering of students. The president of the student body presented the King with an Augustana jacket adorned with the King's monogram. The King presented a work-out suit to the students.

Shortly after noon, the King and his party of nine and a group of twelve Swedish journalists left the Augustana campus for a private visit to the farm of the brothers, Wayne and Forbes Nelson, located near Joy, Illinois. At the farm, the King had a hamburger, potato salad and corn-on-the-cob luncheon and took a ride on a fifty-thousand-dollar tractor. Next the King visited Bishop Hill and Jenny Lind Chapel at Andover.

In the evening the King and his party were guests of Deere and Company at a dinner at its Administrative Center in Moline. Lyal and I were included among the invited guests. Later that evening the King and his party left by plane for Detroit, the next stop on his American tour.

We had been honored by the King's visit. It had been a memorable day for many of us.

The visit of the Swedish princess, Desiree, in the Quad-City area on May 2, 1976, was in sharp contrast to the whirlwind one-day swing that her brother, King Carl XVI Gustaf, had made twelve days earlier.

There wasn't any security guard in sight and no fuss made as she and her husband, Count Niclas Silvershiold, arrived. They were accompanied by an agricultural study group of thirty-five Swedish landowners. The schedule for their visit was similar to that of the King.

Arrangements for their visit at Augustana College were made by the college and the American Scandinavian Foundation. The party was welcomed to the campus by Dr. Bergendoff. Lyal and I attended a dinner in their honor at the House on the Hill.

COMMUNITY AFFAIRS

As I look back to my early years at the Augustana Book Concern, it seems quite natural that I became involved and active in the life of the community. I joined the Rock Island Kiwanis Club in 1928. Mr. J. G. Youngquist of the Book Concern was a member, and Dr. Gustav Andreen, president of Augustana College, was a charter member of the local club.

I became active in many projects sponsored by the club and served on a number of committees. I was elected president for two one-year terms, 1932 and 1933. Other officers were Franklin Wingard, vice president; J. A. Dodge, trustee; Robert Gilloley, treasurer; and E. F. Burch, secretary.

Our membership was not large, only fifty-five. In 1932-1933 we were in the depth of the depression, yet these Kiwanians, though discouraged, were faithful in attendance at our Monday luncheon meetings at the Fort Armstrong Hotel. As a club we were active in youth work through the YMCA, the YWCA, Boy Scouts, Girl Scouts, and all kinds of community services. The club sponsored several successful farm-city dinners each year in neighboring towns, such as Preemption, Joy, and Swedona. I remember especially a chicken dinner in Viola High School in July 1932, where 250 of us met as neighbors.

I also remember a donkey baseball game described as the funniest sport in the world. After a player had batted the ball, he had to mount a donkey and ride the bases. This humorous and unique game was played by members of the Kiwanis and Rotary clubs at Douglas Park. I quote the *Argus* of August 6, 1934:

> The Kiwanis drew first blood in their grudge tilt with Rotary. Birger Swenson, circulation manager for the Augustana Book Concern, "donkeying" around the bases after much difficulty in the first of the second frame, a tremendous roar went up from the Kiwanis bench when his mount's hoof touched the "rubber" as neither had been able to score previously.

This comical game drew an attendance of 3,600.

At this writing, April 1978, I have been a Kiwanis member for fifty years. The membership of our club has grown to 150. I look upon my years in Kiwanis as most rewarding. I appreciate the fellowship and friendships I have enjoyed through the years.

KIWANIS APPROVES BANK PLANS

The depression caused some banks to close and brought problems to others. Locally, protective measures were taken by our two Rock Island banks, which eventually led to a bank holiday and the formation of a Citizens' and Depositors' Committee. The first plan proposed by the State Bank of Rock Island and the Rock Island Bank and Trust Company was to require a sixty-day notice for savings account withdrawals. Our Kiwanis Club endorsed the plan with the following resolution: "We the members of the Rock Island

Kiwanis Club in meeting assembled this 27th day of December, 1932, hereby commend the action on the part of our local bankers and also express our utmost confidence in the stability of our two banking institutions that they will continue the enviable record that 'no depositor ever lost a dollar of deposit in a Rock Island bank.' "

This action was followed by another resolution passed by members of the Rock Island Kiwanis Club on January 16, 1933: "Whereas it has again become necessary for the directors of the State Bank of Rock Island and the Rock Island Bank and Trust Company to take further steps in protecting their customers by instituting a two weeks' bank holiday, we, the members of the Rock Island Kiwanis Club commend this action."

After the inauguration of Franklin Delano Roosevelt as President, a national bank holiday was proclaimed by him.

The principal activity of our Kiwanis Club during 1933 took the form of valuable cooperation in the movements to reopen the State Bank of Rock Island and the Rock Island Bank and Trust Company. The chairman of the Citizens' and Depositors' Committee to reopen the State Bank of Rock Island was Kenneth L. Popplewell, a Kiwanian. He was also the vice chairman of the committee to organize the drive to open the Rock Island Bank and Trust Company. The purpose of the drive was to ask depositors to sign a waiver. This action gave the bank permission to withhold seventy-five percent of a depositor's money until the bank would be able to reimburse in full. Both drives were successful. Many of the volunteer workers were members of the Rock Island Kiwanis Club.

That our effort as volunteers in the Citizens' and Depositors' Committee to reopen the two banks was appreciated is evident by quoting from the following letters I received:

State Bank of Rock Island
Rock Island, Illinois
March 18, 1933

Dear Mr. Swenson:

Before a general announcement of the opening of the State Bank of Rock Island is made, I am addressing this letter to you and other members of the Citizens' and Depositors' Committee. The bank will reopen Tuesday morning.

Your committee and its individual members have performed a

service in the weeks just passed that will prove of enduring benefits to Rock Island. Your devotion to the cause and your ceaseless efforts are an inspiration and a matter of sincere appreciation by this bank.

We bespeak of continuation of your friendship and regard for this bank. It will be our effort to merit both.

Sincerely yours,
I. S. White
President

****

June 23, 1933

Mr. Birger Swenson, President
Rock Island Kiwanis Club
Rock Island, Illinois

My dear Friend:

I cannot refrain from just a brief word of appreciation to you as head of your organization for the thoughtful endorsement and assurance of support of the campaign being carried on by the Citizens' and Depositors' Committee of the Rock Island Bank and Trust Company.

With such loyalty and earnest wishes, we cannot—must not—fail.

Yours sincerely,
P. A. Dahlen
Chairman, Citizens' and Depositors'
Committee of the Rock Island Bank
and Trust Company

COMMUNITY ORGANIZATIONS

As a resident of the Rock Island YMCA from 1930 to 1943, I became involved in many of its activities. I served on the YMCA board of directors for thirty-four years and as president for three years, 1957-1959.

Opportunities for laymen to work in the YMCA organization were many. I found professional and businessmen willing to devote time and to serve on its board of directors and on committees. A few who served with me were Melvin McKay, Earl H. Hanson, Leslie C. Johnson, and John H. Hauberg. General secretaries who served the local YMCA well and were active in community affairs were Clinton C. Lane, W. P. McCaffree, and L. V. Burch. The physical director was Robley Biehl; the boys' work secretary was Dale F. Holmgrain.

After I resigned from the board, I received this letter:

June 27, 1967

Dear Birger:

May I take just a few minutes to express my sincere appreciation for your years of service to Rock Island YMCA while I have been your general secretary.

I can truthfully say I have missed your counsel and guidance the past few months and really appreciate the many years of friendship and support.

Your humor as well as your practical advice is missed not only by me but by all the board members.

I would like to close by saying that I have valued your friendship, your counsel, advice, and support more than I can put into words. Best of health and happiness!

Sincerely yours,
L. V. Burch

The Augustana Book Concern held membership in both the Rock Island and the State of Illinois Chambers of Commerce. I served a number of years on the School Relations Committee of both chambers. After my retirement, I continued my interest in the local chamber and served on the Membership Relations Committee. I had time to give; therefore I was quite successful. The Chamber president, Morris Muhleman, and the general manager, Warren J. Hobson, offered me a job and a desk, which I declined. I wanted to be free for opportunities to travel. At the next annual meeting of the Rock Island Chamber of Commerce, I was honored with a life membership as a tribute to my many years of service.

I was appointed by Mayor Morris E. Muhleman in 1965, to the Zoning Board of Appeals of the City of Rock Island. Later I was reappointed by Mayor James Haymaker. In all I served ten years.

Rock Island Memorial Park Cemetery and Mausoleum has a beautiful location on 30th Street overlooking the Rock River. It is operated as a non-profit institution under a board of directors of six members. I have served as a member of the board for a number of years and have enjoyed the fellowship very much. Our manager and treasurer is the able and genial Roy C. Schourek.

FUND CAMPAIGNS

Fund raising campaigns came quite regularly during my active years in the community. I still look back with fond memories to some very unique and interesting experiences.

In April 1939, 200 Augustana College friends attended a dinner at Andreen Hall. They had been invited to participate in a twin-city campaign to raise ten thousand dollars for new concrete bleachers, a dressing house, and other improvements on the Viking athletic field. The effort met with success. President Conrad Bergendoff, Vice President Knut Erickson, and Coach Harold V. Almquist were delighted and most grateful.

In the spring of 1939, I became a member of a citizens' committee for a new Rock Island City Hall. We were not to solicit money, but to obtain pledges of support from voters and taxpayers. This new City Hall proposal was approved. A new municipal building was erected that reflected credit upon Rock Island.

A YWCA building appeal was launched in February 1952. The men of the city were ready to assist. The goal of $250,000 was promptly raised. A similar amount had been given by John H. Hauberg and his family. Lyal served as chairman of the building committee.

A major fund drive for the new Rock Island Franciscan Hospital took place in May and June of 1966. The campaign went over its $1,500,000 goal with a total of $1,911,735 pledged. The Franciscan Sisters, as well as the community, expressed appreciation for the success of the campaign.

The Rock Island County Heart Association had a fund appeal in February each year. The proceeds of the drive were used to support research, education, and community service activities of the Heart Association. I served as county chairman two years, 1968 and 1969.

A Rock Island Community Chest Appeal was an annual affair. Many of the workers became well-known to each other as they participated year after year. Earl H. Hanson and I served as co-chairmen of the initial gifts section for a number of years. We were cheer leaders at times and led an "I promise to do it now" yell to climax the meeting. We were often asked to give pep talks. In such a talk, I said that it takes salesmanship to put the fund raising campaign over the top. To achieve success, we must believe in the fund, think about it, and work for it. It's like playing a game. We must play hard and play to win.

One year I was asked to serve as master of ceremonies at our report meetings. Working with a committee, we hit upon the idea of conferring the order of the green paper hat upon each chairman of a division that had reached its goal. The Davenport *Daily Times* of October 15, 1958, had this to say relative to our stunt:

A NEW DEGREE

Workers participating in Rock Island's Community Chest drive, which was successfully concluded Friday night, have wondered all week what Birger Swenson, master of ceremonies, had originated in his initiations for the 100 percent club as he kept repeating the words, "Doctor of Honoris Laboris Causa," as his final gesture at the ceremony.

The secret got out Friday night when he explained that the degree meant *Doctor of Labor and Honor*, a title copyrighted only for chest "sparkplugs."

I have many fond memories from these community fund drives and from the men and women workers. All believed in the fund appeals, believed in their community, and were willing to serve as well as give for a better Rock Island.

Birger and Dr. Conrad Bergendoff at Augustana convocation,
June 2, 1958, at which Birger received an honorary L.L.D. degree

Birger, King Carl XVI Gustaf, and Dr. Conrad Bergendoff
at the royal visit to Augustana, April 20, 1976

Lyal at the world famous Taj Mahal, Agra, India

Lyal and Birger at the Cheops Pyramid and Sphinx, Giza, Cairo, Egypt

Lyal goes shopping in Hong Kong

Lars Eric Lindblad, founder of Lindblad Travel and builder of the *Explorer*

Lindblad *Explorer* in ice on the west coast of Greenland, July 1974

Birger's subject, a Gentoo penguin, Antarctica

Lyal and Birger make friends with a sled dog
at Scott Station, Antarctica

Birger stands at the equator, Kenya, East Africa

XI
TRAVELS FAR AND WIDE

Travel began for me the day I emigrated to the United States. I traveled for many years as a newspaper subscription salesman and later as a field representative for Augustana Book Concern. My years at the Book Concern involved travel both in this country and in Europe.

Believing with Benjamin Franklin that "travel lengthens life," Lyal and I do enjoy travel. Since my retirement in 1963, we have visited many distant lands including the seventh continent, Antarctica. In January 1964, a week after my retirement, we boarded the *M. S. Kungsholm* of the Swedish American Line in New York for a three-month cruise around the world. Other cruises on the same line took us to the Mediterranean, the Greek Islands, and the Black Sea; to the North Cape, all five Scandinavian countries, Leningrad and Moscow, Germany, Holland, Belgium, France, England, Ireland, and around South America to the South Pacific Islands, Australia, and New Zealand.

The most unusual and educational cruises have been made on the Lindblad *Explorer,* an icebreaker built in Finland in 1969 and operated by Lars Eric Lindblad Travel, Inc., and the Swedish American Line. This ship has taken us to Antarctica twice; 2,500 miles up the Amazon River in Brazil and Peru; to the Viking ruins and Eskimo villages in Greenland and Ellesmere Island, Canada; and to Alaska, the Bering Sea, and the Aleutian Islands.

Enjoyable auto and bus trips have been made through Mexico, Canada, and the United States.

We have written a travelogue after each trip, which because of length cannot be included here; however, we would like to share the following account of our world cruise:

AROUND THE WORLD IN 88 DAYS

It was 11:30 a.m. on January 11, 1964. At pier 97 at the foot of New York's West 57th Street, there was orderly confusion. It was sailing day again for the Swedish-American liner *Kungsholm,* queen of the Swedish merchant fleet.

After the last farewells had been made and after the last colorful streamers had been tossed toward the pier, the 330 fortunate passengers crowded the rails of this trim, white, and shining vessel to see the straining tugs pull it slowly out into midstream of the busy Hudson River. This was not an ordinary sailing, for we were off on a cruise around the world.

Life aboard the *Kungsholm* was truly elegant. It revolved around the public rooms on the veranda deck, where one enjoyed concerts and dancing to the music of the finest of orchestras. Other favorite pastimes were lectures covering ports of call, horse races, bingo, films, and the ever popular bridge games and tournaments. Still other activities included gymnastics, deck sports, and swimming in the inside or outside pool. There were dancing and bridge lessons, travel forums, and shopping hints. There were also fun nights and contests. Birger participated in the state talk fest in which he was chosen by the twenty-six passengers from Illinois to extol the virtues of the Land of Lincoln in a three-minute talk.

As well as exciting days at sea, this eighty-eight-day cruise offered countless rich experiences ashore for its passengers. Our first port of call was Palma on the beautiful island of Majorca, off the coast of Spain, noted for its superb scenery, healthful climate, attractive white sand beaches, quaint villages, and unspoiled folklore. Of special interest was the beautiful secluded village of Valdemosa, with its ancient Carthusian convent, where the famous composer, Frederic Chopin, lived during the winter of 1838 and composed some of his preludes.

In Palma, the capital of the island, the principal architectural attraction is the thirteenth-century, Gothic-style cathedral, which dominates the city's profile. It is a treasure house of many religious works of art, and one of its rose windows is the largest in the world.

Our second port of call was Naples. We found Capri to be a tourist paradise. Its unique scenic attraction is the Blue Grotto, a remarkable cavern reached by motor launch. After transferring to a small skiff, one enters the narrow opening only four feet high. Once inside, one sees that the cave widens into a large chamber, forty feet high and two hundred feet long. The sun's rays penetrating the narrow entrance fill the interior with an indescribable blue light.

About 800 feet above Capri is the mountain village of Anacapri, reached by a steep mountain road. Of special interest to us here was the Villa San Michele, built by the famous Swedish physician and author, Axel Munthe, who built his home "as a temple to the sun." It is a reconstructed villa designed by Dr. Munthe, containing priceless relics. From this villa one has a commanding view of the island of Capri, considered one of the most beautiful sights in the world.

At Pompeii there is the celebrated excavation of a one-time flourishing city, buried in 79 A.D. under innumerable tons of volcanic ashes and mud during the most damaging eruption of Mount Vesuvius. Walking along the lava-paved streets, one sees the ruins of one- and two-storied houses, stately mansions, gardens adorned with marble and bronze statues, and fountains, the Forum, the Palace of Justice, and the Temple of Apollo.

From Pompeii, we proceeded by automobile through orange, lemon, and olive groves to the picturesque coastal town of Amalfi on the Gulf of Salerno. From here we followed the exciting and world-famous Amalfi Drive between cliffs and sea to Sorrento, a town strung out on a series of terraces about two hundred feet above the sea.

From Naples, we crossed the blue Mediterranean to our third port of call, Alexandria, Egypt's principal seaport. En route to Cairo by train through the great Nile Delta, we saw from our car window a passing parade of interesting sights: Farmers in their fields with toiling camels, donkeys, and oxen, flat-bottomed boats on canals, lazy adobe villages with scores of children waving to us, women working in the fields or carrying everything imaginable on their heads, little boys and girls carrying a baby brother or sister, people in ancient dress, an ancient water-lift, and a water wheel.

One is hardly aware of modern civilization until he arrives in teeming Cairo where modern luxury hotels are but a stone's throw from native quarters. From our window in the Nile Hilton Hotel overlooking the river, we had a commanding view by day of the Great Pyramids outside the city, and by night of the 500-foot high illuminated Cairo Tower as reflected in the Nile.

At suburban Giza, on the very edge of the Libyan Desert, an exciting experience was riding camelback to the pyramids and the sphinx led by an attendant in native garb. At night we returned for the spectacular performance of the "Sound of Light" program in which the history of the immortal pyramids and sphinx was presented.

A tour of the city of Cairo took us to several mosques, including the beautiful mosque of Mohammed Ali in the Citadel of Saladin; to the native quarters and the bazaars where one is expected to bargain for the countless attractive articles offered for sale. At the Egyptian Museum we saw the world-famous treasures discovered in King Tutankhamen's tomb as recently as 1922.

We flew to Luxor. From our plane window, we saw the Nile with a ribbon of green on either side where irrigation is possible. Beyond there is nothing but desert. In Luxor, on the site of the ancient city of Thebes, we visited several tombs in the Valley of the Kings, one of which was that of King Tutankhamen. In the Valley of the Queens, we saw the Temple of Queen Hatshepsut, where the filming of "The Ten Commandments" took place. At nearby Karnak is the Temple of Amun, the sun-god. In one of its huge halls is a forest of 134 immense stone pillars built over 3,000 years ago. Here we found also the famous Avenue of Sphinxes.

After a three-hour train ride from Cairo through the desert, we rejoined the *Kungsholm* at Suez. From here we sailed through the Red Sea on our way to Aden, connected to the mainland of Arabia.

The old city of Aden is in the crater of an extinct volcano at a height of 1,800 feet, providing strong natural defenses and guarding the entrance into the Red Sea from the Indian Ocean. The modern city, called the Crescent, is located outside the crater. In the old city we found bazaar after bazaar, all eager to sell their wares, and numerous beggars. Legend tells us that the grave of Abel, killed by his brother Cain, lies near the main pass which leads to the crater and that Noah's ark was built at the harbor, one of the oldest shipyards.

LANDS OF CONTRAST

Traveling 2,500 miles by train through India permitted us to see in this amazing land startling contrasts between the East and the West, the ancient and the modern, the primitive and the sophisticated. Here we found a variety of cultures and religions, and gentle, thoughtful people, who are, in the main, more interested in the spiritual than the material. Nowhere was this impression more pronounced than in Benares, the holiest city of all India.

There on the banks of the holy Ganges River in the early morning, we saw numberless pilgrims bathing in order to wash away their sins and carrying brass pots filled with holy water to offer to the gods in two of the most sacred temples in all India, the Golden Temple and the Monkey Temple. A short distance from the bathing ghats were the burning ghats where, we were told, about fifty bodies are cremated each day. To a Hindu, a pilgrimage to Benares is a "must," at least once in his lifetime.

The long ride on the train gave us a panoramic view of this vast land: dusty villages with thatched-roof houses and dry adobe huts, colorfully dressed women gracefully bearing burdens on their heads, groups of men squatting around their waterpipes, and throngs of children. We saw the need of water for irrigation and of more progressive farming methods. Poverty was evident everywhere. On railway platforms people huddled together to sleep for the night, perhaps their only beds.

On the other hand, India presents some uncommonly beautiful sights. The capital city, New Delhi, only thirty-five years old and modeled on Washington, D.C., is a beautiful city of wide boulevards, lovely parks, homes, and gardens, and enormous public buildings. One of the most modern structures is the American Embassy. Especially impressive is the Raj Ghat, the memorial to Mahatma Gandhi, built on the site where his body was cremated.

The Pink City of Jaipur is so called because the buildings were tinted pink at the command of a late maharajah who grew weary of the color disorder in the city. Here we rode an elephant up a rocky road to a palace in the deserted city of Amber, an architectural masterpiece of perfect proportions.

Doubtless our most memorable experience in India was viewing the Taj Mahal at sunrise and again at midday. It is impossible to describe adequately the beauty, grace, and exquisite workmanship of this white marble memorial erected to the memory of the beloved wife of a seventeenth-century Mogul emperor, whose body lies beside that of his queen. The interior walls and the tombs are decorated with incredibly beautiful inlay work of precious stones in flower designs carefully inserted into the smoothly polished marble surface.

Lying just south of India, but separated from that great land mass by a narrow strait, is Ceylon, considered by many to be one of the loveliest of all tropical islands (now named Sri Lanka). After the arid, dusty conditions of India, it was indeed refreshing to drive through lush, green tropical countryside, through coconut, banana, and breadfruit groves as well as rubber and tea plantations.

On our way to Kandy, a city high in the green hills of Ceylon, we stopped frequently to photograph roadside scenes: elephants carrying logs by their trunks, women in fields harvesting rice, men tapping rubber trees, people washing clothes in a river, painted oxcarts covered with palm branches, azure-washed houses with thatched roofs, men in checkered sarongs, women in aquamarine and sharp pink saris gracefully carrying burdens on their heads. A visit to a school gave us the opportunity to photograph children with their teachers at work in a pavilion-like building without windows, unnecessary in this tropical climate. Everywhere we were welcomed by these warm-hearted Sinhalese, who presented us with gifts of flowers and spices.

In the city of Kandy, we visited the famous Buddhist Temple of the Tooth, where is enshrined the sacred tooth of the Buddha. At this most revered place of worship in all Ceylon, one sees monks and priests in saffron-colored robes and with shaved heads. At the Queen's Hotel we enjoyed an exhibition by Kandyan dancers in gorgeous costumes, who had developed a style all their own.

On our tour of Georgetown, the capital of Penang Island, we saw wide, clean streets and spacious tropical homes painted white or a pastel shade and with tiled roofs. Of special interest were the Malayan stilt houses with thatched roofs. We visited the Snake Temple, so called because snakes, which are sacred to the Buddhists, are permitted to move about freely. They are harmless because of the incense. At another temple there is a colossal reclining Buddha, whose figure extends over the entire length of the temple.

On the steps leading up to the temple, we found the usual beggars with their begging bowls and many, many stalls where one could buy countless souvenirs. Before we returned to the pier, we took a short ride in a tri-shaw, a three-wheeled bicycle taxi.

Singapore, a gay cosmopolitan city of 1,750,000 inhabitants, known as the "crossroads of the East," has long been one of the important commercial centers of southeast Asia. Here more than one hundred ships from all ports of the world call each day. Founded in 1819 by Sir Stamford Raffles as a trading port for the East India Company, Singapore still thrives on trade; consequently it has a unique mixture of eastern and western influences.

Driving about the city, we saw an international procession of people, a large proportion of which were Chinese. Here were old men walking slowly in traditional long robes and soft shoes, young students in western dress, women wearing the blue cotton tunic and trousers of China, still others in newer styles. We saw turbaned sikhs, women in saris and veils, Americans, Englishmen, and people in just about every type of dress. At How Par Villa we saw a priceless collection of jade, one of the best in the world. We were impressed by the many varieties of orchids at the Botanical Gardens.

EXOTIC PORTS – BANGKOK AND HONG KONG

It was early morning when we boarded a tender for the thirty-two mile ride up the Chow Phya River to the wharf in Bangkok. During that trip we saw the sun rise, a huge coral ball against a slate blue sky, changing color until it shone in pure brightness. The river is a wide lazy stream winding through dense jungle.

Bangkok, the capital and leading city of the ancient kingdom of Thailand, has a population of nearly two million. A center of Buddhist religion, it has more than 300 magnificent golden temples that glitter in the sunlight, the most impressive of which is the Royal Temple, containing the Emerald Buddha, carved from a single piece of jasper, decorated with gold and studded with diamonds, rubies, and emeralds. Of special interest are the doors of the temple, inlaid with mother-of-pearl, and the many small bells along the eaves tinkling in the breeze.

In addition to this temple of the Emerald Buddha in the walled-in Royal Palace grounds are other impressive structures, most outstanding of which is the throne room. Another unusual stucture, in another part of the city, is the Temple of the Dawn, 240 feet in height, broad at the base and tapering to a pinnacle. This temple, like others, is decorated in a striking manner with shells and pieces of broken porcelain set into plaster over brick in beautiful flower designs.

A pleasant break in our busy sightseeing schedule was a specially arranged performance of Thai classical dancing, sponsored by the Public Relations Department of the city. The dancing was graceful and lovely; the costumes were resplendent with color, gold braid, and jewels; and the girls were the most beautiful we have seen anywhere. After the performance we were served tea on the roof garden of the Public Relations Department Auditorium.

Bangkok, often spoken of as "the Venice of the East," has a network of canals extending out into the countryside. An early morning cruise up and down these canals, called klongs, was a memorable experience. We saw the life of the people whose living quarters were open to the canals. Healthy youngsters, as well as grown-ups were having their morning dip; housewives were doing their laundry and washing their breakfast dishes off their canal-washed steps; small boats were carrying chattering children to school; barges loaded with water jugs, sand, and lumber passed by; a coffee-shop boat stopped to sell a bit of breakfast to a farmer, floating in his boat; another boat served a more substantial meal, a bowl of rice with trimmings. In this floating market, we saw boats filled with all kinds of vegetables, bananas, coconuts, pineapples, papayas, oranges, and beautiful flowers. All this activity indicated that Thailand is a land of plenty.

We saw a million lights glow as the *Kungsholm* entered the harbor of Hong Kong after nightfall. There were floodlights of vessels at anchor, the glare of flashing neon signs—some in familiar English and others in mysterious Chinese characters—and the lights of luxury hotels and apartment houses reaching to the top of Victoria Peak on Hong Kong Island.

By day, this harbor presents an equally enchanting sight. Ancient junks and sampans, modern ocean liners, peaceful tugboats, water taxis, and even armed war vessels make a constant flow of traffic. In the cove of Aberdeen fishing village, we saw a floating community where whole families live out their entire lives cramped into small quarters—sleeping, cooking, working, marrying, giving birth, and dying. It is said that the floating population numbers 140,000.

Hong Kong is a British Crown Colony, consisting of the island of Hong Kong, Kowloon Peninsula on the mainland directly across the bay, and the New Territories. The whole area, comprising approximately 400 square miles, has a population of three-and-a-half million of which over ninety-nine percent are Chinese. In the capital city of Victoria on Hong Kong Island, en route to the tram station, we saw the crowded waterfront from which rise ladder streets lined with shops and dwellings with balconies from which hung multi-colored fabrics.

From Victoria Peak we had a magnificent view of the surrounding area and the harbor, the principal deep-water port and distributing center for South China. The harbor is lined with enormous docks, warehouses, and giant cranes for moving heavy loads off ships. Fruit, fish, squealing pigs, vegetables, and quacking ducks are unloaded here from junks.

In Kowloon on the mainland, the Colony's main industrial and trading center, we passed countless government resettlement houses—vast concrete blockhouses giving each family a single room and access to water and toilet. From the windows and balconies of these many houses flapped laundry as it was drying. On the rooftops were kindergartens, and on the ground floors were primary schools, sponsored by charitable and religious organizations. We saw several medical vans operated by various missions.

Much of the area in the New Territories, a section of the mainland leased by Britain in 1898 for a period of ninety-nine years, is occupied by refugees from China, who have swelled the population from 750,000 to three-and-a-half million in four years. Our drive took us through many small villages of make-shift huts of refugees waiting for resettlement in the government housing facilities. Along the way we saw bee farms, duck farms, rice paddies where women labored wearing hakka hats, vegetable farms where workers used ancient methods of watering and tilling the soil. There were fish hatcheries, oyster beds, and cooperative markets. We also noticed many cemeteries with rows of jars containing the bones of the deceased.

We passed through very old Chinese villages surrounded by walls that originally enclosed the homes of a single family—all the in-laws and various generations of relatives. At one point we looked across the border to Communist China, carefully guarded and edged with barbed wire.

One of our memorable experiences in this fascinating colony was dining at one of the restaurants floating among the fishing boats at Aberdeen. Their neon signs flashed out Chinese characters across the water, and at our approach by launch a display of fireworks welcomed us. There, using chopsticks, we enjoyed a superb dinner of genuine Oriental cuisine.

Undoubtedly, more than any other city we have visited, Hong Kong is a shoppers' paradise, where one finds a variety of wares for sale at reasonable prices since the colony is completely tax and duty free. Many articles that were formerly made in China are now made in Hong Kong by skilled refugee craftsmen from behind the Bamboo Curtain.

In these many shops, one finds excellent buys in linens, embroideries, mandarin coats, camphor wood chests, carved jade figurines, Chinese furniture, excellent British woolens, soft cashmeres, rich silks and brocades, Swiss watches, cameras, antique Oriental treasures, and articles of ivory.

Skillful Chinese will take one's measurements and deliver within twenty-four hours a dress, a suit, or a topcoat at a cost considerably less than that in the United States. Only in Hong Kong may one hire a rickshaw boy, as we did, to take us from the pier to the shopping area in Kowloon.

SEVEN MEMORABLE DAYS IN JAPAN

Kobe, the second largest seaport in Japan, was the starting point for our visit in this unusual and attractive land. We traveled by bus to Kyoto, a former capital of Japan and a center of Japanese culture. In this quaint and most picturesque city, we were introduced to Japan—a land of shrines, ancient temples, palaces, gardens, and pagodas.

At one of the temples, Higashi-Hoganji, we saw worshipers meditating and heard shaven-headed priests chanting the service. Here, as at all shrines and temples as well as in homes, one must remove his shoes before entering. The Heian Shrine is noted for its beautiful garden, a typical Japanese garden where showiness is avoided and simplicity is achieved in the use of rocks, greenery, and water. In March there is little color, only an occasional blossoming peach or plum tree. There is an abundance of cherry trees which were not yet in bloom. While we were at this shrine, we were fortunate to see a bridal couple in traditional attire. Another temple, the Golden Pavilion, has its entire structure covered with twenty-two karat gold leaf.

The Nijo Castle, a residence of the Shoguns built in the early sixteenth century, has long corridors and formal rooms lined with elegant screens and paintings, depicting trees, bamboo, animals, birds, and flowers. One of the most fascinating features of the palace is its nightingale floor that sings as its visitors step on it. It was so designed originally to warn the Shogun of approaching enemies.

A most pleasant experience was our four-hour ride on a limited express train, the Kodama, on the Tokaido main line between Kyoto and Numazu. It is without doubt the most efficient, clean, and comfortable train we have seen or ridden. It has a smooth road bed, wide windows, spacious seats and racks, automatic sliding glass doors, delicious food (sizzling steaks for lunch), and tea and snacks served by green-clad Japanese girls.

Leaving Numazu for Lake Kawaguchi by motor coach gave us another unusual experience. We traveled up the mountain in a heavy snowstorm, and were late arriving at the Fuji View Hotel. That evening it was fun to squat on a rush-matted floor to watch the kimono-clad girls prepare a sukiyaki dinner, a tasty dish of thin slices of beef and vegetables cooked in a soya sauce and served with a Japanese wine called "sake," made from rice, and drunk hot. Once again we had the experience of eating with chopsticks.

Later we were entertained by Geisha girls dressed in colorful silk kimonos, with their hair adorned with jewelry and combs. They sang and danced to the music of lutelike instruments called "samisens."

As we opened the screens of our window the next morning hoping to see Mount Fuji, we saw instead a veritable fairyland. Every twig on trees and bushes was laden with freshly fallen snow· Birger hastened to capture with his camera much of the scenery of the lake and the area surrounding the hotel.

Soon we were off again by bus and train for Tokyo. From our train window we had matchless views of the countryside—terraced hillsides, snow-covered mountains, lakes, streams, and fields dotted with sheaves of harvested grain hung on long poles to dry, or more usually stacked in the shape of a tower.

Here we had a good opportunity to view Japanese houses, which are constructed of wood with tiled roofs in urban areas and with thatched roofs in rural districts. The floors of the rooms are covered with thick rush mats, and paper screens or sliding doors serve as partitions between rooms. Not a drop of paint is used in typical Japanese houses, for the Japanese prefer natural beauty and particularly that of the natural grain of wood.

Tokyo, the capital of Japan with a population of over ten million, is now the largest city in the world. A focal point of interest at our hotel, the Tokyo Hilton, was the lovely Japanese garden with its stone steps, stone lanterns, rocks, greenery, and water basin. Facing this garden is the Tea Lounge, where in quiet elegance the Tea Ceremony is performed each afternoon. Based on sixteenth-century rules, it is a ritual usually practiced by young women as a means of cultivating grace, poise, and mental composure.

On our two-hour ride on the limited express to Nikko, we had a magnificent view of snow-capped Mount Fuji. As we returned that evening, we saw it again in an impressive purple haze. It has been said that if one hasn't seen Nikko, one hasn't seen Japan. After our visit to this Alpine-like village, we readily agreed with this statement, for here one finds not only superb natural scenery—crystal lakes, towering evergreen forests, waterfalls, and mountains—but also magnificent man-made beauty.

Located here is the most beautiful shrine in all Japan, the Toshogu Shrine, built in 1636. The first landmark seen on the way to the shrine is the Sacred Bridge, vermilion-colored in the shape of a crescent, which spans a stream. At the entrance to the main shrine is the Yomeimon Gate, famed for its gorgeous decorations in the form of lions, birds, flowers, and dragons. The gate is often called "the gate where one tarries all day." At the Sacred Stable one sees, carved on the only unpainted wooden building in the shrine precincts, the statuary of three monkeys: "Hear no evil," "See no evil," and "Say no evil" monkeys.

Continuing up the mountain on a road of innumerable hairpin curves, we reached Lake Chuzenji, more than four thousand feet above sea level. At this charming mountain highland resort, we visited another lovely little shrine, Futura San. There we saw the Kagura, a kind of religious dance of Shintoism, said to be the dance to comfort the gods. The dancers were young women wearing white robes and scarlet skirts. Each dancer held bells which she jingled as she danced to dispel evil spirits. Two priests, using drums and flutes, gave the musical accompaniment. The dancers also used swords as symbols of destroying evil.

In the quiet seaside town of Kamakura, we saw the famous great Buddha. This huge bronze image, measuring 42½ feet in height, was cast in 1252. It was originally enclosed in a large building which was carried away by a tidal wave in 1495. Ever since the bronze Buddha has remained in the open.

After seven memorable days in Japan, we rejoined the *Kungsholm* at Yokohama. We regretted that we could not linger in this fascinating and progressive land of courteous, friendly and energetic people.

During the voyage of 3,397 miles from Yokohama to Honolulu, we crossed the International Date Line. As one crosses the Date Line going eastward, his watch remains the same, but the date changes abruptly to one day earlier; therefore, the traveler repeats a calendar day. We had two Tuesdays, March 17, 1964. St. Patrick's Day was celebrated on the second Tuesday.

Reaching the Hawaiian Islands brought us from winter to

summer and to an ideal vacation spot. Although Hawaii lies in the tropics, trade winds and nearness to the cool currents of the Bering Sea provide these islands with a mild and temperate climate.

Although our Hawaiian visit was of only two days' duration, we visited such historic places as Iolani Palace (the only royal palace on American soil), the Royal Mausoleum, the statue of King Kamehameha, and the Queen Emma Museum. Also interesting was the visit to a Buddhist temple, its Caucasian priest, and its Japanese garden of stone, lanterns, rocks, and greenery. Buddhism is the strongest Oriental faith in Hawaii. Our drive took us through the Nuuanu Valley to the Pali for a superb view of the "windward" side of the island of Oahu. We saw the Upside-down Falls, where the spray comes over the cliffs and is blown up by the winds.

Another natural wonder is the Blow Hole, a sort of geyser made through a hole in the rocks by the incoming waves. The drive through the lush tropical countryside took us past an abundance of hibiscus, bougainvillea, and tropical trees, by miles of sugar cane and pineapple plantations, and papaya, banana, and coconut palm fields. It may be of interest to note that Hawaii annually produces a million tons of sugar and seventy-five percent of the world's canned pineapple.

Doubtless the highlight was our tour to the U.S. Naval Base at Pearl Harbor with its large and widespread installations. Here we visited the impressive *U.S.S. Arizona* Memorial, dedicated as recently as Memorial Day, 1962. It is an enclosed memorial bridge that spans crosswise the hull of the sunken *U.S.S. Arizona.* It encloses an assembly area large enough to accommodate 200 people. It also includes a carillon and a shrine which has a marble wall on which are inscribed the more than 1,100 names of those who lost their lives on December 7, 1941. These men are still entombed within the rusting hulk of this battleship.

Shortly before departure of the *Kungsholm,* the cruise members enjoyed a performance of Hawaiian songs and dances by a native dance troupe. As the *Kungsholm* gently slipped away from the dock, we heard the strains of strange Hawaiian music and song. The farewell to us was as sincere as the welcome had been enthusiastic. We remained on deck until we were opposite Diamond Head, a world-famed landmark, a huge rock precipice. There all of us cast our leis overboard, for legend says that if one's lei reaches Diamond Head, he will return to Hawaii. All of us agreed with Mark Twain, who called Hawaii, "the loveliest fleet of islands that lies anchored in any ocean."

Our one-day call at the port of Los Angeles was made especially enjoyable by a visit with relatives—our sister-in-law, Rosa Westerlund, her son, Perry, her daughter, Phyllis Toshikian, and her grandchildren, John, Shiela, and Amanda. We proudly showed them the *Kungsholm* and entertained them on board.

The distance between Los Angeles and Panama is approximately 1,500 miles. About halfway of this distance on the western coast of the Mexican mainland is located Acupulco, a city of 70,000 often called the Mexican Riviera. It is situated on an oval-shaped bay of deep blue waters, surrounded by mountains of jungle growth. Within this area are miles of white sand beaches and modern luxurious hotels from some of which we had striking views of the ocean and mountains. Our cruise members had a busy day. In addition to sightseeing, some of them went deep-sea fishing; others roamed about the shops filled with colorful crafts, especially articles of silver, a staple product. A high point of the day was having dinner at the El Mirador Hotel, where we were seated in an open-air, terraced dining area at the edge of a cliff overlooking the Pacific Ocean. There we were thrilled by the spectacular performance of native boys, who, bearing lighted torches, dived from a high cliff into surging waters below.

It was with great anticipation that we entered the Panama Canal. We had read and heard much about this great engineering feat which reduces the distance from the Atlantic to the Pacific by 7,000 miles. Ever since the Spanish explorers first saw the Pacific, men dreamed of a canal through the narrow Isthmus of Panama. After a survey by the Spanish in 1534 and later surveys by the French and the British, the first attempt to dig a canal was made in 1882 by the French. This attempt failed not only because of insurmountable natural obstacles but also because of the plague of yellow fever which took the lives of thousands of workers. In 1904 the United States took over the project of building a canal which was completed in 1914, during which time many formerly unconquerable barriers had been overcome, including the scourge of yellow fever.

The Panama Canal, unlike the Suez Canal which has no locks, is a lock-and-lake type of canal. Ships are lifted and lowered eighty-five feet in three steps on each side of the isthmus. Gatun Lake, to which the ships are lifted, has an elevation of eighty-five feet above sea level and is the second largest artificial lake in the world. Strange as it may seem, the Atlantic end of the canal is twenty-seven miles west of the Pacific end. The Canal Zone, which is a ten-mile wide strip stretching fifty-one miles across the isthmus, is the largest economic asset of the Republic of Panama. This national income is derived from wages of Panamanians working in the zone, cash spent by the United States personnel stationed there, and an annual rental paid by the United States, which has control of the Canal Zone until the year 2,000.

Nearing the end of our 36,000 miles of adventure, we cruised in the Caribbean toward our next and last port of call, New York. During these three months the *Kungsholm* had been our home away from home where every need and desire had been met.

The commander of the *Kungsholm,* Captain Henry Sölje, friendly and able, came from Råå, Skåne. He was a twenty-seven year veteran of the Swedish American Line. It is interesting to note that the Bostrom family, who founded the line, came from Värmland (Birger's home province). It should also be noted that the crew and the staff outnumber the passengers. The cruise manager, Mr. Herbert Colcord, and the social directress, Mrs. Helen Frailey, spared no effort in making the cruise members comfortable and in providing entertainment. Outstanding events were the golden anniversary of the Swedish American Line, Washington's and Lincoln's birthdays, Valentine's Day, St. Patrick's Day, Easter sunrise service on deck, gala smörgåsbords, a Hawaiian night, a Caribbean fiesta, a barn dance and two captain's dinners (one before Los Angeles, the other before New York). Every cruise member observing a birthday was presented flowers, a cake, and a favor and was honored by the dining room staff's singing "Happy Birthday to You" in English and "Länge Må Han Leva" in Swedish.

It was with mingled emotions that we approached the end of our cruise. We were happy to return home but sad at the thought of parting from the *Kungsholm* and the many new friends we had made. We had traveled approximately twenty-six thousand miles by ship and another ten-thousand miles on land. We had visited many strange new countries, observed many cultures, religions, and customs, and had met people of many nationalities. The world cruise was over, but memories lingered. Truly it was a cruise of a lifetime.

AFRICAN WILDLIFE SAFARI

By Larry Heintz
of the *Argus*
January 18, 1969

British Overseas Airline's Flight 530 left New York's Kennedy Airport at ten in the morning on October 7, 1968. On board were soon-to-be participants in the fifth annual East Africa safari sponsored by the Cincinnati Zoological Park. One of the members of the zoological park group was a Rock Island man, Birger Swenson, who related,

"East Africa is famous the world over for its fabulous wildlife. Nowhere else on earth can such spectacular communities of wild animals be seen together. This is particularly true of the large mammals. But the birds are scarcely less remarkable.

"It is hardly possible to overestimate the importance of its wildlife to the Africa of the future; in its preservation for generations to come, plans for its bird life are no less important than plans for lions and elephants, rhinos, and giraffes."

The trip did not start auspiciously for Swenson. Somewhere between the Quad-City Airport and Kennedy Airport, a bag containing the 300-millimeter telephoto lens for his camera was lost. Swenson continued,

"We were asked to travel light with just one bag and a flight bag . . . I had to buy a new bag and some clothing in London. The airlines have reported my bag as still lost."

There was a ten-hour, non-stop flight from London to Entebbe, the Ugandan city built on a peninsula into Lake Victoria. North on the Victoria Nile is Murchison Falls, the 130-foot falls in the heart of the national park which was the first stop for Swenson and his group. He said,

"For three weeks, we traveled in specially built automobiles with hatches in the top so that a person could stand to view the game. It was very different from any other travel I have had.''

Swenson has traveled in Europe, South America, in Mediterranean countries and has made one round-the-world trip. The safari was headed by Ed Maruska, director of the Cincinnati Zoological Park. It visited in Kenya and Tanzania in addition to Uganda. Swenson continued,

''As we traveled through prairie, bush and forest, we saw a great variety of wild animals. There were antelopes of many kinds—the dik-dik, barely over a foot in height, the smallest; the eland, the largest. Herds of elephants marched like soldiers. There were rhinoceroses—both white and black, large herds of buffaloes, zebras and giraffes.''

In the group were eleven travelers, six men and five women and three guides. They traveled in three Land Rovers. Heading the guides and the safari were Gordon Harvey and Karl Pollman. Harvey is a former game warden who left that job unhappy with the leniency shown toward poachers. Swenson added,

''The parks we visited for game viewing were Murchison Falls and Queen Elizabeth National Parks in Uganda; Nairobi National Park, Amboseli Game Reserve and the Treetops in Kenya; Lake Manyara National Park, Ngorongoro Crater, Serengeti and Masai-Mara Game Reserves in Tanzania.

''In the crater we visited a Masai village. Here the chief of the natives tried to bargain for our director's wife whom he referred to as 'Nancy Ohio.' ''

Most of the animals are used to seeing cars, but not people on foot. The animals do not like the sound of the human voice, Swenson said. He continued,

''Early one morning we came upon a pride of lions that had killed an antelope and were having their breakfast. We drove the Land Rover as close as ten feet and sat there for an hour watching them. We saw lions and leopards sleeping in trees like kittens. We saw one tree with six lions in it.''

One evening when Swenson left Keekerok Lodge in the Masai-Mara Game Reserve for his near-by cabin, a security guard armed with a rifle accompanied him. The next morning at breakfast, he learned that a lion had killed a large antelope behind his cabin. He had heard no noise, but a guide explained that an animal attacked by a lion is unable to make a sound because of nerve shock. Swenson related,

"One night was spent in the Treetops. This is a hotel built on stilts with accommodations for sixty guests. During the night, in artificial moonlight achieved by many floodlights, we could sit and watch a variety of wild animals coming to the water hole and also licking salt that had been sprinkled on the ground. We were warned to keep windows to our rooms closed because many baboons were climbing all over the place."

During the three-week safari, the group covered two thousand miles by auto. It crossed the equator six times. The entire trip was more than twenty thousand miles. The travels included a boat trip on the Victoria Nile where herds of hippopotamuses lie all day with only ears and noses visible and where crocodiles were in abundance.

AMONG THE PENGUINS AND SEALS
THE SWENSONS IN ANTARCTICA

By Julie Jensen
of the *Times*
March 6, 1973

The Birger Swensons of Rock Island have felt the lure of Antarctica so strongly that they've visited the seventh continent twice in the last three years.

It all started when they read a National Geographic article about the ultimate southland, and Swenson says, "No tourists had gone there very much until the year before we went the first time."

Lars Eric Lindblad, a native of Swenson's home province in Värmland, Sweden, had just the trip for them. Mrs. Swenson says, "If you want to go anyplace unusual, he'll take you. Siberia, Outer Mongolia . . . "

Lindblad had an icebreaker built in Finland in 1969 for his Antarctic excursions. Birger Swenson describes it as "built without a keel. It rolls and kicks a lot, and you use safety belts for sleeping. But after three or four days, you get your sea legs."

Birger Swenson, retired manager of the Augustana Book Concern, adds, "We were warned to take medicine along for seasickness." Mrs. Swenson is well-acquainted with the rolling action of the ship, for it caused her to lose her balance and break her wrist on one voyage.

On the first trip in 1971, the Swensons flew from Los Angeles to Sydney, Australia, and embarked for Antarctica from Hobart, Tasmania. The ship carried eighty-eight passengers and sixty-five crew members from fourteen nations. The passengers were issued red parkas to make them highly visible in the frozen south and knit caps and face masks. They brought their own heavy boots and gloves from home.

"We sailed straight south until we reached McMurdo Base, the American research station which is the largest on the seventh continent.

"We also visited Macquarie Island, a small island where an Australian research station is based. Fifteen men stay there fifteen months at a time, and they were happy to see us. They were disappointed that the women were so bundled up because they hadn't seen a feminine leg in fifteen months."

McMurdo has a complement of 1,000 men during the Antarctic summer when the Swensons visited the base. The Navy brings them supplies and personnel replacements. During the perpetual daylight of summer, they work at building in three shifts. The entire population of the base (250 in winter) is housed in a single building with club rooms, sleeping quarters, cafeterias, library, and lecture rooms. All the necessities of life are brought in by Hercules planes.

The U.S. research stations in Antarctica cost the American taxpayers $33 million a year. Swenson considers it a good investment for its return in the findings of biologists, ornithologists, marine geologists, and meteorologists.

Since 1959, the twelve nations, with research stations in Antarctica, have agreed that no part of the continent will be claimed by any country for a 30-year period.

The United States has six stations besides McMurdo, including the South Pole base, Scott-Amundsen, which is ninety-five feet below the ice.

Swenson says, "The seventh continent is about the size of the United States and Mexico combined. It is the highest, coldest, windiest, and driest continent on earth. At the South Pole, precipitation is only two inches a year, and snow of thousands and millions of years has packed to form the ice. The continent is covered with a depth of at least two miles of ice. If the ice should melt, it would increase the water level in the oceans about 200 feet, inundating New York City and lapping at the nose of the Statue of Liberty."

Most people go south in the winter to get warm, but the Swensons found Antarctic summer brisk, to say the least. Lyal Swenson says, "The wind is strong, and at the freezing point, the chill factor was 40 below."

Swenson adds, "When I was a boy in Sweden, our parents told us when we were out skiing to rub ice or snow on the frostbite, but in Antarctica, they told us to hurry back to shelter for a warm application."

No tale of Antarctica is complete without mention of Capt. Robert Falcon Scott, the great British explorer. Swenson says,

"In 1901 Scott hoped to reach the South Pole, but the ice didn't break for three years, and he was stranded until 1904. He came back in 1911 and landed thirty miles farther north at Cape Evans. He had Siberian horses with him and hoped to reach the Pole with them. One can still see the bales of hay for the horses and even the fat in the frying pan in his hut, which is now an historical shrine.

"Scott set out for the Pole with his Siberian horses, but they died, and when he reached his goal, he found the Norwegian flag planted and a letter from the Norse explorer, Roald Amundsen, describing the good dinner with champagne and cigars to celebrate the discovery. Scott was a month late.

"On the way back, Scott and his party camped eleven miles from a supply station and told each other good-bye when they went to sleep that night. They knew they would freeze to death before the morning. Their bodies were found a year later. It was decided to leave them where they were. They were covered with canvas and are forever buried in ice.

"The words Scott left behind were these, 'I do not regret this journey. It shows that Englishmen can endure hardship, help one another, and meet death with as great a fortitude as ever in the past.' His widow had this statement carved on Scott's monument in Christ Church, New Zealand."

Swenson says Amundsen succeeded where Scott failed because he had one hundred dogs and food for them. "Whenever a dog was sick, he killed it and fed it to the others."

The Swensons were awed by the scenic beauty of Antarctica. Birger Swenson describes a particularly spectacular iceberg:

"Bright aqua water around the base, a heavenly blue in the crevices as if it were illuminated from within. The beauty of some icebergs was enhanced by a backdrop of exquisite sunset against clouds of pastel blues, greens and grays."

On the second trip in 1972, the Swensons saw the other side of Antarctica, sailing out of Capetown, South Africa, to the land of penguins and icebergs. Swenson says, "The seals were getting a free ride on an ice floe, which looked like a sardine sandwich."

He explains that no four-footed animals can live in Antarctica, and there is no plant life at all. Only flies without wings and penguins live on the fringes of the continent. Swenson continues,

"There are seventeen kinds of penguins, and the king penguin is the showiest. We saw nesting albatrosses with a twelve-foot wing spread. They weigh from twenty to thirty pounds."

They visited South Georgia Island, where many factories for boiling the blubber from whales once operated. All are closed now, as only Russia and Japan still take oil from whales.

"There were glaciers and a great deal of snow on the island," Swenson says, "as well as penguins, elephant seals, petrels, terns, and some reindeer the Norwegians had brought there. This island is famous because Sir Ernest Shackleton, an English explorer, lost his ship in a storm and rowed 800 miles to South Georgia in an open boat with three men. They approached the wrong side of the island, climbed the mountains, and came down to the populated side, where people at the whaling stations thought they were ghosts.

"When Shackleton died in 1922, his body was taken to Montevideo for return to England, but his widow decided that he belonged to Antarctica. He was buried at the Norwegian whaling station, Grytviken, with a quote from Browning as his epitaph: 'I hold that a man should strive to the uttermost for his life's set prize.' "

Antarctica inspires lofty sentiments, for Scott's memorial cross bears a quotation from Tennyson, "To strive, to seek, to find, and not to yield."

The difference between the North and the South Poles is this, according to Swenson: "The North Pole is located in the sea surrounded by land, and the South Pole is located in the center of a continent surrounded by water. In the Arctic, four-footed animals are at least 2,400 miles from the Pole."

At one time the only fresh water supply at McMurdo Station was melted snow, now a nuclear plant transforms sea water into consumable liquid. It also gives light and heat.

The Swensons' delight in Antarctic beauty was undiminished when they visited the Russian, Chilean, and Argentine side of the seventh continent. Lyal Swenson comments on "forests of ice formations—fantastic arches and cathedrals!"

They visited the Falkland Islands, British possessions with a population of two thousand. One of them, West Point, held only one family.

Swenson adds, "When we reached Argentina's Tierre del Fuego, 'Land of Fire,' we visited a 50,000 acre ranch, Harberton estancia, which was given to a missionary, the grandfather of the man who lives there now. Their nearest neighbors are twenty miles away, and they communicate by two-way radio. The rancher married a girl from Ohio. Their life on the ranch was featured in *National Geographic,* written by Natalie Goodall, the wife of the owner.

Though Antarctica has been frozen since the memory of man, it was a tropical region years ago. Birger Swenson brought back rocks and petrified wood that pre-date the ice age.

"They think the seventh continent was part of either South Africa or Australia," Swenson says. "It broke away and drifted out. The closest land is South America, 700 miles away."

After such an adventure, where will the Swensons go next? They'll probably be consulting Lars Eric Lindblad. Birger Swenson smiles as he says, "If he had lived in the age of Eric the Red, Lindblad, not Leif Ericson, would have discovered America!"

AMAZON MEMORIES

By Julie Jensen
of the *Times*
February 16, 1977

A Rock Island couple's amazing adventure aboard an ice-breaker (equipped like a floating college). They traveled the Amazon River in South America, visiting ancient cities along the way.

Lyal and Birger Swenson of Rock Island have come to regard an ice-breaker called the Lindblad *Explorer* as their home away from home on numerous adventuresome holidays, but in the bitter cold days of winter, 1977, they find recollections of their trip up the Amazon on the ice-breaker more congenial than memories of two trips to Antarctica and one to Greenland on the same craft.

In late September, 1975, the Lindblad *Explorer* made its way from the North Cape, Iceland, and Greenland to Bermuda to start the Amazon expedition. The ship is actually a floating college, with marine biologists, ornithologists, and oceanographers aboard.

The group visited St. Lucia Island and Trinidad on the way to Belem, where the Amazon venture would begin.

Birger Swenson says, "We had quite a discussion about the Bermuda Triangle. A plane was lost there not very long ago, and it may be some magnetic situation that scientists have not been able to explain."

The *Explorer* experienced several days of rough weather. As the ice-breaker has no keel, it rolls and kicks, and safety belts are available at night.

Belem at the mouth of the Amazon is a city of 800,000 founded by the Portuguese in 1620.

"The Mississippi at Rock Island looks large," Swenson says, "but the mouth of the Amazon is 208 miles wide, farther than from here to Chicago, and the Amazon has more than 1,000 tributaries.

"A fifth of all the fresh water in the world comes from the Amazon, and it flows with such force that it drives salt water back into the Atlantic 200 miles. Enough fresh water flows from the

Amazon in one day to supply New York City for nine years."

The Amazon flows through a rain forest that was a prehistoric lake, and 8,000 different kinds of trees can be found there.

The weather is hot and humid, 100 degrees fahrenheit or more and 100 percent humidity. The Swensons and others in the party were grateful for the air-conditioning aboard ship.

Birger Swenson says, "Every morning we were awakened by the expedition leader, who said, 'Good morning! It is now 5:30. Coffee awaits you in the Penguin Room, and zodiacs (inflated rubber rafts) will leave every 15 minutes.' These rafts held 15 to 18 people. We explored lagoons and tributaries for two hours before breakfast. After about 8 a.m., it was too hot to be outside."

The rest of the day and evening was spent listening to lectures and dining in cool comfort.

Two of the zodiacs were for fishing, and others were for bird watching, visiting river villages, and just exploring.

Lyal Swenson says, "The rain forest is completely silent at midday because it's so hot, but in the early morning, the birds and monkeys make a lot of noise."

Her husband laughs at the memory of long-tailed squirrel monkeys, saying, "You could hear them half a mile away!"

The river is the habitat of at least 200 different kinds of fish, including the dreaded piranha, which Birger Swenson describes as "a beautiful red and silver fish the size of a man's hand." Lyal caught a couple of them, and the guide told her not to take them off the hook, for they might bite her finger off.

"We caught about 35 of them one morning and put them in a tank aboard ship, but after three days, they had to be put back into the river. They were getting hungry enough to eat each other."

The stingray, the electric eel, and the huge anaconda snake that grows 30 feet long are other dangerous species. A Greek from Tarpon Springs, Florida, was willing to wrestle the anaconda on land, but not in the water.

The Swensons swam off a beach that the marine biologist knew to be safe.

The main stream of the Amazon is milky, murky water from the high Andes, but some of the tributaries are almost black, and black streams can travel unmixed for great distances.

Manaus, about 900 miles up the river, is a city of 500,000. It was a rubber boomtown early in the century. The opera house was imported piece by piece from Europe, even to the wavy paving stones from Portugal. The Manaus market building was designed by the same architect, Eiffel, who created the famous tower in Paris.

The party moved on to the Rio Negro, where dozens of native dugout canoes were anchored for fishing. A black streak from the black river flowed for about 200 miles in the milky Amazon. They visited two Indian villages and found the inhabitants to be primitive but friendly and pleased to be photographed. At one Yagua village, Birger Swenson disembarked from the zodiac into knee-deep mud. When he returned to the ship, he took a shower in his clothes and shoes to get rid of the mud.

The leper colony at San Pablo is operated by a small group of Canadian Franciscans. *Explorer* passengers donated more than $200 plus medicine, fruit and candy to the eight male lepers and their families.

The expedition was fast approaching its goal, Iquitos, Peru. The next day the party flew to Lima. There they reflected on Pizzaro, the Spanish swineherder, who became a general and conquered the noble Incas. The following morning they flew to Cuzco, where the altitude makes one short of breath.

They reached Machu Picchu by bus, train and mini-bus, doubling around the mountains for nearly four hours to travel 80 miles.

The lost city of Machu Picchu was never discovered by the Spanish invaders. In fact, it was not found until July, 1911, when Hiram Bingham, an American professor, came upon it. The ruins of its palaces and temple still hold evidence of grandeur, and the great stones are held together without mortar.

"The fortress of Sacsahuaman near Cuzco is one of the greatest engineering feats ever attempted by primitive man," Swenson says. "At an elevation of 12,000 feet, it is more than 1800 feet long and honey-combed with tunnels. Some of the stones weigh more than 200 tons. How were the Indians able to get them there? What tools did they use? Nearby we saw a contemporary man pitching hay with a pronged tree branch."

They went on to Arequipa, the most Spanish city in Peru,

where they were entertained by the deputy mayor. (The mayor was recovering from an airplane accident.)

The Swensons flew home from Arequipa, leaving the steamy equator and the brisk high Andes for the late October weather of the Midwest.

In five and a half weeks, they had traveled 4,770 miles by ship and a similar distance by air. They had enjoyed the mystic rain forest, the haughty llamas of the Andes, the friendly Indians, the bright birds, the lush foliage and the unusual fish of the Amazon. They had eaten duck wrapped in manioc leaves which the people of Para call Pata Tucupe, and they had learned a great deal from the floating "faculty" aboard the *Explorer*.

The Swensons plan to take the same ship next June from Nome, Alaska, for a cruise in the Bering Sea, the Aleutians, the Gulf of Alaska, Glacier Bay and the Inside Passage. They will visit the famous Pribilof Islands, observing thousands of fur-bearing seals and visiting eskimo villages.

THE SVENSSON FAMILY, 1979

In the beginning of my life story, I stated that there were nine children in the Svensson family. I have already mentioned the deaths of my brothers, Robert and Sven. The deaths of others occurred as follows: Amanda in 1971, Ragnar in 1972, Annie in 1973, and my twin sister, Signe, in 1974.

The three remaining members of our family had a most enjoyable reunion in September 1977, at the time of my younger brother Rickard's eightieth birthday. The celebration was held in the home of his daughter, Margaretha, and her husband, Brian Magnusson, in Moline. Rickard, his wife, Greta, and daughter, Marianne, had come to the United States for a month's visit. Our sister, Hilma Nordstrom, then eighty-seven, her daughter, June, and her son, Fred, and his wife, Doris, came from the Chicago area. Brother Ragnar's widow, Frida, and her daughter, Anita, came from California. Ragnar's son, Robert, and his wife, Elsa, and family came from Chicago.

Another death occurred in the fall of 1978. My sister, Hilma, died on November 4, at the age of eighty-eight. Now only two children remain: my brother, Rickard, and I.

APPENDIX A

HOME AT LAST

Never before had I felt such a longing for home. Never before had life as a soldier seemed so gloomy and monotonous. Visions of Mother and her dear countenance appeared constantly before me. Oh, if I were only home again, home again — with Mother!

Visions of the little red cottage with its white trimmings and its newly laid tile roof rose before me as it lay there imbedded in the garden like a playhouse. There I had seen the first light of day. There I had enjoyed the innocence and peace of childhood. There I had received the caresses and admonitions of Mother.

"Love not only your friends, but also your enemies," were the parting words she sent with me as a guide on my journey through life.

Now I sat alone and forsaken in a foreign land, a participant in the most horrible war that the world had ever seen. The conflict had at first been a great delight to me. The thundering cannon, the clattering of the machine guns, and the whistling of bullets had been music to my ears. I had had no time to think of home and of the dear ones. I had often written to them, but longing for home had been something foreign to me.

But now as I sat there, an attendant in the Red Cross tent, gazing over the desolate landscape, a deadly longing for home came over me. Everything seemed monotonous and disagreeable. The verdure of nature, which in the morning had been bathed in the most glorious sunshine, had been overshadowed by heavy, leaden-colored clouds. The bright day had turned into dark night. The mountains and the forest had lost their outlines and were changed into a hazy mass. The wind came sweeping down from the narrow pass between the mountains, shrieking as it forced its way through the trees. I rolled down the canvas covering and huddled up on my box in order to dream in my loneliness of home.

The roar of cannon could be heard in the distance; only a few miles away death was reaping its triumph. The enemy had met the American division at Chateau Thierry. The battle was now in full blast. Already the ambulance began to come back with the wounded.

Friend as well as enemy was carried into the tent to receive first aid treatment.

A German was lying near me. His head was bandaged. Wound fever had already set in. He was delirious; he threw himself to and fro in his bed. He was crying and talking about his mother. He reached out after her hand as though she were standing at his side. He raised himself up, groping wildly in the air. Then he opened his eyes and stared confusedly about him.

"Where am I?" he asked. I bent over him and tried to console him, but he only stared into the empty air.

"Oh, if I only were home with Mother!" he moaned. There was anguish and despair in his voice. It showed an overwhelming longing for home, a longing which made him forget everything else and rendered him unable to realize that he was in a hostile country.

"You are home, home with your mother," I consoled him. I understood that he had not long to live. His countenance brightened; a cheerful smile played on his pale face. He whispered to himself like a small child ready to fall asleep.

His home was in the neighborhood of Mainz by the Rhine River. There at the oak-covered banks of the river, he had spent his happiest childhood years. Everything had been peaceful and beautiful. The loving care and affection of his mother had been inexhaustible. She had carried him in her arms while he was an infant, watched at his bedside when he had been sick, had consoled him, and had dried his tears with kisses. She had protected him and loved him as her own life. Both home and mother had been inseparable to him. Then the war came and they had to part. How bitter had the parting been! But the law of war must be obeyed.

Two years had passed since he had been called into the army, and during this time he had visited his home only once. This was in June 1918, and the visit was very short. Rumors that the American troops had taken their place on the western front had forced the Germans to reinforce this line. All those who had been home on leave had been recalled. Max's regiment belonged to the reserved troops that were stationed at Chateau Thierry. They had camped there for days, for weeks, and waited.

But now the battle had come. The Germans pressed forward in order to cut off the way and had thrown themselves on their new enemy. Time and again they had tried to press forward but had been compelled to retreat. It had been a more severe battle than the Germans had expected.

Finally they had found it impossible to break through the American line. Therefore, a small group, a patrol of six men led by Max, had been sent out to reconnoiter in order to find a possible way of surrounding the enemy. As soon as they had come out, the Americans had opened fire on them. Max had sought shelter in a hollow in the ground, and then as he was trying to raise himself up to see if there was any possible way to continue, he received what seemed to be a deafening blow on the head. A bomb had exploded nearby and a splinter had entered his head. Almost deafened, he had drawn his hand across his face. He had felt blood running down his forehead. He staggered forward and with a faint cry, "Mother! Mother!" he fell to the ground.

Now he was lying there in the tent, rescued but a prisoner in an enemy's country. At first he had spoken incoherently, as if he had not known where he was. He had believed himself home with his mother. Toward the end he spoke more clearly.

Now he raised himself in bed. His hand groped nervously over the edge of the bed. His eyes stared feverishly. His face grew ashen gray.

"No, I am not at home! Oh, if Mother were here!" He tried to raise himself on his elbow but he sank back in bed. He closed his eyes; a smile played on his burning lips. What was it? Did he believe himself home again? His heart throbbed with joy. The gloom disappeared and his face was radiant. With a trembling voice, he whispered, "My home, my Mother!"

There was a sudden convulsion, and then he lay motionless.

The sound of cannon became duller and its thundering died away to a rumbling in the distance. Max was dead. He had found his home.

Then I saw written with fire, in suffering and want, the meaning of home. "Home, home, sweet home," was no longer a meaningless phrase; it sounded like the chiming of bells in the evening, a peaceful invitation from the Almighty's own heart.

APPENDIX B

WESTWARD THE COURSE OF EMPIRE TAKES ITS WAY

Evening had come. The sun was shedding its last rays about me as a parting to a beautiful spring day. Shadows were slowly gathering in the deep ravines of the old Indian campground nearby and the old Watch Tower where I stood was taking on a hue of purple reflected from the sunset in the west.

It was historic Rock Island County, a bit of the grandiose Mississippi Valley, that composed the picture, a region known for its singular scenery, cliffs and valleys, hills and prairies, majestic rivers, clear and sparkling rivulets.

From the east the Rock River was winding its way on its westward journey, making its highway through fertile fields and stately forests. Here and there numerous islands lay resting on its bosom, some low and sunken as if imbedded in the water. Others rose far above the surface, clothed in a foliage of green trees. Among the islands, light canoes were sailing back and forth, and merry laughter echoed across the water as happy couples passed each other in joyous races. On the bank of the river, a little town lay dreaming in the twilight, and great stretches of prairie were reaching out into the far beyond. Farther to the west, the river divides itself into several arms, each one hurrying down the rapids to join the great Mississippi, forming a bond of union with the Father of Waters which remained throughout their long journey southward to the Gulf.

The sun had now totally disappeared beneath the horizon, and the glowing purple of the sunset was shifting into pink and white, while in the east the bright full moon began sending its messengers of light over the landscape. The happy songs of the birds had ceased except for the occasional plaintive cry of the whippoorwill. The river below was peacefully sleeping. The scene had at once changed to a tranquil resting place.

I sat down on the hillside in order to enjoy more fully this glorious evening. I saw nature clothed in such a harmonious manner as never before. I saw the green fields, the forests, the shadows of the woods. Each breeze was filled with the fragrance of wild flowers and of lilies of the valley. I felt the spring of youth in my veins, and memories of days long gone by began to play before my eyes. I was dreaming.

I dreamt that another era—long since passed—had come back to reenact its scenes in this peaceful valley, an era when the proud and liberty-loving Sac and Fox Indians paddled their canoes on the river and camped on its beautiful shores.

I saw the red man and his squaw prepare the campfire on the shore. I saw them gather fruit from the wild orchard, eat and go to sleep. I saw the flower-strewn earth, their resting place, and the blue skies, their canopy. The faithful kept watch against wild animals. There were no other enemies for them to fear. I saw the mighty Sac and Fox nations encamped at Watch Tower. Their village was beautifully situated on the bold, high bluff overlooking valleys unsurpassed in beauty, high above the clear sparkling Rock River. It was a village full of life and happiness. Row upon row of wigwams covered the hillside, occupied by a healthy, happy and contented people, peacefully performing their tasks, raising corn, beans, and tobacco while at home, and bravely pursuing the wild beasts while on the hunt. Here was their burying place where the brave went to sleep to wake up and meet the Good Spirit.

Oh, how happy and fortunate you were, red man, who lived and died before Joliet and Marquette came from France to force a strange faith upon you! How free you were! You knew no enemies before the English came with their blood-thirsty men, armed with guns and lances in order to hunt you. Hunt you, you proud and peaceful people, as a hunter his game, from your territories in order to prepare the way for civilization.

I saw Chief Black Hawk, sitting at the lookout in council with his family, tall and dignified in his movements, possessing intelligence far beyond his race. His face had something of the Grecian cast, and his mind and character were more those of a great general than of an uncivilized warrior. He was loved by his people, admired and revered by those who sought his counsel, a great mediator and orator, always fighting for the rights of his people. And now! Now! He was lying in chains there on his beloved Watch Tower, broken in spirit, a prisoner looking for the last time at his home, the fertile fields, and the land for which his fathers and his braves had fought and died. Now he must part with it all. The white man's civilization had reached his country on its steady way westward.

> Indian! Thy camp fires no longer are smouldering,
> Thy bones 'neath the forest moss long have been mouldering;
> The Great Spirit claims thee. He leadeth thy tribe,
> To new hunting grounds not won with a bribe.
> On thy Watch Tow'r the pale face his home now makes,
> His dwelling, the site of the forest tree takes.
> Gone are thy wigwams, the wild deer long fled.
> Black Hawk, with his tribe, lies silent and dead.

Behold! I am no longer dreaming. What do I see in the northeast? A large dome is towering toward the sky. The pale moon is throwing her rays over its cupola. It is the new Watch Tower on Zion Hill, built by the descendants of the sturdy Vikings from the far North, soon after the Indians left old Black Hawk's Watch Tower. Long has it stood there, majestic, beautiful, and impressive, not a lookout to detect approaching enemies, but a beacon spreading light in every direction. It is a center around which populous cities have sprung up, transforming this grand region so rich in legend and old time mystery to a great commonwealth. Huge factories now line the banks of the Mississippi, imposing business structures beautify the downtown districts; stately mansions, beautiful schools, churches, and hospitals cover the hills. The valleys are teeming with life.

We live in the present. The past is but a dream. The days of the mighty Chief Black Hawk and his warriors are but memories. Years have passed, years of continued westward progress which have slowly brought the white man's civilization to the Mississippi Valley, to the great prairies, to the Rockies, and even to the great sea beyond, for always westward the course of empire takes its way.

APPENDIX C

THE FUTURE OF THE BOOK CONCERN

Lifted from Birger's article in the final issue of the *Augustana Annual, 1962:*

The question has often been asked—What of the future of the Augustana Book Concern and what place will it have in the merged church, the Lutheran Church in America? There are three publishing houses in the merger which will become one large publishing house: Augustana Book Concern, Rock Island; United Lutheran Publication House, Philadelphia; and Finnish Lutheran Book Concern, Hancock, Michigan. All these are strategically located; therefore the operation can be divided to serve the new church more efficiently than any one of them did previously.

Many of the facilities presently offered will be enlarged and made available in fields of special service. The ecclesiastical arts department will include a complete tailor shop for the manufacture of stoles, paraments, and other appointments. A woodworking shop will be staffed with craftsmen in the field of church furniture. The music department will include an enlarged program of publication, as well as stocking and distribution of music of other publishers. The audio-visual department will include expanded service in the field of production, rentals, as well as sales of equipment, films, slides, and film strips. Rental libraries of films and slides will be located at various centers.

All three publishing houses in the merger have printing plants. These may have to be enlarged in order to serve a greater constituency. Publication of new books may increase four-fold. The long-range program will tax the capacity of these plants inasmuch as several years will be required to put the new lesson materials into production and use in our churches.

The present branches of the Augustana Book Concern and the United Lutheran Publication House in Chicago will be merged. Besides sixteen existing retail stores, new branches in other parts of the Church will be established to help distribute printed material and to serve local congregations more efficiently. Mail order distances to congregations will undoubtedly be shorter than they are now. The greater percentage of our church members will be close enough to one or more of these branches to enable them to visit one of our retail stores more often than in the past.

For the last three years or more, the staff members of the three publication houses in the merger have met in order to work out a consolidation of publication work. The spirit of working together in this common project has been most encouraging. There are many problems yet to be solved, but these are not insurmountable. We eagerly look forward to a new merged publication house with a family of six hundred devoted employees who will endeavor to serve Christ and His Church through the *printed page.*

A new name will undoubtedly be chosen to designate the new publishing house. Whatever that name will be, it will spell a new era and open a field for greater service to the Lutheran Church in America.

The new name chosen was The Board of Publication of the Lutheran Church in America.